A radical new look at
how creativity is born

ReAwakening of Art

A radical new look at how creativity is born

By
Meera Hashimoto

Perfect Publishers Ltd

ReAwakening of Art

A radical new look at
how creativity is born

ISBN 1-905399-03-0

Cover design by **Hamido Frank Kardell** at
hamido@web.de
Cover photography by Sammy Hart

PERFECT PUBLISHERS LTD
23 Maitland Avenue
Cambridge
Cambridgeshire
CB4 1TA England
www.perfectpublishers.co.uk

*Awareness plus action and you
will attain reality immediately*

Osho

Contents

Life is a mystery.
How to touch it? How to hear it? How to speak it?
Every night, we die a little bit.
Every morning, we are born again, we wake up...
a little bit.
This cycle of birth and death, waking and sleeping,
Is just the breath of nature.
It is automatic.
You may call it a dream.
The story of waking up from this dream,
The story of a second awakening,
Of re-awakening through painting,
Is the story of this book.

So, what is left after re-awakening?
Everything...
As play... as art... as laughter...
As Meera's Dance.
Start at any point of this book.
You will receive a taste of it, Meera-style.

Günter Nitschke (Swami Anand Govind)
Author of "The Silent Orgasm" and "Japanese Gardens."
Director, Institute for East Asian Architecture and Urbanism,
Kyoto, Japan.

Acknowledgements

So many people have contributed to my life and influenced the way I paint and lead painting courses that it is impossible to mention everyone. I will have to be content with naming just a few.

I would like to thank my mother, for always encouraging my creativity, in whichever direction it took me, and my father for the financial support that allowed me to study art for so many years.

My sister Taeko, for opening my eyes to simplicity and a deep appreciation of nature.

Masanari Murari and Reitaro Fuji, my art professors at Musashino University, Tokyo, for teaching me the basics of painting.

Govind, for introducing me to a synthesis of East and West, and for bringing me to Osho, my spiritual Master.

Geetesh, my wild artist friend, for triggering in me the overwhelming urge to create.

Sagarpriya and Svagito, for introducing me to the group leading process as a tool for transformation and meditation.

Svagito, my life partner; through living together with him and sharing daily life I am learning so much about love – both the giving and the receiving.

The Tolmo Group of artists in Toledo, Spain, especially Aroldo, a painter to his very bones, who showed my how an artist can survive in the material world.

Victor and Marina in Toledo, for feeding a hungry artist when she had no money left to buy bread. Gloria and Ricardo, also in Toledo, for loving my work and photographing it so much.

Sammy Hart, Anubhav and Premendra for their photography work.

Doris Jheel, my loyal, patient and conscientious secretary in Munich. Saagara, Shako, Patricia, Richa, Vedam and Gayan, for organizing my trainings in Europe.

Sharone, for his enthusiastic support for the publishing of this book.

Mukta, for fulfilling Osho's vision of a jungle-like garden and caring for it over the years for us to paint.

My dancing teachers, Navanita, Viram and Birgitt.

Hamido, for his support over 15 years and his three videos of my work.

Nirvano, my translator and fellow traveler, who has always fanned the flames of my desire to create.

All my friends and helpers in the Master Painter Trainings in Pune, especially Fulwari, Ekin, Henna, Bhaven, Rishiraj, Nirvikalpa and Devena. These trainings are not just my doing. Without the love and devotion of our team members they would not exist.

Subhuti, who participated in a six-week training and who met with me every evening to review the day's events. While sipping tea and watching the river flow, he listened to my comments, understood my perspective and then put it in written form.

This book is dedicated to Osho. The effort in my groups and trainings is to translate Osho's work into painting, because I know that painting is one of the most powerful methods of working on people's consciousness.

Meera Hashimoto

Foreword

Meera's love affair with art embraces method and mystery, creativity and chaos, outer dance and inner silence. Hence, it is difficult to write about it.

When Meera asked me to help her put together a book, it was obvious to me that we could easily create a self-help manual on how to awaken the creative impulse in people. After all, this is what Meera does so well in her groups and trainings.

But a user-oriented book, with exercises and instructions, geared toward guiding the reader through a step-by-step process, would of necessity sacrifice much of what makes Meera's approach so dynamic, spontaneous and unique.

For one thing, the most essential element in the process would be missing, simply because it is mysterious and unsayable. It cannot be forced into language. It can be communicated, being to being, but not rationally explained.

The people who participate in Meera's courses emerge as revitalized, creative, confident painters, and they know how to carry this new and precious outpouring of creative energy into other dimensions of their lives. But exactly how this happens, I doubt if any one of them can say.

So I have chosen instead to describe Meera's training as it happens, using this as a foundation for the book, while at the same time weaving around it anecdotes from her personal life plus her views on art.

Some people say the book reads like a novel, with all kinds of unexpected twists and turns in the story. If so, it's rather like Meera herself. She has the mercurial ability to be totally immersed in one thing, then suddenly shift to something entirely different and seemingly unrelated – like a leaping particle in quantum physics.

Through this way of writing, I hope to convey the character and quality of Meera, the depth and delight of her being, thereby helping the reader to trespass into those dimensions beyond words where the real source of creativity lies.

Even if this can be communicated only partially, the book will be a success.

Swami Anand Subhuti

Introduction

Art is the longing of the individual to be bridged with the whole of life; to connect with and give expression to life itself.

Thousands of years ago, in the caves of Altamira in Spain, long before any art schools were born, ancient tribes of hunters depicted bison and other animals with great sensitivity and accuracy.

Their art was not the product of some carefully learned technique. It was a pure prayer of human expression.

In a similar way, while reading this book, you may suddenly remember your own thirst to express, even if you are not a trained artist.

This thirst can be remembered easily, because creative expression is nothing but your own life energy – it's like invisible blood running through your body.

The intelligence to create is hidden in us and can flow out like a spring bubbling from a snow-covered mountain top. It is endless, abundant and delightful.

In our contemporary society, art is being treated more and more as a separate entity, something reserved for specialists, like any other profession.

This is a pity, because painting not only is everyone's birthright; it is one of the greatest tools for awakening one's consciousness and awareness.

In the long tradition of Zen, many different spiritual methods – including art – have been dedicated to a single aim: to recognize the inner space known as "No Mind," or "Isness."

Zen masters developed all kinds of strange devices to bring disciples to a place where the normal, thinking mind has nothing to grasp, no foothold on which to stand. In this gap, suddenly the disciple is directly confronted with existence, with life.

This book invites you on a similar kind of journey, on a search to find yourself and the source of your original expression.

Painting can be a mirror to look deeply into yourself. When you paint with awareness, whoever you are, whatever you are feeling in this moment, will find expression on the paper and be captured there, reflecting yourself back to you.

All that you need to do is stay open and watch.

In this way, through awareness of each moment, a revolution in consciousness is possible, because the mind has no space to get into old habits of commenting, judging, criticizing or instructing.

Living each moment means giving space to intuition and spontaneity. Once you learn this secret, painting is sheer joy and playfulness. You are accepting the invitation of life energy to flow through you.

My hope is that, by reading this book, you will get so turned on that you will also want to look inside yourself and discover how painting can open all the doors and windows of your creative intelligence.

Meera

Illustrations

A book about painting without artistic illustrations is something of a novelty, but there are many vivid images hidden in these pages that will evoke your creative imagination.

In fact, for me, this book is filled with paintings. The descriptions of my work and trainings are awash with bright colors and so are the anecdotes from my life.

Perhaps later, when I have the time and resources, I will bring out a lavishly illustrated, coffee table edition.

Meanwhile, if you are curious to see samples of my work, you can browse through the 'gallery' and 'posters' sections of my website: www.meera.de

In this book you will find mentions of many artists, from Vincent Van Gogh to Paul Klee. I also mention specific paintings that had a formative effect on me, like Edvard Munch's 'The Cry,' and William Turner's 'Rain, Steam and Speed.'

The works of these artists are easily found on the internet, and you may wish to view them as I talk about them. If so, I particularly recommend the Artist index of WebMuseum, Paris: http://www.ibiblio.org/wm/paint/auth/ and poster websites like:www.allposters.com

You can also browse the websites of art museums like the Tate in London and the Guggenheim in New York, or just enter the artists' names in your favorite search engine to find them.

Chapter 1

Primal Painting

This is a strange place in which to create a revolution in contemporary art. In fact, the artistic revolution that is growing here goes way beyond contemporary, because nothing like it has happened in the whole history of art, except perhaps in the Far East, centuries and centuries ago.

Also, I have to be honest and say that this revolution will go unrecognized for at least fifty or a hundred years. That's just the way things go, and, in fact, it's always been like that. In any field of creative expression, the real revolution happens long before most people realize it.

Those who believe they are the pioneers of modern art today will continue to lead people down a blind alley until one day they will turn around and see that, years earlier, art had gone in a totally new and different direction. They will be left stranded and not a little embarrassed, rather like railway workers, laying track across a virgin land, who misread the map, took a wrong turn and went into a desert.

Of course, this sounds very egoistic and fantastic, but I can't help it. I have to say the truth. I have to straighten up the whole direction of modern art. That's the main reason why I'm writing this book, and it will take a little time to explain, so please be patient with me.

What makes it strange is that, in this place, where I mostly live and work, the artistic revolution in which I am involved is just a by-product. It's not the main focus of what's happening and the people who know about it are not particularly impressed. They smile, give me a hug and say,

1

"Oh really? That's interesting. Keep it up, Meera!" and go about their business.

Meera is my name. Painting is my game.

And now you will have to excuse me because I have to go and pick up the participants in my annual painting training who are waiting in the plaza.

I walk in through the back gate of the meditation resort in my black robe and, with a wide, toothy grin and a "Hello! Good morning!" refuse to show my pass. You see, I have some kind of authority-thing with gates and passes.

The guard, a middle-aged Indian woman with tied-back silver hair has been through this with me many times and, without lifting a finger to stop me, complains indulgently, "Meera! Sometimes you have to show your date sticker to me!"

To which I respond with a cheery wave and a few Japanese words thrown back over my shoulder, for I am already through the gate and walking down a narrow path, lined with tall bamboos and black-painted buildings, heading towards the heart of the resort.

Further along the path I catch a glimpse of myself in a blue-tinted, floor-length office window and stop for a moment to take a longer look. Once in a while, it's good to remember what others are looking at, especially at the beginning of a long training program like the one that starts today — Meera is going to be onstage for the next six weeks.

I look a little wild: long, shiny, dark hair with a few grey ones hidden in the depths, bangs cut low across the forehead, a classic Asian face with olive skin, brown sparkling eyes, a broad nose and a sensual mouth. Put a fur cap on me and I could be a nomad from Tibet or Mongolia. Let me slide into a kimono and I could surprise you as an elegant geisha hostess. See me crack up in a smile or laugh and I look like a little girl from a fishing village on the East coast of Japan, which is in fact where I was born, some fifty-four years ago.

2

Now I am coming into the plaza, a large, square-shaped assembly area, floored with dark green marble and bordered by gardens on three sides. Today it is crowded with people, most of whom are wearing maroon-colored robes and looking for the right place to stand, because at least three courses are starting this morning.

Mine has 25 participants, eight helpers, three translators, two assistants and one co-leader. The participants come from all over the world, from Greece, Italy, Israel, Scandinavia, Russia, Switzerland, Japan, Taiwan, Brazil, Australia, Mexico, the United Kingdom and the United States.

There is a sign marking the assembly point for each group and mine says "Master Painter Training," but some people have difficulty reading English and aren't sure where to go, so the general effect is one of a colorful chaos, like some kind of international, spiritual train station.

The full name for the plaza is Osho Multiversity Plaza, which is part of the Osho Meditation Resort in Pune, India. This is where I conduct my annual painting training, as well as some shorter courses, and this is where I choose to spend a big chunk of my life.

The plaza is where visitors sign up for a variety of programs, ranging from Primal Therapy to Vipassana to Shamanic Healing. The short programs last 1-3 days, but trainings like mine are much longer.

As I mingle with the crowd, a few people come to me and say they are still unsure whether they want to commit so much time, energy and money to the painting course. In the past, I would have tried to charm them, seduce them into signing up with me, but this time I don't try to pull them in.

I say to one, "If you can't decide, it means you're not meant to come."

I don't want people to come to me accidentally, on a whim, because in life you can't get everything at once. If you're not getting what you need here with me, then I trust that you can get it somewhere else.

Another thing I often notice is how people tend to put creativity aside. People come to this place because they want to explore themselves, they want to embark on an adventure of self-discovery through meditation, therapy, education in esoteric arts, all kinds of workshops. There's so much to choose from that it's like a laundry list, with creativity too often at the bottom.

"Yes, Meera," they say, "I'd love to spend some time painting with you, but first, I have to do some serious therapy, dig deep into myself, look into the dark corners of my being, heal the pains and fears, find my true nature.... Then maybe one day I can be creative." That's a common understanding of creativity.

I want to assert that this approach is wrong. If you really want to see into all your dark corners, you need a lot of energy, you need a lot of light inside so you can face the problems that you are going to encounter. Creativity does this part, supporting the beautiful side in you. Once this side is supported, you are ready to look at the dark corners with joy, not with a heavy heart.

Start from creativity, which is linked to the discovery of your inner child, linked to spontaneity and sensitivity. Then you are not crushed down by darkness, but instead you say, "Aha! So this is what I have to look at in order to grow." It's a totally different attitude that you bring to your growth.

Well, now you see that I am being carried away by my own prejudices. If I take a few deep breaths and calm down, then I can tell you the truth: you can start your inner journey from anywhere, from the dark or the light. It doesn't matter. If you are sincere and intelligent in your search, you'll find your way.

It's just that I get annoyed when people assume that the way of joy and creativity is less valuable than suffering. To me, it's a product of thousands of years of religious indoctrination: be sad, serious, and you are on the right path: be joyful and playful and you aren't a sincere seeker.

In the plaza, we have a problem. One Italian woman doesn't have a translator and this is unusual because

4

normally we organize very well with translators – there is no shortage of volunteers, since translators get a free ride through the whole training. They do the course, but they don't have to pay. Then I remember: two people applied for the job and I sent them away because I didn't feel they would fit.

Groping for a solution, I think of Vardhan, an Italian woman in her forties, who is training with me to be an instructor. Here, I should explain that, side by side with the painting training, I run an instructor's training for those who want to learn how to lead these kinds of courses. There are five people signed up this time.

"So Vardhan can be the translator," I decide. It's a good challenge for her: when translating she will need to be very accurate in what she is hearing and observing, otherwise the person who cannot understand English will miss much. And with my very special way of speaking English, it's easy to miss what's being said.

I check with Vardhan; she likes the idea, so the problem is quickly solved and we are ready to move. We all walk together, participants, helpers, assistants, translators, along the path that leads to the back gate of the resort and across a public road to a cluster of large, handsome-looking black pyramids that were built several years ago at the suggestion of Osho. Who exactly Osho is and what he has to do with creativity and painting is something I prefer to explain later on.

We enter the largest pyramid, named after Naropa, an enlightened mystic in the tradition of Tantric Buddhism who lived in India about a thousand years ago. All the buildings in the resort are named after enlightened mystics from different countries, different periods of history and different spiritual traditions: Lao Tzu, Krishna, Jesus, Meera, Rinzai, Kabir… and so on.

We climb the stairs and enter a very large room with glass windows on three sides and a high, pointed, pyramid roof. Many group leaders don't like this room. They say it's too big and the energy of their groups gets lost in the huge

5

space, but I love it. I need lots of space for my work. I could take over the whole ashram for my painting training if they'd let me.

Normally, I start my groups by inviting everyone to sit down in a circle and introduce themselves – their names, where they've come from, why they want to do the group. But with so many people and so much feeling of chaos in the plaza just behind us, I feel the energy is not settled enough to do it.

By the way, please excuse me when I talk about "energy," especially if you are one of those people who hate New Age terms. Actually, I must apologize twice, three times, because I am going to use it a lot. Energy is my pulse, my heartbeat. It's central to my work. It's the wind in the sails of the ship that we have all just boarded and in which we are going to voyage together for the next six weeks. I can't tell you exactly what energy is, but perhaps you'll get the idea as we go along.

Anyway, as far as introducing people is concerned, when the situation is not settled and you try to meet people too quickly, right away, the chances are that you will meet only the head. By which I mean a superficial mental and social layer that we use for meeting and dealing with people day to day: "Hello, my name's Rosemary, I come from London, I'm very happy to be here…" etc. Nice, polite, comfortable and boring -- a bit like an English tea party.

So instead, we start dancing to some upbeat music from my mini-disc collection. One of my main tasks in this course is to bring people from the head to the heart and from the heart to an even deeper level inside themselves, and for this the body is a much more direct route than discussion.

Picking up the microphone, I invite people to focus their attention in the sensations of their feet as they dance. Usually, we are not aware of our feet or legs, unless they have been bruised, cut or damaged in some way. Most of the time, we take them for granted – just a mechanical means to transport the rest of the body around from place to place.

This is a mistake. The feet and legs contain many secrets. For example, one of the most important Buddhist meditations is Vipassana, which was developed by Gautama the Buddha about 2,500 years ago. This meditation has two parts: first, sitting cross-legged with eyes closed, watching your own breathing rhythm. Then, walking slowly with eyes focused on the ground, putting your attention on the sensations in the soles of your feet as they touch the earth.

That's the whole meditation: sitting and watching your breathing, walking and feeling your feet. By focusing attention in this very simple and relaxed way, a flame of awareness, or consciousness, slowly grows inside the meditator.

I myself studied a form of classical Japanese dance based on the Noh tradition, in which there is strong emphasis on being aware of your feet – your feet and your back. If I had time, I'd tell you about Kantomoe, my dance teacher, a rare woman who escaped from near-slavery as a young geisha girl and refused to marry anyone, choosing instead to devote her life to dance. She must be nearly eighty now and still teaching.

Through Kantomoe I imbibed the real spirit of dancing. Through her, I know that dance is an effective method to get people more grounded, more rooted in their bodies, more present and alert, more alive and energized.

Next, I ask the participants to begin to relate with each other as they dance, but only through the feet – allowing the feet to meet, touch, say hello and dance together. Again, it's a simple and effective technique, because when you come into a group and meet new people face to face, there tends to be a sudden contraction in your energy.

Immediately, your mind starts forming opinions: "I like this person... I don't like that person... I want to do the exercise with this person... I want to avoid that one." But with the feet, with the legs, you can stay relaxed and choiceless because it's more impersonal. It's really a very innocent part of our body.

After a few minutes of playing footy-footy, I slowly include more and more parts of the body, until it's easy and natural to move to the final stage: "Dance freely, moving from partner to partner, making eye contact."

Even though I'm the leader, the course facilitator, I can't stand aside and watch other people. I love dancing so much, I have to be a participant. So I am dancing around the room, meeting these people – some strangers, some well-known faces – when I see Pilar, a young woman from Spain. I know her from a previous workshop. Now, she's five months pregnant.

I notice she is crying. I go to her, look softly and inquiringly into her eyes and she tells me, "Meera, I'm sad." This touches my heart, because it is said with child-like simplicity, with no attempt to cover it up. I hug her, she is still crying and we are gently dance together. I don't ask why she is sad; there is no need.

Pilar gives me inspiration what to do next, because everybody is carrying feelings inside, different feelings, and I want to encourage people to say 'okay' to these feelings, whatever they are. Usually, we think we have to present some image to the world, like a social mask, which doesn't show what is going on inside. But then we can never be authentic and true to ourselves, and then you can forget about painting anything worthwhile except maybe your kitchen door.

"Connecting with your body, tuning into the body and its movement as it dances, is a very good way to become aware of your feelings," I tell the group, after saying goodbye to Pilar and picking up the microphone. "Close your eyes and explore your feelings. Express them through the movement of your body."

When they have got the idea, I ask them to expand the feeling, to exaggerate their expression, and then open their eyes and continue. "If you include this whole pyramid space and the people dancing around you, what happens to your feeling? Is it the same feeling, or is it expanding or changing?"

Some people are happy, some sad, some look grumpy or angry – the usual range of emotions that we carry inside us. Some like to share their feelings with others, dancing together, while others prefer to dance alone. After a while, most people slip into a light and playful mood, because that's the basic atmosphere in the room, created by the music and the new situation – a group of strangers meeting for the first time, dancing in a big, beautiful space.

With these simple exercises, we have all 'arrived' in the room. We are present, with our minds, emotions and energy, and we can begin the first sharing session.

The music ends and we sit in a big circle. Looking around at all the different faces, I remember why I love this training in Pune: I lead courses all around the world, but here I get the widest range of nationalities, the biggest ethnic and cultural mix.

Without having to go to all these different countries, I am visiting them, getting to know them. And even though these participants are coming from different cultures, different professions and walks of life, whenever we share about creativity the same issues come up again and again. This makes for an international oneness. Everybody is ready to look at the same thing.

With this in mind, I invite the participants to come with me on a journey into the past. I ask them to close their eyes, sit comfortably, and spend a little time recalling memories from childhood – moments of happiness or sadness around the issue of creativity. Then, after a few minutes, I ask them to focus on one unhappy memory.

"I don't want just a simple introduction… your name, country, occupation, and so on," I explain. "Instead, I invite you, when it is your turn, to recall some wound or difficulty that happened in your childhood, related to your creativity, and to share it with the group."

It looks like quite a challenge, to start in this way, digging back into the past, but, as I anticipated, the childhood memories and stories come quite easily. For most of the participants, it's not difficult to remember such

9

painful moments, because even if they sound simple and childish, still, they have left a deep impression on our psyche.

By the way, you have to remember, too, that all of these people have traveled thousands of miles to be here, ready to put up with the discomforts of India in order to embark on a journey of self-exploration. So they have a level of commitment and willingness to participate that you won't find in your local seminars and workshops.

Vardhan begins the sharing, recalling a time as a young girl when, one summer day, she saw her mother picking flowers in the garden. "They looked so beautiful and when I went to school I tried to paint those flowers in my art class. But there was no appreciation and my painting wasn't chosen amongst the best ones that the teacher put on the wall. In fact, my paintings were never chosen."

This became a wound in her creativity.

After a few other people have shared, we come to Dipti, a beautiful and petite woman from Taiwan. Interestingly, she had the opposite experience, telling us that her paintings were always chosen by her teacher to hang on the classroom wall, but deep inside, even as a child, she felt that she was not being at all honest. She was afraid that she had learned to be nice, to paint nicely in order to be accepted by others, to gain their approval.

"Through this, I felt my falseness," she confesses in a soft, tiny voice.

Here, you see how vulnerable children are and how easily the creative impulse gets damaged: one, because her paintings were never chosen, the other, because they were. In neither case was the child supported in her individual expression. It's just that Dipti, realizing the situation, decided to produce what the teacher required in order to be rewarded.

Moving round the circle we hear other stories, like for example, how left-handed children were forced to be right-handed by teachers who had no idea that many children with artistic talent naturally use their left hand more.

Alexandra, a big, blonde from Athens with lots of energy and charm, has one of the most dramatic stories. She tells us that, when she was a child, she could play for hours with color and paints, happy to be alone, needing nothing. But then one day she stole her mother's lipstick and hid it. Her mother was very angry, but Alexandra would not give it back. Then her mother, in frustration, told Alexandra, "If you don't give me back my lipstick I'm going to rip up all these paintings!"

Alexandra didn't believe her, but her mother did it. She ripped up everything. This created such a shock in her – to see her paintings destroyed – that it damaged something inside. After that, she could still paint, but never again could she connect with that feeling she had as a child – that it was really coming from her guts, her creative source. Now she wonders whether that magical feeling will ever return.

Telling the story, she begins to cry deeply and I appreciate her courage. Sharing like this is one of the most essential aspects of the training, because once you really get in touch with a wound – even though your first instinct is to push it away, forget it, hide it, even from yourself – you bring the past into the present. You re-experience the pain you felt all those years ago. Instead of being hidden, festering away in some dark corner of the mind, you bring it into the light of your awareness and understanding. Then, naturally, it starts to heal. Unless you relive such painful experiences, getting in touch with the essence of creativity is not possible.

I am careful not to try and make everything okay, like a quick fix, putting band-aids on people's open wounds. I don't want to give consolations, because these will prevent the real healing from happening. For example, with Alexandra, I don't do anything except listen with an open heart, and actually that's all that's needed.

She is a strong adult, supporting her 'child' inside. She does not need sympathy or kind words right now, beyond the caring environment of the group itself. She knows that, one way or another, everyone has experienced the same

11

thing. I ask her if she can stay with it, without getting any answer from me, and she nods understandingly.

One more story I would like to report. Again, it is coming from a woman, but please don't think this is a women-only group. There are lots of men here, too. I will introduce them later.

This story is from a silently beautiful Japanese woman in her mid-fifties called Sangita, who lives in a forest just outside Hiroshima. She first heard of Pune many years before, and once visited the resort briefly, but was mainly tied to her home, caring for a husband suffering from Parkinson's Disease.

Finally, when her children made all the arrangements for her to take a long holiday in India, she became fearful even to enter the resort, afraid that the experience might touch her so deeply that her life would change forever. For two weeks she could only come to the gate and look in.

Fortunately, Sangita could not resist coming to the promotional event that I staged for my painting training, held one lunch-time in the plaza, which was a spectacular riot of color, live music, dance, painting and overflowing creativity. Something clicked and she decided to join in.

Now she tells us, slowly, through a translator: "When I was a young girl, I was told to paint a fish in class, on a piece of cloth. This kind of fish is very common in Japan, because whenever a healthy boy is born to a family it is flown high over the roof – flying and swimming in the air – as a symbol that good luck has blessed this house. In May every year, on children's day, all the houses that have a boy, they fly this fish.

"But I was very small and to me the fish seemed very big. The only thing I could really comprehend was its eye, so that is what I painted. I enjoyed it very much. I disappeared into creating the eye. Of course, I got harsh words from the teacher: 'What are you doing? That is not what we are teaching here!' It was such a shock to me and since then I dropped my creativity. I could not paint any more."

Small things have a big impact on vulnerable young minds. The pain of incidents like these is so shocking that it cuts the connection with the creative source, just like, for example, when you get an electric shock from a toaster, or an iron, and then you don't want to touch it any more.

One by one, in this way, we move around the circle until it is complete and everyone has shared something.

Now it is time to introduce people to the paper that we will be using during the training.

This paper is very special: off-white in color, quite thick and made of fabric. It's handmade in a factory just outside Pune – I think India is one of the last countries to make paper in this way, because in Europe, when I go to buy handmade paper, I find that almost all of it is imported.

Last year, when the training was finished, we were so curious about the paper that we rented a minibus and went to see the factory where it is made. The factory workers, about twenty in all, lined up to greet us, treating us like honored guests, happy to see us because normally they never meet their clients. Only a small fraction of the paper is sold inside India.

The paper is created out of linen and cotton. The staff explained to us how they put the layers together with glue and then strain it through water. Then it is hung up to dry. It cannot be produced in rolls, or in very large sections, but only in pieces – we use 1.00 x 0.75 meters as our standard size in the training – because it is so thick and heavy that it would rip and tear while drying on the factory 'washing line.'

We were intrigued. For me, the visit was essential because I can't separate the creativity of painting from other activities. All this background: the process of making the paper, the Indian workers, how they are living, how they are feeling, is also included.

Paper made in this way has a beautiful texture and immediately, as you start touching it, your fingers start remembering some organic quality. It connects you with your senses and with nature.

I invite everyone to take a sheet of paper from the piles that have been laid out on the floor. I say to them, "This piece of paper is your whole world at this moment. Your connection is only with this one paper. Just feel it. When there is only one paper in your whole life, how are you going to relate to it? What are you going to do? What is the feeling inside?"

With a little encouragement from me, they start investigating the potential of the situation, bending the paper this way and that, looking at it with the curiosity of a child.

"There is no hurry to reach somewhere, to do something special with the paper," I explain. "One thing you must have noticed is how small children can be endlessly creative with the most simple elements. On a beach, where there is just water and sand, they can play for hours with almost nothing – no video games are needed, no magazines, no TV or web sites to keep them entertained. Just a bucket and spade, or maybe not even that.

"And each moment they feel so excited. I remember when I was a child, I would ask my grandmother to tell me the same story again and again. Even though I knew exactly how the story went, and how it ended, each time it was new for me. This is the quality that I want you to remember."

Some people start wrinkling the paper, crumpling it up into a ball, some are making shapes like hats, diapers, or a dress. Somebody rolls up his paper and makes a telescope, while somebody else makes a hole right in the middle and sticks his tongue through it.

There is no sense of restriction, no miserliness. Old memories about wasting time, or wasting the paper – "look how much it cost and you are tearing it up!" – are cast aside. This is another attitude about creativity that frequently comes up in my groups: the social economics of money, time and energy, because creativity is always connected with wasting time and effort: "It's not practical, there's no purpose, you're throwing away hard-earned money, it's good for nothing, and so on."

But the child-like atmosphere that we have created here knows nothing of economics.

Now it is time for me to take the experiment one step further and invite people to connect and play with each other. Almost immediately the energy takes off and the place becomes a huge nursery, a romper room.

I watch as a Japanese guy makes mats for an Italian girl to step on by putting a piece of paper on the floor in front of her. She smiles, steps on it and starts dancing. He takes another paper, makes another mat and she jumps to that one, and in this way he guides her through the whole room, faster and faster. I like how they play this game: the girl dancing, the man creating the pathway for her.

So now, in this moment, people are becoming really relaxed and freely spontaneous, creating whatever comes to mind. Without knowing it, they have in their hands the key to the whole creative process. At first, it does not seem easy. Just a piece of paper? Nothing else? Usually, even in kindergarten, you are given more outside support – scissors, glue, paints and pencils to help – but here, instead, you have to feel the quality of creativity coming from inside, and that is my intention.

What I like is that, even though the participants don't know each other well, the oneness of an international playground is happening. People are tearing paper and throwing it around like snowflakes, making big airplanes and flying them across the room. I see birds, houses, a Hawaiian grass-style skirt, telescopes, masks of all kinds and some sheets that are totally wrinkled and becoming soft, like papier mâché.

When everyone has thoroughly enjoyed themselves, I invite them to stop and put their creations together in the middle of the room. We stand in a circle around the pile and, when the excitement has died down, I say, "Spend a little time soaking up all the creativity that you see here, all the creations in front of you, which will never come back again, because soon we have to clean up."

15

It is fascinating to me, because what we see before us is basically one square piece of paper transformed into dozens of shapes and, when you put them all together, it becomes even more interesting, like one huge creation, one big piece of crazy architecture.

"When I was a kid we used to have so much snow in our village in winter, and I used to make a house and all kinds of things with the snow," I tell the group. "I remember this feeling now because, as you can see, the light through our windows is hitting our paper and it really looks like a snow landscape.

"Now you know, from your own experience, that you really don't need many things to be creative. You can open your heart and it unfolds on its own. So just let it in, and then we will take this feeling, this understanding, to our other painting room."

It is one of the luxuries in this year's training that we have been given two big spaces in which to work. One is the Naropa pyramid; the other is a large space on the roof of Krishna House, in the central part of the resort, where I have been holding painting trainings for many years. It's high up among the trees, protected from the sun by a temporary roof but open on three sides, so you look out on a jungle-like world of branches, leaves, creepers and birds.

The location is close to Buddha Hall, the resort's main meditation space, where each day a program of different meditation techniques and other activities is offered to the public. Most of these techniques last an hour and many of them are accompanied by music, so throughout the day there is a continuous background of music, which I welcome as a valuable addition to the atmosphere on our roof.

Of course, when we forget ourselves and play loud dance music, our contribution is not so welcome down in the hall, especially when they are doing some silent meditation like Vipassana. But on the whole, we live in harmony during the weeks of the training.

Maybe I should mention, here, that this is the last year in the life of Buddha Hall. It is being replaced by a new, pyramid-shaped meditation hall, fully enclosed and sound-proofed. No amount of loud music from Meera will penetrate its thick black walls or disturb those who meditate within.

By the way, it may seem odd to call this place a 'resort,' because normally you don't see people walking around in long robes and meditating in holiday resorts – the usual use for this term. You could also call it an 'ashram,' but then you don't usually see people dancing, dating, playing tennis and having fun in such holy places in India. In fact, it's an ashram and a resort – a unique mix that defies easy categorization.

The roof on Krishna House has been carefully prepared for us. Places are set out for everyone, with a cushion, a large piece of handmade paper – in fact, two pieces glued together to increase the size – and a box of paints and inks, with brushes, sponges and a small plastic bucket filled with water. The spaces have been arranged in clusters of four, so that when you sit down you have someone sitting beside you, and also someone opposite you.

The room is longer than it is wide, so two big painting areas, each containing roughly half the group, fill both ends of the room, while the middle remains empty, available for dancing, sharing, any kind of activity that does not require the paints and brushes. Underlying both painting areas is a thick layer of green plastic, our valiant but ultimately hopeless attempt to prevent spilled paint from staining the linoleum flooring.

There is one aspect of the training I take so much for granted that I have almost forgotten to mention: we don't paint standing up, with an easel in front of us, in the conventional way that most painters and artists do. We paint sitting or kneeling on the floor. Why? Because in this way more of the body is involved and there is more chance to keep an organic quality in the painting process. When you're standing, there's more chance of your energy rising upward and taking you into your head, into your mind.

For fifteen years I painted standing, but since I got in touch with this new way of painting I dropped the whole thing. I never went back.

I invite everyone to find a place to sit. Then, before even touching the paper or the paints, I ask people to close their eyes and, very slowly, with as much sensitivity as possible, to gently touch their own faces.

This looks odd. I am supposed to be teaching painting and here we all are, stroking our cheeks with our fingers.

But there is a method in my strange behavior. Painting is a visual art. It is appreciated by the mind through the eyes, with no other senses involved. It can therefore easily become cerebral, disconnected from everything else, and in fact that's how modern art has lost its way. It's become entirely a creature of the intellect.

So for me, the challenge is how to bring a more organic quality to painting, with no separation from the rest of nature and from yourself – yourself as something bigger than your intellect. The truth is that, unless painting happens from deep inside, from your guts, it has no meaning, because you are not in touch with your originality.

Anyone can paint through techniques, through learning how to do this, how to do that – the way it has been taught in art schools and universities – but it's rare to see the organic quality I am talking about.

"I want you to start from zero, from 'I don't know,'" I explain to the group. "You think you know your face because you have seen it in the mirror. You can describe it. You can say 'I have blue eyes, a pointed nose, thick eyebrows...' But to really meet yourself, as a direct experience, without naming anything, is not easy.

"You may remember, when you were a small baby, you were experiencing everything through touch and taste, putting it in your mouth, touching it with your hands. Everything was touch and taste. Unless you come to this stage again, consciously, as an adult, all talk about creativity is just soap bubbles."

From the face, I guide people to touch the whole of the head, the crown, the ears, the neck, the shoulders, the chest, down to the stomach, legs and feet. "Notice the areas that you are not touching," I say, after a while. "Are you ignoring your sex center? Is it forbidden to touch there?"

One of the things I have learned, as a disciple of Osho, is that sex energy is the source of all human energy. Energy is sex, sex is energy. It's the starting point, the source, the well of life that springs up and spreads out through the body, changing form and quality as it moves. When this energy is ignored, or not lived, you can't expect much from human beings. They live castrated lives. And it's no secret that most great artists, down through the ages, have been very sexual people – their creativity is an overflow of their sexual energy.

"Nothing is wrong in touching yourself, so don't discriminate," I say into the microphone. "To say the chest is a good part of your body and sex is a bad part is a really funny idea. Before you were stopped as a child, there was no discrimination. You must remember, seeing babies touching their genitals in the same way that they touch their feet or any part of themselves. They don't make any distinction. Slowly, slowly, this innocence is taken away.

"But now, with eyes closed, you are not afraid, you feel protected, you feel nobody is watching you, nobody is judging you. You can be natural."

When the whole body has been touched, I move to the next step.

"Now, slowly take your hands away from your body and, with your eyes still closed, let your arms reach up and out in front of you, as if you are trying to touch or reach something – maybe you don't even know what it is, but that's okay. Stay in the unknown, in the not knowing. It's just a feeling, a deep feeling of longing. Let yourself become this longing."

It's a symbolic gesture and for each person the experience can be different. For example, you reach out, eyes closed, and suddenly a memory surfaces from your childhood. You are reaching out to your mother, who was not there when you needed her. You wanted to be held by her, cuddled and loved, and for some reason it could not happen. Or you are reaching to your father, or a lover, or some other person who was significant for you.

For others, it can be more spiritual, symbolizing a longing for something beyond themselves. And for others, especially in the context of my group, it can be the longing to be creative, to express beauty. Perhaps some people cannot even formulate what it is, but through this position of reaching out everybody connects with the same quality, the same feeling.

"With this feeling, with this longing, bring your hands slowly down in front of you until they touch the paper on the floor."

This has been my experience, working with hundreds, even thousands of people, that when you walk into a room, sit down and look at a blank piece of paper with the idea that you are going to paint, something inside becomes frozen with fear. Because you again remember how your creative impulse was stopped.

Your parents were hoping you would become the next Pablo Picasso, hoping you would excel in whatever you did, including art, and the pressure of their ambition, their hopes and dreams, crushed your enthusiasm, your spirit. You knew you could never hope to meet their expectations, so you dropped the very idea of painting.

But here on the roof, with eyes closed, making contact through the basic, primal sense of touch, with no idea of painting anything, it's a different experience.

Slowly the sea of hands before me in the room is coming back to earth, like petals falling through the sky. They do it very slowly, eyes closed, until the first touch happens on the paper.

"As you touch, you may find that different parts of your hands experience the paper differently," I say, as guidance. "Touching lightly with your fingertips, pressing with your palms, stroking with the back of your hand...

"You may find the sensations in your right hand are different from those in your left. You may start making certain movements, patterns with your hand, a circle or a diagonal stroke; perhaps a very slow and graceful touch, or perhaps a speedy movement."

I also guide them to touch the edges of the paper, because here, normally, is the boundary line where one world ends and another is starting. I want people to explore beyond the line, as if there is no difference between the paper and the floor on which it lies, between a painting and the whole of existence that surrounds it, between the inner feeling of the painter and the outer expression of his work.

After a while, I invite them to experiment with opening their eyes, to see if some change happens in the sensations in their hands or feelings. "Notice whether the velocity of your hand movement changes, whether the sensation you are feeling stops, or not. Can you maintain a quality of innocent exploration, or are you pulled back into your adult mind?"

This is a delicate moment. When people open their eyes, they can easily become self-conscious and lose the thread of spontaneity – 'What am I doing? What will others think about me? What am I supposed to do now?'

"If you feel you are losing your connection with yourself, then close your eyes again. There is no hurry," I tell them. But looking around the room, I see that the spirit of child-like curiosity predominates. With eyes open or closed there is no difference and, with my encouragement, the experiment goes further.

"Notice what is available next to your paper: the paints, the inks, brushes, sponges and water. Without naming the colors – this is green, this is blue, this one I like, this one not – start opening the bottles and getting in touch with the materials. Just explore the sensation."

Each person has about twelve bottles of bright acrylic paints in small plastic containers, and five ink colors.

Here, I need to explain a little bit about my choice of media. Acrylic is a synthetic paint and when it dries it is permanently fixed. With watercolor, even when it is dry,

21

you can wet it again and take it off. With acrylic you can't do that. In this way, it's a very interesting material to work with because when it is dry there is no way to go backwards. You can only go forwards and this is really encouraging for the painter.

It's like life: there's no rewind button; you can only go forward into the future, not back into the past.

Acrylics are a modern addition to painting, developed in the 1950's out of a group of resins that can also be used – so I'm told – for manufacturing clothing, carpets and windows. It's the first new painting media for over 500 years and is similar to oil painting, with two added benefits: it dries very fast and it's water soluble so you can clean up easily afterwards. No smelly turpentine needs to be rubbed over oil-stained fingers and brushes.

For all of these reasons, it's a good medium for beginners. When we use acrylics in the training, we can endlessly paint over what we have created, bringing in new shapes, emphasizing or changing old ones, splashing on new layers of color as the old layers dry. The paper is thick and strong, and can take a lot of punishment. It won't disintegrate under the weight of the paint.

The ink colors have a twofold quality of being intensely bright, yet at the same time transparent. You can throw them on top of the acrylic and still see through to the color underneath. In this way, inks give depth to a painting, opening new dimensions and creating different moods. Used rightly, they can open your sensitivity.

Now I invite people to begin to play with the acrylic colors and inks on the paper in front of them, but not all at once, because again, the same tendency is there. As soon as you think about using the whole range of colors, again these impossible questions come in: 'What am I going to do? What combination of colors should I use, and in which order? Will I achieve anything worthwhile?' and so on.

We need to move in small, easy steps, so I tell the group, "Connect with one color that you like; one color you are really attracted to."

With just one color, it's a safer situation. You quickly gain a sense of intimacy and familiarity with it. Then it's not such a big jump when I add, "In any way that you like, with a brush, with a sponge, with your fingers or even with your feet, start putting the color on the paper in front of you."

In my own experience, once one color is thrown onto the paper, some remembrance in your system starts happening. The next color comes in a natural way, like a response to the first one, rather than through thinking. It's like a cellular memory, painting from instinct rather than from the mind.

After a few minutes, I ask them to stop, close their eyes, and reconnect inside to the child-like space we have been creating during the morning. "Remember, any time you feel that you are losing this connection, you can stop, go inside and reconnect."

I do not try and guide the participants into a particular way of painting, into some kind of structure or technique, because this will be a disturbance. But I do ask them to connect with a feeling of longing, especially for beauty. Even if you are immature, imperfect, not gifted in painting, everyone has the same longing to manifest some kind of beauty in their lives, and I want to encourage and support that.

This is a very basic and primary stage in my approach to painting – to support the innocent child inside who feels the creative impulse to do something and who does not want to be restricted. Only when this impulse is satisfied will the child be ready to accept structure and direction. This is why I call the first part of my training 'primal painting,' because we are going back to childhood, to innocence, reconnecting with a lost impulse and beginning again.

Usually, when they're invited to paint in this way, many people begin by drawing an object: a house, a tree, a rabbit or cat, a landscape, the sun, moon, stars. This is natural, but also quite limiting. Once you have drawn it, you realize that you have confined your creativity to a specific form and this makes it difficult to continue.

If you stay with the abstract, enjoying the movement and play of color without form, it creates a more open, flexible and unlimited situation.

I notice that, even though I have said nothing, very few people are painting form. This may be because some of them have already done courses with me, while others watched our introductory demonstration in the plaza, where we were covering huge areas of paper with abstract painting.

Now I sit back, play some relaxing, upbeat music, and let people enjoy themselves for about half an hour. That's the time limit, at this early stage of the game, before people get too much carried back into the intellect.

I take the opportunity to walk quietly around the room, looking at the paintings, watching how people are using their freedom. Even at this early stage, it's a chance for me to see where people are at – what direction they take, how they explore their creativity.

The atmosphere in the room is one of absorbed attention. I can feel, through my sixth sense acquired from leading many courses and trainings, that everyone is being carried on the same wave of energy. Nobody is left behind, frustrated, spacing out, restless or lost. They are all involved, absorbed with putting colors on the paper.

It's a good start to a long, long journey. Through a series of modest steps, we have arrived at the threshold of a new approach to painting – the beginning of a revolution. There are many steps ahead of us, and my challenge will be to try and share with you the significance of what we are doing, while we are doing it, and the impact this can have on the world of art. It is a challenge worth accepting, but whether I can find words to express the full implications of what I have discovered is something I will know only when this book has been written.

Right now, it is a mystery. But, like working with the acrylics, there is no way to go back. Like life, there is no rewind button. I can only go forward.

Chapter 2

Pillars of Freedom

Vincent van Gogh, Pablo Picasso and Jackson Pollock are the three pillars of modern painting. Many other painters can claim to stand as high, and many of them have made important contributions, but for me, these three are the most important. They are the Everest's of the modern movement.

Perhaps it is not an accident that the genius of Van Gogh and his Impressionist colleagues blossomed at more or less the same time as the invention of the photographic camera. I don't think any of them saw the connection – at least, I never read about it in my art studies – but it is one of those mysterious coincidences that happen in history from time to time.

Up until that moment, painting had been used as a method of historical record. Kings and queens, emperors and conquerors, nobles and wealthy merchants could not have their pictures taken on film. The only way for them to survive their own deaths was to be painted on canvas, on a mural, on a wall, or to have their likeness carved in stone or cast in metal. Great battles, epic victories, turning points in the lives of nations, these also had to be recorded – sometimes by pen and ink, sometimes by sculpting, often by painting.

The other important job that painters had to do was to serve religion, especially in Christian Europe, decorating churches and cathedrals with dramatic religious themes like creation, damnation, judgment day and scenes from the life and death of Jesus Christ and the saints. These paintings, too, were pictorial in nature. They were mythical, divine, but represented by conventional forms – clouds, skies, bodies, wings, rainbows, trumpets – and therefore subject to the same painting techniques.

But with the invention of the camera, the job of the painter as a visual recorder of history was over. Something more accurate had been invented to depict not only human events but also the world around us: landscapes, trees, oceans, clouds, and sunrise – it could all be captured in astonishingly accurate detail by the photographer. And with the decline of religion as the central focus of society, it looked as though the painter was out of his two main jobs.

Then, with Van Gogh, a radical change happened. He, too, painted nature – the sun, the stars, trees and fields – but it was not at all the usual way of looking at things. It was not a literal translation of 'reality.' His trees were like arrows of longing, reaching to the stars; his stars were spiraling madly in the sky, his fields were restlessly circling within themselves like wind-blown seas.

He painted a dynamic existence and he painted it from within himself. It was his personal vision, his impression, his heartfelt expression of how life really is. Of course, because it was personal – and because it was a new approach to art – nobody understood him. Perhaps even Van Gogh did not understand himself, because although he was acutely aware of his driving need and passion to paint, he does not seem to have had much insight into the underlying dynamics of what was happening to him.

"It is those who love nature to the extent of becoming mad or ill who are painters," he once wrote, in a letter to Johanna, the wife of his beloved younger brother, Theo. And later, in his final letter to Theo, written just before he shot himself, Van Gogh said about his work, "I am risking my life for it, and my reason has half foundered because of it."

In his longing to express what he saw, he disappeared into the object. There was no longer any separation between the inner and outer existence, no more division between the painter and the painted, between himself and the trees, the

26

sun, moon and stars. He took the whole existence into his being. That's why he was so free to paint the way he did.

But he paid the price, because the depth of his art was developing more and more, day by day, and he was losing his ability to make any distinction. In other words, he was losing his mind, because it is through the mind that we distinguish between what is inside and outside, what is subjective and objective, what is real and unreal. His stay in an asylum and his decision to end his life are testimony that he could not handle the situation.

One more thing I'd like to say about Van Gogh. If he had been born in the East, in a country like India or Japan, where meditation is part of the cultural atmosphere, there is every possibility that he could have achieved the same goal – going beyond the mind and becoming a great artist – without going mad. Because this, really, is the art of meditation: how to go beyond the mind, and yet still be a fully conscious, centered, balanced human being.

Now comes Picasso. For me, Picasso represents all art. If you have to leave one person behind on this planet to record what is art then maybe you will have to choose Picasso, because in his life and in his painting he spanned the whole era of transition from traditional to modern art.

From where did Picasso find his inspiration to break free of traditional forms? Because Van Gogh, even though he painted a totally different kind of nature, still, his nature was recognizable in its basic forms. His trees were still trees. His men and women were still proportionate figures. It was Picasso who broke the rules of form, logic and reason, fragmenting his images, making painting look like an exercise in geometry, giving life a Primitive, Cubist or Surrealistic twist, and he got his inspiration from the paintings of children. He copied their innocent approach – it started from there.

Perhaps you have had this experience when watching children draw or paint. You ask, "What are you painting?" And perhaps they say, "Mummy." And you can't figure it out, because the nose is above the eyes, the ears are on top

27

of the head, and so on. It doesn't look anything like a woman, but the children can see it – they are so certain that what they are doing is a faithful representation of the mother. It comes from their freedom. It's the power of innocence, pure energy of expression.

Of course, Picasso was not just copying. He was an artistic genius. Even when he was a child, his talent was so obvious that his father, himself an artist, simply gave up painting in order to help his son. So when he took inspiration from children and developed it into an art form, it revolutionized the art world.

But Picasso could not embrace the quality of child-like innocence in his own life, which in book form reads just like any other personal drama: love affairs, broken hearts, fights and quarrels, and an admission, close to the end, that he compromised his genius by supplying what the public demanded. In other words, his personal life was not a great work of art.

Now, Jackson Pollock. His work is a kind of refinement of Picasso and there are a few things that touch me deeply about him. First of all, I had no idea that he painted on the floor, like me, until I saw a movie documentary about his life. I'd seen his work in museums and assumed that he painted on an easel, or on the wall, which was a little naïve of me – I should have immediately understood that those splashing, dripping colors would have run right off the bottom of the canvas.

But I had an excuse: I'd grown accustomed to the idea that all western artists paint standing, and knew that the tradition of painting on the floor belonged to the East, to China, Korea, Japan. It has a lot to do with understanding the way energy flows – especially the energy of water. It's a basic law of water: always moving to the lowest available point, so naturally it makes sense to put the paper on the floor, where water can rest and be still.

One more thing: painting on the floor, from the Eastern perspective, creates more space for relaxation so that accidents can happen, and this is exactly what happened to Jackson Pollock.

He was painting like Picasso's late work, with divisions and lines, brush strokes here, brushstrokes there, outlining forms and filling in the colors. In that particular moment, while he was painting on the floor, he had a can of paint in his left hand and a large stick-like brush in the other. He was so focused on thinking about what he was going to do with the stick; he did not notice that color was already dripping from the can onto the canvas in a very natural way. Then he saw it, the effect, the possibilities, and understood the power of a spontaneous event that is not planned, that is not coming from the past, that happens without intention.

By intuition, Jackson Pollock had found his way, his personal style, and this became his breakthrough. Art became even more abstract, even more free from form. With Pollock's 'action painting,' the last barriers had been removed.

Even though he denied that anything was accidental in his art, I'm sure it happened in this way. Because in an accident, when you have enough space inside yourself to receive the unplanned, the unexpected event, then you are being carried by life in a new direction, you are entering new art.

That's all Jackson Pollock did.

But then he ran into difficulties. He developed a new style, but himself became a victim of that style – a prisoner of his own creation.

It's worth understanding. When you have a breakthrough artistic experience, then of course, in the beginning, everything is fresh, new and exciting. But if you continue to paint that way, day after day, your innovative approach gradually develops into a fixed pattern or style.

Pollock could not afford to change his style, because it was bringing him fame, making him a celebrity. Newspapers and magazines were jumping on his new approach to art and calling him 'the shock trooper of modern painting.'

The galleries that were selling his work started making their own demands: "Why don't you do it this way? Why don't you use these colors? Why don't you make hundreds of painting like this, so that we can promote you better?"

If he had been an artist of integrity, he would have said, "Thank you, but painting is my hobby, my deepest passion, and I'm not going to sell myself." But he was too poor and also, naturally enough, he had an ego that enjoyed the publicity and controversy.

A deep conflict arose between the demands of his promoters and his soul as an artist, and one evening, at a big dinner party, he simply swept the whole cloth – dinner and all – off the table. When I saw this scene in the movie I was touched by his anger and rage, and I also I felt pity for him, because he could not find a way to live in harmony with his art.

Any artist who becomes successful, even modestly, is going to experience this conflict. Here, I want to mention Salima, a talented woman in her early forties from Sydney, Australia, who has worked for many years as a graphic design and commercial multi-media artist. She did a workshop with me about eight years ago and has returned to Pune for the training this year.

After her first workshop with me, she went home to Sydney, developed her talent as an abstract artist, exhibited in several major galleries and to her surprise and delight her paintings started becoming popular with art collectors and wealthy patrons.

That's when the trouble started, because soon the galleries started giving her feedback: "Please don't use bright red, because this may remind our customers of blood and then they won't buy your paintings. Please use more of this range of colors, because that's what our customers like the most..." and so on.

"Slowly, I became aware that the general public likes to buy paintings that match their living room furniture and their bedroom suites," Salima told me, with a wry smile. "I don't blame them for it – it makes sense for them – but naturally, for the artist, it creates a dilemma: do I go for commercial success or for my authentic creativity? The temptation is to find a winning formula and just stick to it."

Van Gogh never had this problem. His tortured genius remained unrecognized by the public during his whole life, so he was spared any temptation to compromise. Picasso came to terms with public opinion and taste, while Pollock allowed it to destroy him.

Looking at the work of Van Gogh, Picasso and Pollock, you can pick out a few qualities that are essential to creativity and artistic expression:

1) Dissolving boundaries between inner and outer experience.

2) Painting from a state of child-like innocence.

3) Allowing the spontaneous expression of energy, in the moment, without prior intention.

There are many more qualities that you can find in these geniuses but for me these are the most important. Why? Because these qualities are not just keys to creative expression – that in itself would be valuable enough. But their roots go even deeper, into something even more significant, something that is fundamental to the nature of human consciousness itself. Something that explains why Meera, this gypsy-artist who has traveled the world and studied so many different styles of painting, chooses to spend so much of her time in India.

But I'm not going to talk about that now. This is not a lecture in the history and theory of art. It's just that, when I try to explain what I am doing, I have to put things in a certain context otherwise no intellectual understanding is possible, and then there is no point in writing a book.

Now, we can return to our painting training. Today, we are going to invoke the spirit of Jackson Pollock and also, I hope, show how it is possible to overcome one of the difficulties he encountered.

By the way, when I say 'today,' I am referring to one of the early days in the training. I don't want to be more

31

specific. I don't intend to describe the exact sequence of exercises that we follow, day by day, throughout the course. The way I teach is flexible. No two workshops are alike. No two trainings follow the same sequence. So, in this book, I will simply try to cover the main points, giving you an overall impression of how my work develops.

It is my experience that as soon as people pick up a brush, dip it in paint and touch a blank sheet of paper before them, the controlling mind immediately enters with all its attitudes, opinions, beliefs and presumptions. It starts giving orders and telling you where to go, what to paint, how to achieve your goals. Then your freedom is lost.

So, this morning we begin again with dancing in the Naropa pyramid. It will seem strange to outsiders that we spend so much time *not painting* in this training, but in my experience it is essential to keep people rooted in their physical bodies, connected with the earth, and at the same time full of energy and vitality. Dance does all of this and more. It is also an easy way to generate a cheerful mood, which acts as a general atmosphere, or backdrop for our working together.

Then I invite everyone to sit in a circle and we conduct a short sharing session in which people relate their experiences from the day before. I won't go into detail on this particular session. Later on, you will become familiar with the way these sessions happen, and their value.

Then it is time to head for Krishna House roof and, when all the participants are sitting down in front of a fresh, blank sheet of paper, I say to the group: "Today, everything is allowed. Only one thing you cannot do. You are not going to touch any brush on the paper. If you want to use a brush then you can drip the colors from the air. Sometimes, you will feel helpless, because in this way things are constantly happening which you didn't plan and you can only watch it unfold. So welcome the unexpected, the accidental, and stay open to any new direction."

Some people follow my suggestion, holding the brush above the paper and dripping from the air. Others forget about brushes completely and started using their bare hands, daubing the paper with painted fingers. Some use their feet. In this way, they stay in touch with an organic, sensuous feeling that belongs more to the body, less to the mind, more to a childhood state of innocence and playful exploration.

It is satisfying for me to see the totality and enthusiasm with which everyone is participating. When you do things without any real structure it gives you a certain power. You are not following orders, you are allowing freedom and spontaneity, and so, of course, the energy of the group is going to take off and get very high.

We add some lively music and the atmosphere in the room becomes joyous, ecstatic. This is something of a mystery that cannot really be explained: how, here in Pune, people discover the ability to move quickly into states of high, positive, overflowing energy. It must sound a bit strange to those who have never been here, but I hope, as this book progresses, you can fathom the reasons for it.

"Yes, stand up, dance, shake, walk around, do whatever connects you with your energy, your ecstasy," I say, encouragingly. "Then, when you are ready, go back to your paper and continue to paint. Just explore, try it out."

It is a beautiful session. Each person's expression is different and everyone is absorbed in the experiment. There is nothing stale, bored or borrowed, and this reminds me of something that I noticed in the movie about Jackson Pollock. If it was an accurate portrayal of the artist's life, he did not reach this state of ecstasy and freedom. Even if he broke away from the conventional rules of art – doing his 'drippy, drippy' thing in the air without touching the canvas – still there was calculation in his work: this color goes here, that color goes there. He was not totally empty.

After a while, of course, he got bored – for how long can you do 'drippy, drippy'? – and then, in his frustration, he dashed out all his energy on the canvas in a kind of catharsis. That's one reason why people were touched by his paintings, because of this quality of sudden expression. Modern man lives such a restricted and regulated life, hemmed in by so many rules and timetables, naturally, he feels attracted to an artist who seems to have broken free of restraint.

Jackson Pollock offered the right thing to the world with his action painting, only he couldn't continue beyond it. To me, this is perfectly understandable: action without awareness, without consciousness, is bound to run into a dead end. He started drinking heavily, because he needed inspiration from somewhere, but for how long can one be inspired by alcohol? There is a limit. And when the effect of the alcohol is over, what are you? Just a bum.

One thing I have learned over the years is that if art is going to fulfil you it has to have deep roots inside you, because only there can you connect with the fountain, the well, of your unique expression. It can't be just a mental concept, a clever idea, or an emotional catharsis. And the problem is that modern art has become exactly this: a succession of clever ideas. That's why I gave it up and started looking for something deeper.

Many years ago, I used to belong to a group of artists in Spain called Tolmo. We had a gallery in Toledo – it still exists – and we were leftists, which was rather risky at the time because General Franco was still alive and imposing his fascist dictatorship on the whole country.

We viewed ourselves as a sincere and dedicated group of 'modern artists,' and even though I eventually left the Tolmo group, I still carried the feeling in my heart that I was part of a worldwide radical artistic movement. This feeling stayed with me until just a few years ago, when I decided to visit La Biennale di Venezia. The art exhibition staged by La Biennale is a huge event, with invitations to artists from all over the world, and I was eager to see what they were presenting.

But that exhibition finished me. It destroyed the idea I'd been nursing inside me that I was a 'modern artist,' part of an international movement that had something valuable to share with the world.

It felt so empty, so meaningless. For example, at the exhibition I saw this huge video screen showing a sandy beach with trees blowing in the wind, and suddenly two women came onto the beach and started beating each other. That's all that was shown: just these two women beating each other. One fell down, stumbled, tried to get up and was then beaten back down again. Blood was oozing from their faces. It was so sad.

Another thing I saw, by a famous conceptual artist, was a canvas oozing with a mass of thick brown liquid. Next to the canvas was a photo of some men killing a cow. The artist had thrown cow's blood onto the canvas and that's what it was all about. That was his statement.

I was shattered by what I saw, because these two exhibits were not exceptions. They were typical of the general approach.

"So this is the direction that modern art is taking?" I thought to myself, and in that moment I lost interest.

This was years ago, but the trend over the last few decades has not changed. It's not always so violent, so depressing, but it stays in the realm of mental ideas.

For example, recently I heard that in London somebody won the annual Turner Prize – described as "one of the most important and prestigious awards for the visual arts in Europe" – with an entry of a vacant room. In this room, the lights go on and off at regular intervals. On for five seconds. Off for five seconds. That's it.

A few years earlier, a well-known British artist, Damien Hirst, won the same prize for a sheep that he had cut in half and preserved in formaldehyde. In other exhibits, he did the same with cows. I don't know what it is that these modern artists have against cows! Such peaceful creatures, yet they seem to attract the worst forms of behavior.

So I gave it up, that whole world, as well as my image as a progressive artist, because everything continues to go in the same direction: tooth and nail competition to come up with the latest bizarre idea, the newest conceptual twist, the biggest shock.

Moreover, these artists don't try to share new insights with their audiences. Instead, they combat the public: if you don't like my work then it simply shows you are stupid – you don't have enough intelligence to understand it. Naturally, no one wants to fall into that category so, like the old, old story of the king's invisible clothes, everyone tries to appreciate the genius of the modern artist.

Well, as you can see, I have returned to the lecture hall in spite of my good intentions to stay out of it. But please don't misunderstand me. I'm not saying that all art has to be joyful, beautiful and ecstatic. I'm saying that art, as a fulfilling and creative experience, needs to express something deeper than clever concepts generated by intellectual and neurotic minds.

So, then, the question arises: how to find this depth? How to help people experience something more than the mind? I could try and explain my whole approach right now, but as I said before, I'm afraid it would end up sounding like another theory, or another clever idea. So instead, I ask your patience and return to the group room.

At the beginning of the next session on Krishna House roof, the participants are supplied with another fresh sheet of paper for another new beginning. It's an important quality of my training to give people permission to use as much paint and paper as they need, creating an atmosphere of freedom and abundance.

"Now I invite you to remember your inner longing for beauty and your desire to express it," I tell the group. "You can paint in any way that appeals to you, using whatever colors convey your sense of beauty."

I don't explain why I am emphasizing beauty at this point, because this will spoil the surprise. The truth is, I want them to create something to which they feel personally attached, so that they can experience what it is like to transcend the attachment, by giving the painting to someone else to work on.

Up to now, their paintings have been wild and chaotic, so there is not much personal investment. You can easily give

36

away something like that. But when you bring in the longings of your heart, your attempt to connect with beauty and express it, an exercise like this has a much stronger impact.

There is another, equally important, reason for introducing this exercise. Even now, at this early stage of the training, with so much freedom to explore, people are revealing their personal tendencies, developing routines and habits – the way they move the brush, the type of colors they use, the kind of shapes and forms they create on the paper.

Giving your painting to someone else cuts through such tendencies in a direct and dramatic way.

I let them paint for about an hour, then ask them to stop.

"Please stand up and look for a moment at what you have created."

In the next moment, I am going to ask them to exchange paintings with the person opposite, but before I can do so a young American woman, Rajani, starts crying.

When I ask her what is happening, she says sadly, "I was really excited at the idea of painting something beautiful. I went with my energy, but it didn't turn out the way I expected. I got lost, then I felt sad, because I realize... I don't know how... how to do it."

This kind of situation is typical in my trainings. Here I am, carefully setting up an exercise with the intention of giving people a certain experience and then, suddenly, another issue pops up and the whole direction shifts.

Personally, I welcome unplanned changes. I have no difficulty with them. It keeps the training alive and full of surprises. But it does create problems when trying to make a coherent record of my work in written form.

In the past, many people have asked me to write a book and to make some kind of manual – a training manual – so that those who don't do my groups can follow the stages and have the same experience.

But, as you may have noticed, life does not come with a manual. It does not follow logical steps. It keeps changing, mutating, in unexpected ways. One moment you're happy.

Next, you're so sad. One moment you're in a love, think life is wonderful and this time it's going to last forever; next, you're nursing a broken heart and wondering what went wrong. One moment you want to paint, next, you feel paralyzed and you don't even know why.

In this context, I can't say to Rajani "Okay, well, thank you but we'll have to deal with this later on because right now I have something else in mind."

Her emotion, her tears, are manifesting here, now. This is the moment to catch them. Later on, if I say, "Now Rajani, what was it?" then her tears may be dry, her mood changed, her focus on something entirely different. And I know from years of experience that the frustration Rajani is expressing is very, very common, and it will be challenging for our group to look at it.

So the planned exercise goes on the backburner, I invite everyone to leave their paintings, come and sit in a circle in the middle of the room, and I address Rajani.

"We have very fixed ideas around creativity – what is creativity, what is beautiful – and we don't realize that all of these ideas are cultivated and borrowed," I explain. "They are not authentic. They're not coming from your original source because that source has been ignored. Instead, we've been trained since childhood to adopt external values.

"The way you are taught to look at things... Even in children's books, you're given a very structured way to understand the world. You're given pictures with names, labels: this is a cat, dog, tree, apple...

"Before you can even think for yourself, you are loaded with information, taught in a very black and white way: this is a good person, this is a bad person, this is a good thing to do, this is a bad thing to do; this is beautiful, this is ugly.

"Just now, you started off enthusiastically, in a very innocent way, with lots of energy: 'Wow! Now I'm going to do something really beautiful.' But as soon as you started painting, all these old ideas and judgments came flooding into your head and soon you felt crushed by them. Then you

38

were no longer able to do anything, thinking 'I'm no good at this.' Something like that, right?"

Rajani nods and I decide to do a little improvised gestalt therapy. I'm not really a therapist, in a clinical sense, but unless you have some basic know-how about working with people's psychology it's not possible to run a group like this.

Painting is such a mirror. It reflects your whole psyche, and takes you back to those formative years of childhood when you were so vulnerable, so easily hurt, so open to other people's attitudes and ideas. The impressions and wounds from those early days rule your unconscious mind and have to be faced, acknowledged and healed. That's why I call the first stage of my group 'primal painting.'

I invite Rajani to close her eyes and identify two main characters within her: the person who is innocent and the person who is the judge, the critic. This she does quite easily. Then I place two cushions on the floor in front of us. I ask her to pick the one that represents the innocent person and invite her to sit on it, becoming this person.

Pretty soon, I can see that she is relaxing, her heart is being touched and her energy is expanding. It's a child-like space, which Rajani can access easily, being so young and naturally enthusiastic. She has that youthful quality of 'get up and go' so common among Americans.

Next, I ask her to move to the cushion representing the critical person, who, not surprisingly, turns out to be very familiar – her father. He is dominant, always judging the behavior of the innocent child, always thinking that he knows what's best for her.

As I guide Rajani into experiencing the two characters, a key theme emerges. In the father's view, it's very important to know what you're doing, all the time, in every activity, including art.

"You've got to stay on top of it, stay in control," says Rajani, giving him a voice.

In his view of the world, even a creative past-time like painting needs to have an assembly line quality, running towards a certain goal, a certain accomplishment or end product – like patenting a new invention.

But when Rajani sits on the cushion of the innocent child, it's a very different experience.

"The main feeling is one of not knowing," she says, simply.

"Good. This is a very precious quality that I want to encourage and support," I reply. "Almost all of us have been trained to think like your father. But the creative process doesn't work like that. In fact, creativity cannot happen unless you get in touch with the space of not-knowing, which is a mystery, a gap, a kind of drowning into the isness of the here and now…"

Sometimes, when I hear myself speaking, I really wonder where these words are coming from. English is not my native language, but still the most extraordinary things come out of my mouth. 'Drowning into the isness of the here and now?' If you don't like such terms, I hope you will excuse me, but I can't apologize too much because in fact it expresses exactly what I want to say.

"Out of this mystery, this gap, something new and fresh can emerge," I tell Rajani. "Something not already decided by the mind – that's the beauty of not knowing."

Through the gestalt process, working with the two voices, Rajani comes to an understanding of the struggle inside her, but I'm not yet satisfied. I would like her to feel it on a deeper level. So now I ask her to turn and face the photo of Osho hanging on the wall.

I realize I still haven't explained who Osho is, so it is going to seem a bit odd to introduce him in this way.

"Look at Osho's picture and feel what sentence comes up inside you," I suggest to Rajani.

Please note, dear reader, that I don't say, "Feel what Osho is saying to you."

That would be an entirely wrong approach. I don't see Osho as a religious person at all. It's not like praying to Jesus for help and waiting for his reply.

To me, Osho is a mirror. Somehow, looking into his eyes, you are thrown deeper into yourself. Even though he is no longer alive, looking at his picture can act like a bridge to your own inner world, helping you connect with your essence. Don't ask me how this happens -- I have no answer.

Rajani looks at Osho and, after a while, says "It's okay not to know."

Then she breaks out into a big smile and laughs, and that's when I know she has really got it. She is accepting and supporting the innocence inside herself. She recognizes the value of this quality that she has been pushing down, condemning, and now her whole value system is shifting.

She can see that 'not knowing' has lots of possibilities and potential. It's deeper than borrowed knowledge, it connects more with meditation, mystery and creativity, and its part of a developing journey where you don't necessarily know what the next step is going to be.

I have been in this space myself so many times, because I, too, slip into this old idea that creativity has to have the flavor of doing, achieving, making it – especially when I have a deadline, like getting paintings ready for an exhibition. This 'doing' is all society knows. Nobody is supporting the gap.

And, of course, when people sign up for a painting group and nothing is happening, some of them get really afraid: "My god! I'm not being creative. Look, all these other people are busy painting, producing some great works of art, and I'm not doing anything. I can't make it!"

Here, I really ought to mention Fulwari, the gentle ghost, who has been silently participating in my painting trainings for the past seven years continuously. She can sit for an hour in front of a blank piece of paper, doing nothing, waiting for an impulse to arise. And if it doesn't come, she doesn't paint. She waits. She doesn't care about time or productivity. But she is Japanese, not American, and embodies the Eastern spiritual quality of endless patience… if not in this life, then perhaps in the next.

This year, Fulwari is my main helper.

41

Rajani's issue has been dealt with to her satisfaction, and mine, so it is time to resume the experiment of letting go attachments. "Go and stand beside the painting of the person who is working opposite you," I tell the group. "Look at this painting for a while... take it in... receive it... then, when you are ready, sit down and continue painting."

There are a few murmurs of surprise, one person laughs and someone cries aloud, 'Oh no!' But, willingly or unwillingly, everyone is prepared to face the challenge. I let them paint for half-an-hour, then invite them to return to their own paintings – to inspect the transformation.

"Receive the painting as it is now," I gently guide them. "Check that you are standing in a natural way, shoulders relaxed, not tense, breathing deeply, and receive the painting... Now, close your eyes and connect with your feelings. Do you like what has happened to your painting? Do you have a 'yes' for it? Or do you hate it? Do you have a 'no' for it?"

Next, I ask them to leave everything and follow me downstairs into the basement of the building where there are a few padded, soundproofed rooms especially designed for making noise without disturbing the neighbors or the rest of the meditation resort.

When everyone has arrived, I ask them to find the partner with whom they exchanged paintings and to stand facing each other.

"Even if you think that you had a 'yes' to what was done to your painting, it's not really true, it's basically a lie," I tell them. "It's just not possible *not* to have a 'no.' Even if somebody did beautiful work on your painting, still, it's not you, and when it's not you then you can find a 'no' inside very easily, because this person can never be you.

"So now I want you to ask yourself a question: if you did not find the 'no' just now, why not? Look and see. Is it really because you feel 'yes,' or is it because we have been forced all our lives to say 'yes,' trained to be tolerant toward others, to avoid conflict, like some social formality, like a polite little boy or girl? If this is the case, then your 'yes' has no meaning, no guts, it's not worth a damn.

"I want you to connect with your 'no' and put it out. I want you to face your partner and say: 'I don't like what you did to my painting!' You can say many other things: 'You didn't have any sensitivity, you destroyed my work, you stamped all over it,' whatever comes to mind that supports your 'no.' But keep returning to this sentence: 'I don't like what you did to my painting.'"

This is something I learned from Osho: to be an authentic individual you have to shatter the superficial, social 'yes' and connect with your 'no.' And this 'no' is present in all of us. Naturally, because how many times as a child you had to say 'yes' when you meant 'no'? How many times, even as an adult, you had to stand before some boss, some policeman, some power figure, smile and say 'yes sir' when you wanted to say 'fuck off, you idiot!'

The 'no' is there, and only after expressing your 'no,' will you be able to connect with a genuine 'yes,' not otherwise. The real power and energy of creativity lies in an authentic 'yes,' but unless you can first create space for it with a loud 'no!' it will not be able to manifest itself. It will be crushed under the weight of a phony 'yes' and a fake, diplomatic smile.

The room explodes with noise as everyone dives into the experiment. Some people find their 'no' easily and put it out with full emotion. For others, it's not so easy. They don't want to offend or hurt the other person. As I pass by Alexandra, the big Greek blonde, she says to me pleadingly, "But Meera, it really is okay! I really like what he did to my painting."

Her partner for this exercise is Sakaama, a distinguished-looking Greek man of about sixty. He was a banker in Athens and later retired to become a commercial painter in the Greek islands, where he paints mainly seascapes. He has a heart condition and this, says Alexandra, is another reason why she doesn't want to say 'no to him. She's afraid he can't take it.

43

But I look at Sakaama and he is smiling, very much at ease, centered and relaxed in himself.

"Don't worry about Sakaama, he is perfectly able to take care of himself," I tell Alexandra. "Whether you know it or not, you have a 'no' inside, so take this exercise as an excuse to give it a voice."

"I don't think I can," she implores, but I stand closely behind her, supporting her back with my body, putting my arms around her, my hands resting on her belly.

"Trust the exercise," I tell her. "Find your 'no.' You can let it out now. It's safe."

Almost immediately, a total transformation comes over Alexandra. Where, one moment before, there was a politely smiling adult woman, saying 'everything is okay,' now suddenly in my arms there is a miserable, hurt little girl. She cannot even say words, she simply moans loudly, looking at the man in front of her as if he is her father, or perhaps her mother, who tore up her painting.

The moan is deep, coming from her guts, so I feel the need to stay with her until it is time to change over. Now it's the turn of the other partner to say "I don't like what you did with my painting!"

It is a powerful exercise, so simple yet so strong.

Before changing roles, I invite everyone to be silent for a moment, close their eyes and really ask themselves what it is like to express 'no' to another person, and what it is like to receive it.

"To connect with this feeling is important," I explain. "What usually happens, when we get angry, is that we are responding without any self-awareness. Something triggers us, and suddenly we are consumed by the emotion. Then, of course, the other reacts back. And when two parties are trapped in reaction it's an endless game.

"But if you can receive the anger and listen without any judgment, if you can make space for the other, take it in the 'no,' soak in it, receive it, then something different can happen. Then you are not reacting. Then the one who is angry can feel that his voice is being heard and, when this happens, he has room to look at himself. It's like, 'Hey, maybe I also have to look at something.'"

Personally, I have found this to be a very useful exercise in my own life, in relating to others, whenever I am angry with them, or they are angry with me. It transforms the whole quality of the encounter.

But in this particular exercise the real surprise comes when, after both partners have expressed their 'no,' I invite them to switch to 'yes.'

"Now use the sentence: 'I like what you did to my painting.'"

It's a surprise because, as most people discover, both sentences are true, and both are true together.

Now I am listening to Sangita, the older Japanese woman, who is partnered with Crystal, a 20 year-old American girl. You remember that Sangita told the group how her creativity had been crushed as a girl when she tried to paint the eye of a fish at school.

In the 'no' part of the exercise, which I'd heard briefly before going to help Alexandra, Sangita was using strong language, especially for a polite Japanese lady. She was telling Crystal how, for the first time since her childhood, she'd been able to express what she really wanted to paint and was feeling very content. She'd got in touch with some natural quality of her own through the painting – I remember, it was mainly orange, with many beautiful spots of color and big sweeping movements. It really had some depth.

In a voice trembling with emotion, she said to Crystal, "I really didn't like that you destroyed my beauty. You didn't respect my beauty. You just dumped paint on it – here and there, wherever you thought. I'm really hurt! You had no feeling to listen to my painting. I don't like what you did."

Then Sangita said, "If I had known this exercise would be happening, I would have gone home."

That was strong stuff. Later, Sangita explained to me that she'd made a deep personal commitment to regain her creativity and that's why she didn't leave. It was a big step

45

for her to stay in the exercise, encountering another person, exposing herself, because normally she is a shy, retiring type, always escaping from the crowd, from even the slightest suggestion of disharmony.

Crystal, in her own way, is also a shy type and I could see that her body was shaking while Sangita was saying these things, but she was staying open and receptive. When it was her turn to express her 'no,' she also had lots to say.

"You destroyed the whole feeling of my painting!" she complained. "I poured so much joy and love into it and you ruined it!"

The 'no' was a strong experience for both of them. But what touches me now is the shift that happens when the 'yes' part starts entering, when we use the sentence, 'I like what you did to my painting.' The same reality changes in a miraculous way.

Sangita explains to Crystal that she has discovered something more important than the superficial appearance of her painting.

"I was touched by your quality of warmth," she says softly. "When I saw what you had done, I felt your hand was an extension from your heart and you gave this quality to my painting. So when I received it back, I felt the warmth of this person, the joy of this person. Somehow it has entered my painting and I am happy."

Crystal, when it is her turn, describes how the colors Sangita had thrown around the edges of her painting had somehow made it united, becoming a whole, integrated painting – not just scattered elements.

"I'm happy to get to know you through exchanging our paintings," says Crystal, with genuine warmth. "I feel your presence beside me all the time."

In a way, both of them are saying the same thing: they met through energy, through warmth, through presence, realizing they have similar qualities: shyness, caring and a longing to meet. It was a beautiful session for both of them.

In the group sharing that follows, several people point towards the same experience: the painting doesn't change by

46

saying 'yes' or 'no,' but the gestalt changes, because what you think the other has destroyed can also be seen as a valuable addition – a quality that was missing in your painting. It may also reveal some quality you were avoiding, some denied part in yourself.

"This is not superficial acceptance, swallowing what the other did with a phoney smile," I explain to them. "It's broadening your vision as a painter, seeing what's missing, seeing a quality that you were denying and rejecting as 'no.'"

This exercise is one way to solve Jackson Pollock's predicament of getting stuck with a certain style, because the artist stays open to unexpected influences.

For me, the creative process is all about discovering new perspectives and this is one way to find them – by exchanging paintings. I am constantly trying to open myself to the new, because I know that one of the most fulfilling experiences as a painter is to discover and express a quality, a value that nobody has seen before. You have discovered it, only you can see it, and now you want to share it with others.

I'm going to explain it in a different way: you go to a bookshop, or gift shop, and look at a display of pretty postcards. There's a certain formula about commercial beauty: one third is ocean and waves, one third is sky, clouds and sunsets, the rest some nice gardens and cute animals. This is a common, predictable kind of beauty. Everybody knows it.

As a creator, I want to transmit a feeling of fresh beauty, fresh discovery, like uncut diamonds. And everybody has this possibility, this potential, because everybody is different, everybody's creative expression is unique. What you can discover, nobody else can discover.

That's why a group like this is so interesting, because everyone is pouring their unique contributions into one pool, broadening their own understanding, being provoked by others to discover new things within themselves.

It's like an artists' commune in nineteenth century Paris. Or perhaps I should say, like a romantic's idea of such a commune, because apart from those artists who joined the Paris communards in the revolutionary uprising of 1871 – when Paris declared itself as separate from the rest of France – no such commune really existed.

Many brilliant artists banded together in times of adversity. For example, some of the best Impressionists – Claude Monet, Edouard Manet, Paul Cezanne, Antoine Guillaumin, Camille Pissarro, James McNeill Whistler – campaigned vigorously together when their works were rejected by the jury of the 1863 Beaux-Arts Salon in Paris, resulting in the famous Salon des Refusés. Many of them, too, painted together for a while – Van Gogh with Gaugin, Cezanne with Pissarro – but there was never a commune.

Artists, generally, are too prickly and too proud to stay together very long. And when Van Gogh invited Gaugin to Arles, in the south of France, with the intention of forming such a commune, his mercurial and unbalanced temperament proved a danger to them both – first he threatened Gaugin with a razor, then he mutilated his own ear.

Looking back over the centuries, one can see that artists, by and large, have been a lonely and isolated bunch of individuals. Alas, it seems easier for people to be brothers in arms than brothers and sisters in art.

That's one reason why I love my painting courses and trainings so much. Because for a little while, for a few days or weeks, all these strangers become a group, a commune, an organic unity, discovering together the joy of artistic expression and, paradoxically, through this togetherness, finding their own individual uniqueness.

These apparent opposites, togetherness and individuality, contain a hidden harmony, a secret dance, and this brings me to the theme of the next chapter.

Chapter 3

Dance of Opposites

White and black.
Light and dark.
Good and bad.
Beautiful and ugly.

As children, we are taught to believe in a world of opposing forces that are fighting with each other: good guys and bad guys, cops and robbers, saints and sinners; the good, the bad and the ugly. Philosophers have an expression for it: 'conflict dualism,' the idea that this whole universe is nothing but a battleground for the forces of good and evil, endlessly at war with each other.

Of course, it is all nonsense. The only war you'll ever find in this beautiful existence is the one that rages inside the human skull, and it is this inner conflict that we project outwards onto the world, onto nature and all that surrounds us.

In reality, nature is one harmonious whole. It is we who are split, divided. We say 'this is good,' and 'that is bad,' then try to cling to the good and reject the bad, not realizing that it is futile because in the first place the division does not exist. As a result, we end up repressing our own energy, destroying our own vitality.

Several of the exercises that I do early in the training are designed to dissolve this idea of conflict between opposites and undo the damage it does to our creativity.

For example, about three days into the training, I invite all the participants to hang one of their paintings on the low wall that surrounds our space on Krishna House roof. I ask them to choose the energy ecstasy paintings they did on the first day, which have more of an earthy, raw, primeval feeling. It's difficult to recognize these paintings as beautiful, because the participants created them spontaneously, moving with their energy, experimenting with being a child again, and that's what I need right now – something not so beautiful.

Many of these paintings are muddy in color, brown, black, dark and heavy, with no meaning, no direction and seemingly dull. But of course people enjoyed that session, when they were allowed to be wild and free, throwing paint here and there – no parents in the house to keep things tidy and under control, so the children can do what they want.

The second painting which they did is more connected with beauty. It can be recognized as beautiful, even after they exchanged with other people. That's why I want them to hang this dirty-looking painting, because, as yet, you can't give any structure or evaluation to it.

I ask each person to stand in front of his or her painting and look at it.

"Address this painting as if it's a person," I explain. "Speak in gibberish, in nonsense language, and put out all your judgments: 'this is not good, this is ugly, this is meaningless, anybody could make a painting like this, this is dark...' All your negative opinions. And do it with your fists closed." I add this because when the fist is closed, then everything inside you is closed and you can connect only with negative judgments. Try it yourself and see.

Within seconds the room is filled with noise, as everyone starts to speak at once. It doesn't look as though anyone has a problem with this exercise; there are lots of opinions flooding out towards the paintings.

I let them carry on for a few minutes, then ask them to stop. "Now, I invite you to locate the part of your painting that you dislike the most," I tell the group. "Go up to your painting, touch this part with your hands, look at it, make sure that in your opinion this is the most ugly part, define it clearly.

"Now take a few steps back and reverse the roles. Let this ugly part look at you. You are not watching the painting, the painting is watching you. Just be soft, passive, receptive and let in whatever comes to you from the ugly part."

This is my personal variation of an ancient meditation technique – I think it may be Buddhist in origin – to shift from watching to being watched. Usually, when you watch, you connect strongly with your mind, its opinions and criticisms.

You must have noticed: just walking down a street, looking at other people, the mind offers a continuous stream of opinions about them... 'this one is pretty, that one looks sad, this one is ugly...' You do not know any of these people, but that doesn't prevent you from instantly labeling them.

You're going out through the mind toward the object, but when you shift from watching to being watched, the whole gestalt changes.

"With eyes open, without blinking and with soft, unfocused vision, soak up whatever feeling is coming to you from your painting. And when you close your eyes, feel it inside your body. It's more like a body experience than an idea in your head. See if you can locate where this ugliness is being mirrored in you.

"If you let your body mirror the ugly part of your painting, what movement does it make? What form? What shape? Allow yourself to explore and then take a position that gives it expression, like a statue or sculpture."

I watch as people slowly contort their bodies to reflect what they are feeling. Many of the human statues around the room are grotesque, as limbs are turned inward or upward in a twisted way, while others are reaching out, or somehow holding themselves. I ask them to freeze in this position, because in this way understanding happens more deeply – not just in the intellect, but in the cells of your body.

This part of the exercise is now complete, so I ask people to melt the frozen statues, come alive again, and shake their hands, arms, legs and heads to break the energy pattern and the mood they have captured.

"Now, please stand again in front of your painting, look at it, and find the part that is the most beautiful. Find a spot, even a small bit will do, or a big area – big or small, it doesn't matter. When you have found it, go up to the painting and touch it…"

In this way, we repeat the exercise. Now it is the beautiful part that watches the painter that is received by the painter, and it is the feeling of beauty that is expressed through the body and its movements.

For this stage, I take more time, encouraging them to enjoy the feeling and explore where beauty can be located in their own bodies, and how the body will express this in the form of a statue.

"When you make a statue in the shape of beauty with your body, open your eyes and look at the beautiful part of your painting. Let the beautiful part of your painting watch the sculpture. So the beautiful painting is meeting the beautiful sculpture."

The body remembers this feeling of beauty, or, perhaps should I say that the body has always had this feeling. It's intrinsic. It comes with the package when we are born. It's just that we have forgotten it. It got lost back there, somewhere, under all the nappy changing and potty training. But it's there, in everyone, and that's why I don't like teaching art techniques directly, because you are imposing something from outside when what you really need to do is uncover something that already exists inside. This is the first thing to do. Techniques can come later.

Right now, imposing any technique is going to disturb a person's uniqueness of expression. That uniqueness has already been disturbed too much. What needs to happen is more like diamond cutting – exposing a jewel inside a rock.

I remember a beautiful story that Osho told many times in his discourses – a story about Michelangelo, the great

Italian artist. He was passing in front of a shop where marble was sold and he became interested in a strange piece that the shopkeeper had been unable to sell to anyone, because it looked useless for sculpting.

It became one of his greatest works of art: the Pieta, where Jesus has just been taken down from the cross and lies dead in his mother's arms. When he saw the completed sculpture, the shopkeeper could not believe it was the same piece of marble and asked Michelangelo how he could possibly have seen the form of the sculpture in such a misshapen piece of marble.

Michelangelo simply said "Jesus cried out to me from inside the rock, saying 'Unburden me!'"

Historically speaking, I don't think Osho's version of the story is accurate. As I recall, it was the marble rock used by Michelangelo for his statue of David that was considered a ruined stone, having been abandoned forty years earlier by another Florentine sculptor. Marble for the Pieta was taken directly from the quarries under Michelangelo's personal supervision and put to immediate use.

But in any case, the way Osho uses the story, it's not about history or art. It's about human beings. It reflects the situation of everyone. That's the point Osho is making: we are all so busy trying to impose things on human beings from outside – religious beliefs, national identities, moral values, all kinds of roles, titles and labels – that we never bother to look inside and see what's already been given to us by existence.

If I am going to introduce Osho in any particular way, this may be the best: as a kind of master sculptor who specializes in helping to release beautiful individuals who are trapped inside common rock. The rock is the garbage that is heaped on us by society; the false identity that is imposed on us from birth: "this is your name, this is your nation, caste, creed, color, political party, football club, social ranking…" and on and on and on.

According to Osho, you cannot hope to be an awakened spiritual being unless and until you break through all this

53

crap and discover your individuality. And according to me, you cannot hope to find your own unique expression of creativity until you discover your individuality. So you see, Osho and I are more or less in the same business.

"Okay, now, move quickly around the room and stand in front of the ugliest painting you can find," I tell the group. "You can choose any painting except your own."

Speed is essential, here, because it does not allow the mind to come in. You are forced to make a snap decision from your guts. Pretty soon, everyone has found a painting and while a few stand singly, most are grouped in front of two or three paintings. Clearly, there is some agreement here about what is ugly.

"Say to this painting, in your mother tongue, 'How ugly you are!' Let it out."

This is my experience: when you keep something hidden in the unconscious part of your mind, not fully acknowledged, not fully expressed – like judgments about ugliness, for example – then it slowly becomes poisonous and cripples your vitality. When you express the same thing totally and consciously, with full awareness, a miracle happens: the feeling dissolves, shifts and transforms. Really, it's just trapped energy that needs to be released, healed, purified.

As far as painting is concerned, that which you judge as ugly can turn into a valuable quality that was missing in your own style of painting. Acceptance and relaxation changes your vision, ugliness suddenly turns into depth, revealing hidden potential and possibilities. One of the main purposes of this exercise is to help people grasp this truth through their own experience.

I repeat the steps we did before, asking people to stop the gibberish after a few minutes, then be silent and receive the feeling from the painting.

"Now find the most beautiful painting in the room – quickly!"

But this time, after they have chosen a painting, I give everyone the opportunity to reconsider. "A quick first impression may be not enough where beauty is concerned," I tell them. "So now you can take your time, move around slowly, find the most beautiful painting."

The group does not have such a clear consensus where beauty is concerned and people scatter through the room, standing here, standing there. Several have difficulty even choosing a painting. When, finally, everyone has picked one, I repeat the steps as before, receiving the feeling of beauty, then ask everyone to return to their own painting.

"Notice if anything had changed in the way you look at your own painting," I invite the participants. Then, after a few minutes, I gather everyone in the middle part of the room, which is covered with mattresses and cushions. We sit in a circle on the floor and I ask people to share what they experienced.

The painting that attracted most judgments from people as the ugliest one belongs to Sivan, a lively, bubbly young Israeli woman in her mid-twenties.

"I knew people would pick my painting as the ugly one!" exclaims Sivan, with a half-embarrassed, half-defiant smile. At the very beginning of the group, during the first sharing, Sivan had explained how, as a child, she had carefully chosen only those activities in which she was the best and, having always considered herself bad at painting, she avoided it. She signed on for this group in order to break her old pattern.

But her painting wasn't bad in the sense of illustrating lack of talent or capacity. It was simply black all over.

Now she tells me, "The other day, we'd been painting a long time, and my painting was full, and then you said 'you have a few seconds left, express yourself, how you feel right now.' And I felt I wanted a fresh beginning, so I just covered the painting in black.

"Today, I come to the roof and all the paintings are hanging on the walls! I thought 'Oh my god, this is the end!' But worse was coming! And when you asked people to choose the ugliest I knew... Then I laughed, because I did what I had to do, I expressed my feeling without worrying

55

what others will think. And I thought: if it's hard for somebody to feel this black and take it inside him, it's his issue, not mine."

Sivan has a point. Black is just a color. It is neutral, neither beautiful nor ugly. The fact that so many people have negative ideas about black says something about our upbringing, education and age-old prejudices, not about the color itself.

As the sharing continues, many people report a change in the way they view their own paintings. Amrita, an Italian woman of about 40, who lives in Brazil with her Indian husband and their small daughter, says she experienced a big shift in the beginning of the exercise, when judging part of her painting as ugly.

"When I became receptive to it, suddenly I felt love and compassion coming to me from that ugly spot. I was almost shocked by the power of it. That was something very surprising and revolutionary," she declares.

"Coming back to my painting after going around the room was also very important for me, because visually I can now see a beauty and subtlety in that ugly part which I didn't see before. Before it was dark and dismal. Now it has depth and mystery."

This kind of feedback is important for me, because it shows the effectiveness of the exercise. If even one person can achieve a visual breakthrough of this kind, it's really great.

Now it's lunchtime and I give the participants a little homework, asking them to take their paintings with them into the resort and show them to at least a dozen people. "Just hold it up in front of them and say, 'This is my painting, I want you to look at it.' Then, after receiving their response, just say 'thank you,' and move on. With this exercise you are exposing yourself, you are declaring your isness, your existence, and you are ready to receive people's opinions and see whether you are affected or not."

I have watched this exercise many times in the past and it's always interesting to see people's reactions. Many people are afraid to share their honest feelings. Instead, they often deflect the issue, changing the subject instead of talking about the painting. Immediately, they will say, "Oh, you're doing Meera's painting group! How is it going? Blah, blah, blah..." They take the conversation away from the point, start talking about something else.

Just as people are leaving the room, Santosh, a young Israeli guy, walks straight up to me, holding his painting in front of him, and says, "Meera, this is my painting. I want you to look at it."

This is a good opportunity to emphasize the strength of the exercise, so I purposely try to crush him by criticizing his painting: too much yellow here, too much confusion there... But his eyes hold steady and he doesn't quit, give up or move away, nor does he start to fight with me. He receives my feedback.

"I just don't get it, what is this painting supposed to be?" I ask him, finally, scratching my head in mock bewilderment.

"This is me."

I am surprised and deeply touched by his answer, so then it is easy for me to switch roles and appreciate his painting: how the yellow sparkles in contrast to the dark parts, and so on.

But it's not always criticism that people find hard to accept. Sometimes praise is even more difficult. For example, the painting that was chosen by many people as the most beautiful this morning was by a little Taiwanese woman called Indu, causing her to practically go into a state of shock.

"I don't believe it!" she kept saying during the sharing.

This is also a typical reaction. We tend to accept criticism more easily than praise because we are accustomed to being criticized from childhood. This brings me to an essential point: praise and criticism look very different to us, feel very different to us – just think, how desperately we seek the former and try and avoid the latter! But they have basically the same function. They give shape to our personalities as

57

we grow up. Ego, the idea of self, who you think you are, is developed in response to these opinions, given by others.

Take away all these opinions, and who are you? That's the root of every spiritual quest, every inquiry into your own true identity.

But I am straying onto a subject that would take a book in itself to deal with. Coming back to the subject of beauty: when ideas about beauty are shared by many people they become collective and this, in turn, creates a specific culture. In the Japanese culture, in which I grew up, beauty was such an intrinsic part of our collective social attitudes that I did not value it at all.

Well, that is not quite true. I still remember, when I was very young, taking my baby sister Taeko by the hand and climbing the stairs of a huge storage house that belonged to my maternal grandparents. It was very ancient, with thick walls to keep out the heat and the cold, thereby maintaining a constant temperature for the umeboshi plums, miso and soy sauce that was stored there in large quantities.

My grandparents were the head family of Noto, a rather wealthy fishing village and one of the chief ports on the Eastern coast of Japan for deep-sea boats heading North to Hokkaido or Russia to catch fish.

But I was not interested in the plums or the miso. I would lead Taeko to the entrance and then, with both of us pushing together, we would slowly open the heavy sliding door and enter a treasure trove of mysterious objects from past generations, like old samurai costumes, complete with armor and swords, hanging like ghosts from the walls.

It was very silent in there and, in among the old furniture and discarded family heirlooms, I found many paintings, most of them done by my uncle, who died in the Second World War. He was painting in oils, something relatively new to Japanese art – the technique was imported around the beginning of the twentieth century – and he'd created an impressive array of seascapes, landscapes and portraits.

The eyes that looked at those paintings were innocent and filled with wonder. I did not know, then, that I would grow up to study painting, nor that I would one day turn my back on the traditional Japanese love of beauty in art – dismissing it as too decorative and superficial – favoring instead the turmoil, intensity and suffering expressed in the modern Western approach.

It is worth telling the story of my development as an artist – I will try and make it brief – because it is also a dance of opposites, spanning two different cultures with dramatically different values. So we will take a little detour, for a while, along the path of my life. It may offer some valuable lessons.

I guess I must have been six or seven years old when I led Taeko on these explorations, and by the time I was ten I was already discarding the culture of my home country in favor of Europe. My father, a seaman working on oil tankers for 35 years, brought the influence of the West into our house, with all kinds of news, gifts, music and fashions from strange and distant countries. I remember when he first danced the Tango with my mother in front of us – something unheard of in our village!

My first adventure into Western art concerned a French ballerina doll, which I loved very much, and this I painted in class at school and was rewarded by having my painting displayed in the school corridor. My ballerina had a short pink costume – I think it's called a tutu – with little pink panties underneath and big strong legs.

I remember standing in the school corridor, looking at this painting and being touched by my own work: what a powerful impression, what big legs, how strongly this child can paint! It was a feeling of watching myself watching my own painting.

But I had not entirely abandoned the Eastern approach to art. Around that time, my grandmother had renovated twelve fusuma – beautiful, paper sliding-doors in our home's guest room – and I was attracted and intrigued by the purity of their whiteness.

Someone had been using a calligraphy set in the room – in those days it was still quite common to write letters in the traditional way, with a calligraphy brush – and had left a big pot of black ink and several brushes on the floor.

I don't know what happened to me. I took a big brush, dipped it in the black ink and went around all the new white doors, the brush dancing in my hands, painting out of pure joy. These days, I'd call it "energy ecstasy painting." My grandmother called it a crime and I had to stand in a corner for a long time as punishment, but inside I felt very satisfied and not at all guilty. Looking back, I can see it had to do with my creativity, a feeling of strength and pride that I'd been able to express something from within, something entirely mine – a spontaneous outpouring of energy in the same way that I teach in my painting groups.

As a teenager, I always got good marks at school for painting, routinely bagging first prize, but I considered myself best at drawing. I used to travel 50 kilometers from my home town to study charcoal drawing with a gifted artist, because I knew I would not be able to pass the entrance examination to art university without it – only one in twenty applicants was admitted to the one I'd chosen.

I had no feeling for colors, or so I thought, until one art teacher, who loved me very much, praised my natural talent at finding aesthetic color combinations. At first, I was angry with him – I thought he was teasing me! But he insisted and gradually it became clear to me that he was right.

That teacher was an unusual man. Unless he was teaching at our school he never got up during the day – much too noisy, according to him – and preferred to live only in the night, going to bed at dawn when others awoke. He created a scandal by marrying a local geisha and she proved to be as strange as he was. As she got older, she used to dress him up in a fine kimono and white socks, and send him off to the local whorehouse to enjoy the delights of younger women. "To be a real man you have to play with geishas," she explained.

I must not indulge in too many anecdotes or I will lose the thread of my tale, but in those early years many of my teachers were eccentrics and I think it is valuable to know

60

such people. They are society's misfits and they broaden one's mind beyond the collective, limited mentality of 'normal life.'

Leaving school, I went to study at Musashino Art University in Tokyo, living in the house of my mother's best girlfriend and her husband. He was an artist and I had acquired a very strong belief – I don't know where from – that in order to study with such people I must serve them like a disciple, even like a servant, so I was always cleaning the house and doing the dishes. Of course, they loved me very much!

I studied for a bachelor's degree, specializing in oil painting, which meant that Western art dominated my studies. Naturally, I learned many things, but the real teaching came from two professors: Fujii and Murai.

It was Professor Murai who taught me not to get too focused on form and technique, but instead to get in touch with my inner creative impulse, my energy, and follow it through to its full expression. He was a modern artist, painting mainly in three major colors, using triangles and squares as basic forms.

Professor Fujii painted only empty chairs. That's all he did, because to him the chair was a challenge to convey something invisible. In his works, even if it was only a chair, you were able to feel – if you were sensitive and alert – the person who had been sitting in it. He painted this way all his life.

He also taught me to be a free spirit, especially with money. He was absolutely generous and a gentleman. He was so generous, he would take us all to a bar, pull out the biggest bill and say to the waiter, "Keep filling the glasses, I don't want any change." He lived like Humphrey Bogart – at least, how Bogart appeared in his movies.

My course also included a class about ancient Japanese paintings and in summer we used to take a trip to Kyoto, one of the oldest cities in Japan. There, in all the temples, they have old paintings, mostly painted on paper doors. This teacher was very sensitive and always took out a handkerchief to cover his mouth while he spoke, because the paintings were not protected – he said the moisture and fumes of our breath could adversely affect them.

One painting that really touched me was by Hasegawa Tohaku. This man painted a triangular cedar with such depth. It's an unusual kind of cedar, with wide branches near the ground and narrowing upwards so that it looks like a triangle, and this he painted with mountain cherry blossoms in front of it, all merging and mingling.

Nobody knows where Hasegawa Tohaku was born, but historians guess he was from my province, Ishikawa – from the place where I was born. He lived in the Momoyama period, during the 16th century, and is now considered to be one of the world's finest artists.

I felt inspired by his paintings. He created such a sense of depth, mystery and vastness of nature in a very beautiful way, even though he often painted in the Sumi-e style, using only black ink on white rice-paper. Just black and white, and yet such amazing pine trees! I got so inspired that since then I have painted many pine trees, in Spain, in Japan, wherever I find them.

But mainly we studied oil painting, Western painting, so after I graduated from the university I decided I must go to Europe, to see some of the great masterpieces. It was 1969 and I was 21 years old. I traveled through Russia, partly to see the Blue Period Picassos in the Hermitage Museum in Leningrad – the city had not yet reverted to St. Petersburg – and partly because I was madly in love with Dostoevsky, Turgenev and the great Russian writers.

Then I went to Oslo to see the paintings of Edvard Munch, a gifted Norwegian artist who helped to develop modern expressionism. In his most powerful work, "The Cry," he's really painted the darkness and craziness inside the human psyche. The main figure, standing alone against an ominous backdrop of red sky and swirling sea, is all eyes and no hair, with pale hands touching the face, either side of a silently screaming mouth – it's really a cry from the depths of human madness.

By now, you can see the direction in which I was headed, with Dostoevesky's dismal view of human nature, Munch's anguish, Picasso's Blue Period... I was falling in love with suffering. I thought art should be darkness, art should reflect those human emotions that normally can't be expressed: deep pain, deep suffering, madness, sorrow and agony. I was not only leaving Japan far behind geographically, but artistically as well. Beautiful flowers and trees? Ha! That's not art. Even my love for Tohaku could not prevent the hardening of my new attitude.

I went to museums and galleries all over Europe – in Copenhagen, Hamburg, Munich, Paris, London and then to Florence, where I thought I would live for a while and start to paint. But first I went to Spain, to see the art of Goya and El Greco, and when I arrived at the train station in Toledo a strange thing happened: I got goose pimples all over my body. I started shivering and suddenly I knew: this is my place. So I dropped all other plans and started living in Toledo, in a pension, a small hotel run by a woman I knew only as 'señora.'

Apart from 'señora' I knew two Spanish words, one was 'hello' and the other, oddly enough, was 'moon' – something I'd remembered from a Spanish TV show that was popular in Japan. Nobody spoke English, let alone Japanese, but I didn't mind. I enjoyed the feeling of being a total stranger.

One day, I was sitting in the main square, making a pencil drawing in a big notebook with all the enthusiasm of a 'real artist' – drawing the houses around me from a top view – when there was big laughter behind me and, simultaneously, a big dog licking my foot.

I screamed, jumped up, turned around and saw a big man with a big black cape, black clothes, black hair, big blue eyes and big nose – everything about the man was big, including his dog.

He was laughing at me, "Ha, ha, ha!"

I got so offended. "Who are you?" I demanded.

"I am an artist.'

"Why are you laughing at me?"

He jabbed a finger in the direction of my notebook. "Are you painting from an airplane or a helicopter? Your perspective is absolutely wrong."

I did not believe him. "If you are talking to me like this, then you'd better show me your own drawings first. Then we can talk."

He took me to his house, showed me his pencil drawings and immediately my newly-born artist's ego fell flat on the floor. They were superb! This was the taste of real art.

Of course, I wanted to learn from him and I thought, "Well, if I am going to be his student I should also be his lover," and sure enough, he very soon fell in love with me. From my teenage years onwards I always knew what kind of man was good for me.

His name was Aroldo and later on he became quite well known in the art world, before switching the main focus of his creative energy to urban architecture and design. He was that kind of man, always reinventing himself, looking for new forms of artistic expression. He was from a Swiss family of artists – his mother was a famous opera singer and his stepfather a sculptor, with pieces in several European museums.

Aroldo and I were in love for a long while. He saw my potential as a painter and was happy to teach me everything he knew, especially about drawing. At the same time, I was modeling for him, because while you are modeling you also learn. He made so many drawings of me, beautiful drawings, mostly nude. I would model for him every day, sometimes for five hours at a single session – nobody does such a thing, normally – because I was so determined to be an artist.

I stayed in Toledo for three years and Aroldo taught me how to bring a new quality to my drawing. His was a modern, existentialist approach. It's not that you copy this and that, or that you understand so much about volume and form, or simplify in the abstract way, but something more mysterious. With his method, the essential 'isness' of the subject is transmitted.

With him, I also learned the beauty of using grey as the dominant color, which later became very important in the self-portrait section of my trainings. I'll talk more about that later.

Aroldo supported my first exhibition in Toledo, in 1971, and introduced me to other artists who formed a group called Tolmo – I talked about it in the previous chapter. They welcomed me as one of them. We had a gallery in Toledo and used to have exhibitions together all over Spain, as well as in Portugal and Switzerland. We also appeared on television. As I said before, Spain was still under Franco, so it was something new to speak up for new directions and new ideas, as we did, without being afraid of the regime. It was really a breath of fresh air.

I was the only woman artist; the rest were men. That's typical of my artist's life; I always felt I had to compete with men and learn from men. Slowly, too, I absorbed their ideology – the need for a new look, a new vision for art. To paint like a photographer was not, they told me emphatically, an authentic artistic approach.

I was drowned into this world, with long discussions and meetings about art, because everybody had his own style, very different from one another, and therefore a different opinion. To be a real artist, you have to establish your own style – this, I learned, is very important from the man's perspective.

So, naturally, I was examining my own work: what is my style? At the time, I was interested in painting like Paul Cézanne, the nineteenth century French artist who is called the father of modern art because he challenged all traditional values. His work grew out of the Impressionist school, but he went far beyond it. His primary concern was the integrity of the painting, emphasizing and analyzing the main forms and structures, and this I translated into my own paintings of Toledo's amazing architecture.

I wish I had more space to tell you more about those exciting days. How poor we were, how we helped each other, exchanging not only ideas about art but also food when we ran out of money. How, too, the local people supported us by buying our paintings – it's a tradition in Spain, even among ordinary folk, to buy original art for your home.

I recall one incident that is typical:

One day, Pablo, a Tolmo member, came to see me while I was painting in my house. After a while, he commented, "It's lunch time, why are you not eating?"

Somewhat embarrassed, I said, "Well, I've run out of money, so I have to skip my lunch."

He shook his head. "This is not possible, that you don't tell me when you are in trouble – this is not friendship!"

Next day, he came by with six Spanish friends, who all bought paintings from me, rescuing me from hunger. In this way, I learned the Spanish attitude: how important it is for friends to take care of each other.

In Toledo, I was poor but I felt rich, because I learned so much about art. It is a unique city, with Muslim architecture as well as Christian and Jewish, because long ago the Moors invaded from Africa and ruled part of Spain, so I found myself surrounded by a wealth of beautiful and challenging subjects to draw and paint.

I lived by the cathedral, on the fifth floor. When I opened my window, I could see a whole panorama of different roofs, spires and wonderful architecture, and when the sun was setting this vista became a golden wonderland, sculptured in dramatic patterns of dark and light, brilliant yellow and gold contrasting with deep shadow.

Now, I really have to break off this tale of an aspiring Japanese artist and return to the group room, because I can see that it is taking too long and will consume the rest of this chapter. But this is a good place to halt, while speaking of opposites, of contrasting darkness and light, because it has been my experience, teaching over many years, that people are programmed by their social education to choose light and avoid darkness.

When you think about it, this is really absurd, because without darkness, how can their be light? Without the contrast of opposites, how can they exist? They are, in reality, two aspects of one phenomenon, inseparable from each other.

Yet I can see, too, how darkness has, since the beginning of time, been associated with fear and danger, starting in the primitive days when man was almost helpless, without weapons, surrounded by wild animals that stalked him in the night. Robbers and all kinds of criminals also used the night to hide their crimes, so even today it is more dangerous to walk in the night than in the day. And, of course, religion capitalized on the situation, equating light with good and darkness with evil, labeling the devil "the prince of darkness."

Acceptance of darkness is difficult for most people because through it they reconnect with ancient fears, with pain, with helplessness and this reflects in their attitude toward painting, regarding black as a dirty, negative color, avoiding dark brown and similar heavy colors. In this way, the colors act as a mirror, because what people are really avoiding is their own depth.

So after the lunch break I take everyone down to the group chambers, under Krishna House, where, since there are no windows, it is easy to create a totally dark environment.

Here are places set out on the floor with a blank sheet of white paper, paints, brushes and unlit candles. Before doing anything else I ask people to stand up, turn and face the padded walls, stretch out their arms and lean against the walls, resting their weight on their hands. Then, when they are ready, to push strongly against the walls.

"Really push the wall," I tell them, switching off the lights and engulfing the room in total darkness. "And as you do so, remember the impossible moments you had in the past, connecting with loneliness, being left alone, maybe

67

abandoned as children, maybe later, as an adult, being overwhelmed by a stronger person, or a hopeless situation…"

Symbolically they are trying to push against darkness and not being able to succeed and so naturally, in their frustration, some people begin to shout and cry and bang their fists against the padded walls, rather like they would in a therapy group dealing with emotional release.

But in this context, I see emotional expression as another way to escape. You are feeling overwhelmed, hopeless, so you want to lose yourself in your emotions. So, after a few minutes, I encourage everyone to stay connected with the feeling without expressing it.

"Just push against the wall and feel it," I say to them. "See the difference between when you are emotional and when you are not. Is there more chance to connect, now, with those unwelcome memories, while you are silently watching what's happening?"

The next step in this exercise offers a very interesting turning point.

"Please slowly turn around and lean with your whole body against the wall. Put your back against the wall and feel supported by the darkness. This darkness is not working against you, this darkness can be a support to you. See if you can relax with it and accept it. Darkness is an eternal quality of existence, a universal principle, neither negative nor positive. And it is always there. From this darkness we come. To this darkness we return."

I wait for about fifteen minutes and then slowly bring up the lights and ask everybody to gather round while I sit in front of a sheet of paper.

"I'm going to show you a little bit of calligraphy," I tell them. "It's going to help you with the coming exercise. In calligraphy, the way you hold and move the brush is important, because it contains all the essential elements: your quality of meditation, your ease of movement, your ability to stay relaxed and centered. See…"

I pick up a brush with two fingers and a thumb, stretch out my arm – without leaning forward, so I remain sitting in a centered and balanced position – and dip the brush into a pot of black ink. I hold the loaded brush above the paper, poised in a neutral position, allowing a gap of a few seconds, and then come down onto the paper with a definite movement, making a bold stroke across the white surface.

"Keep your awareness focused in your hand: which moment your hand wants to move, which moment your hand finishes the stroke and comes back to the neutral position, which moment your hand remains motionless, in a gap," I continue.

"When you are not aware, the result also doesn't come out so well. If you are in a hurry, you don't see the process. If your hand is tense, your mind is tense. But if you are relaxed and aware, you experience each stroke as a meditation, a way of being here and now, in the present moment."

This is the main reason why I like calligraphy, because it teaches awareness. Another reason, relevant to today's session, is that it helps people become friendly with darkness, through using black ink.

The participants return to their seats and I encourage them to experiment with the brush and ink in the way I have suggested. After a while, when I feel they are comfortable with the new medium, I ask them to express, through black paint on white paper, what they experienced in the darkness exercise.

"With this black paint we are taking one more step into darkness, just like going down into an Indian well, with steps circling down inside the walls," I explain.

"Don't try to paint a pretty picture, or feel confined to symbols, but really try and express what you experienced with darkness. Keep your awareness focused in your hand, using the brush in the way I showed you."

After about ten or fifteen minutes, when everyone is engrossed in their work, I turn off the lights "Keep your eyes open and keep painting," I encourage them. "Go deeper into your expression. Let your hand remember the organic quality of touch, surrender to this sensuous feeling of your hand moving over the paper with the brush."

When you do this in darkness, there is more chance that you will remember your child-like quality of touch, because your eyes are taken away. With nothing to see, the mind cannot judge what you are doing, but you can remember, your body remembers, the deeper, earlier and more simple sense of touch. And that's my interest, because everybody has some beauty inside, some child-like qualities, some hidden creative impulse, and these can all be recalled more easily through touch. You are containing them, but you don't remember them through the head.

Then I invite people to experiment: painting with eyes open, painting with eyes closed, both in total darkness. "Look through the painting you are doing in the dark. You can see nothing. You are watching through the darkness, which is not possible. Then close your eyes and continue to paint. What is the difference?

There is a certain difference between the darkness that you see when your eyes are open and the darkness behind your closed eyelids. You can try it yourself. Sometimes, a special darkness meditation is offered in the resort that gives a longer and deeper experience of this, in which you receive the energy of darkness through open eyes. But for now I simply invite the group participants to notice the change.

"Now, keep your eyes closed and I will bring the light in. Don't open your eyes right away, just sense with your eyes closed how even one small light can dispel all the darkness."

This reminds me of one of Osho's observations that struck me very strongly, that darkness has no positive existence of its own; it is only an absence of light. Hence you cannot do anything directly with darkness. If you want to remove darkness from a room you cannot throw it out; instead, you will have to bring light in. If you want to bring darkness into a room you cannot drag it in by the neck; you have to switch off the light.

Whatever you want to do, you will have to do it with light, because the light has existence. Darkness has no existence, and with the non-existential nothing can be done.

Many times, Osho has used this as a metaphor for the spiritual search. You can't do anything directly with the ego, the false personality that prevents us from knowing ourselves. But you can light a flame of awareness inside, becoming more and more conscious, and it is the light of consciousness that dispels the darkness of ego.

I invite people to open their eyes and look softly at the candle, then to light more candles around the room. The atmosphere now has a magical, fairy-like quality, perhaps like a secret birthday party held in a cellar under the house.

"Now take a pot of white paint in your hand, take a clean brush in the other, dip it in the paint, hold your brush in the air and let the white color fall onto your painting," I invite everyone. "You may be surprised, because the light is entering your dark painting without effort."

During the next half-hour, I help people become aware that they can play with light and dark, black and white, in many different ways. Each individual discovers according to his or her likes and dislikes, so they can all experience, in their own ways, without even thinking about it, how the white paint is symbolic of bringing light into darkness.

But this is only half the story. As far as the consciousness is concerned, one has to find a way to move from darkness to light. From the artist's point of view, however, you need flexibility to flow in both directions – from darkness to light, from light to darkness – without getting stuck at either extreme.

In a deeper way, this exercise strengthens your trust that nothing comes to an end, to a full stop. Even if there is total darkness I can bring in the light, even if there's too much light I can bring in the darkness. Thus, without me having to say it directly, an understanding of depth is happening on its own. This is what I want people to discover.

When the exercise is completed, I invite people to sit in a circle and share their experiences. "Sharing doesn't need to be a great thing, so don't stop yourself from speaking just because you're not sure how to put the words together," I say, encouragingly, especially addressing those who's English is poor.

"Try connecting more through the body, through feelings. Even if you don't know how to put it together in words you can start to share from this space, because this is more true, this is more authentic, coming directly from yourself."

Many people share their surprise and also their relief at the experience of suddenly changing from fighting with darkness to feeling how it can be a support. This was an important lesson for almost everyone.

One of the Israelis in the group shares how he identified darkness with a feeling of helplessness about the situation in his home country, and this becomes a trigger for Rafeek, a young German from Bremen.

Rafeek says he feels deep despair about the whole global situation: endless wars between rival nations and faiths, destruction of the environment, poverty, overpopulation... He also feels angry with the politicians and businessmen who exploit these problems.

"Yes, it certainly is a hopeless situation," I agree, trying to push him a little deeper into his emotions.

Rafeek looks even younger than his twenty-four years and is a pretty-looking fellow, blue-eyed and blond; a really nice, angelic choirboy. He's always warm, friendly and helpful, always hugging everybody, so I am pleased when he starts to reveal a hidden side of himself.

"I feel angry with these oppressors!" he exclaims. "They are somehow provoking feelings of violence in me. Yes, there is also a killer in me – I want to kill them."

This is too good an opportunity to pass up, so I guide Rafeek into a gestalt situation, using two pillows: one is the nice guy that we see and meet every day in the group; one is the bad guy, the hidden killer within.

He is eager to cooperate and, when I ask him to sit on the cushion representing the hidden killer, the real situation begins to emerge.

"I feel violent," he says, ashamedly. "I feel like I'm going to do something bad."

"Okay, do it! Let it out!" I encourage him, and when he just sits there, hesitating, confused, unwilling to express what is inside, I ask, "Who is stopping you?"

He sighs, "My mother."

Gradually, it all comes out: how his father left home when he was very young, how he was brought up by his mother, how he wanted her love, even though she had developed a strong hatred toward men, and how he, in response, became a very soft, feminine young man.

So I ask him to sit on the other pillow and play the good little angel, which he does, but reluctantly. He's not happy with this role either. It's become a burden on him.

"You are struggling inside," I tell him, after he has acted the two parts. "You've taken on your mother's hatred towards men. The female part in you never accepts your masculine side, your wildness, your power. So rather than connecting with this quality, which you own, which is part of you, you keep pushing it away, judging it as bad.

"You think it represents violence, a killer, a dominating male who abuses women – all the ideas you absorbed from your mother – but it also contains your male power, your juice, your real guts. This is actually a beautiful quality, which you have been thinking of as a negative quality."

This is a breakthrough moment for Rafeek and illustrates how important it is for me to be spontaneous in these daily sessions. We are supposed to be focusing on painting, but when you go into a simple subject like light and darkness – when you really go into it, beyond any superficial, technical knowledge about how to use them in a painting – then all kinds of hidden emotions and issues start to surface.

I ask Rafeek to sit again on the 'bad guy' cushion.

"Who would have guessed that this little choir boy has been sitting on his male energy all these years in order to please his mother?" I say, provocatively.

He laughs, and suddenly something relaxes in him. The effect is dramatic and visible. As soon as he recognizes his own quality for what it really is – pure male energy – his condemnation of it disappears and he starts to connect with it in a new way.

He starts to enjoy the feeling of being a man, a strong young man, accepting it as part of himself.

"You like it, don't you?" I ask him, teasingly.

He smiles, a little awkwardly, but this time without shame.

"Mmm, yes, I'm getting used to it!" he declares, and the group laughs with him.

"I can feel the male side growing in you," I tell him. "You are sitting more upright, with a new feeling of strength. It almost seems like your body is getting bigger."

Rafeek's new strength is not against his femininity. It's an added dimension. Now he can experience both sides, and I am sure this will enhance his painting, because now the creative impulse of his masculine side will be able to express itself more freely. At the same time, his feminine side will continue to support his sensitivity.

This play between male and female energy is something that I would like to discuss in more detail in the next chapter. Or maybe in the one after next, because right now I need to talk about watercolor.

Chapter 4

Dissolving into Watercolor

It's always beautiful to begin a session with the body. The body is so simple, innocent, uncomplicated, an easy doorway to being natural. In a group situation, starting a day with the body has the effect of bringing everyone here, now, in the present moment, while at the same time awakening energy and vitality.

Your mind is a tourist, never still, never present, always traveling somewhere else – into the past, into the future: who you took to the movie last night, what you are going to eat for lunch, how much money you are going to make… on and on and on. It takes a body exercise to lasso the mind and drag it into the here and now.

So, when all the participants have arrived in the Naropa pyramid, I ask them to close their eyes, check inside for physical sensations and identify that part of the body where they feel the most vitality, the most aliveness.

"Connect with this part of your body and give space to the movement that wants to happen," I invite them. The dance begins from this point. As people begin to explore the movement arising from a particular part of the body, I put on some music to help things along.

"Let other parts of your body follow the movement you are making," I suggest. "Slowly, include your whole body in the movement."

Soon, everybody is dancing, moving with eyes closed. This approach is very different from the mechanical way I see people dancing in discotheques. Really, disco dancing is so limited; people stand, put their hands up and sway in a certain way or they apply learned steps, techniques that are fashionable. It seems like everybody has to follow a certain pattern out of fear that they won't be accepted by their peers.

People are forgetting the organic quality of rhythm and movement, which your body has in its cells. Everybody has a beautiful dance inside but there's no background, no support, nobody to teach it, except in situations like this.

But today I am not going to let people linger for long in solo dancing.

"Choose a partner and dance, connecting back-to-back," I say after a few minutes have passed.

When you start focusing your attention on your back, something magical happens – something unexpected and not apparently connected. The back is not something we are usually aware of, and thus the mind doesn't come in so easily, so, rather than being in the head, you start moving into your heart.

Here, I have to make a mental note to explain my attitude toward the mind and its thinking process, because when you read this book and see all the exercises that I use to distract people from the mind, you may very well conclude that I am against it. But this is a misunderstanding. I'll come back to this point later.

"When your partner touches your back, you are not so inhibited because the back is like an inviting space, where you can relax and be yourself. You don't need to introduce yourself," I say, encouragingly.

"In the back are hidden all kinds of feelings. In Noh Dance, they say if you're not aware of your back, dance doesn't happen. When you connect with your back, it draws out certain movements which usually you don't do."

People start moving together, rubbing their backs this way and that, connecting and feeling more warmth. It's a little bit cold in here this morning and a back rub with a partner is the right thing to get energy moving. In a way, it's like warming-up a car.

Then I say, "Just turn around and look at this partner for a moment. Find a mat, sit down and continue dancing back to back."

One foam rubber mat has been set out for each pair and so everybody sits down and starts again, back to back. I encourage them to explore, move and dance, and almost everybody is fully participating except one or two partners, who are sitting cross-legged, buddha-like, with only a little bit of the upper back touching.

So I inspire them to explore further: "If you expand the quality of dance from this space, what happens? It means you can involve all the other parts of the body; your legs, arms, hands…"

Something wild starts happening. People are giggling, rolling around, putting there feet together in the air, getting on top of each other in a playful ballet. Maybe you can't call it a dance, which you can perform, but there is a natural, organic quality to the body movements – a bit like contact dance.

In this moment, I can see that certain people want to impress their partners, so I welcome this as the next step.

"One person stays off the mat and watches while the other dances alone on the mat with eyes closed," I announce. "Now, it's your territory, your island. You can do what you want. Somebody is watching you, supporting you with his or her presence, giving you warmth and love so that you can really explore your body movements on the mat."

It is a beautiful moment. This technique is based on Reichian methods of energy release. The freedom to be sensual helps people experience body movements that are basically equivalent to ocean waves, letting the body remember orgasmic moments normally restricted by our social sense of proper behavior.

Allowing such movements is dangerous because they are easily connected with sex. But once you don't name the energy as sex, getting caught up in all the taboos around the subject, then it is really just an expression of the life force.

In my work, I have seen how important it is for people to use the body for painting, connecting with their own energy in an organic way, expressing this quality in the way they move the brush. Dance is a good way to get in touch with this organic feeling. It's a feeling that somehow you have invisible roots that you're connected to a source of energy beyond yourself, and this will be especially important when we come to nature painting, because what you feel inside you can also find outside in the trees, flowers and plants.

Nature, too, has this connection to an invisible source, and when the artist understands both – his own roots and those in nature – he can convey something very deep and mysterious. And since nature painting with watercolors is going to be our next step in the training, getting prepared through this kind of dancing can be helpful.

When both partners have had the opportunity to explore dancing while being watched, I say, "Now, let's see if you can put two islands together, so it makes four people sitting back to back, with eyes closed."

Again this is a new situation: how you are relating with others, how your movement changes, how the energy is expanding. Then we come to groups of eight and the final one is sixteen – two big islands with about half the group on each.

While this is happening, I see one woman is getting a little scared, because this kind of physical contact with lots of people may remind someone of an orgy. Even though everyone has their clothes on, just the idea of it is causing her to freeze, sitting awkwardly between two men who are not doing anything to her directly, just enjoying their own movements.

But intuitively I can feel that these movements are reminding her of her own sexuality and I think she is afraid of it. So I gently take her out of the situation and lead her to another part of the group, where she has more room and can sit between two women. Immediately, she relaxes and begins to melt into the group energy.

One of the effects of dancing and connecting in this way is to help people dissolve their personal boundaries and experience the melting and merging that can happen when we forget our ideas about correct social behavior – keeping a safe distance from almost everyone and everything that surrounds us.

This feeling of dissolving boundaries is another key aspect of painting nature, especially with watercolors, which naturally have this merging, melting, disappearing quality.

Before going any further, I'd like to give a little lecture on the history of watercolor painting. It doesn't take long, and has some interesting points.

Watercolor is made of colored pigments ground into, or suspended in, soluble gum, usually gum Arabic. When you have prepared your mixture then, typically, you daub a small quantity onto a palette, mix a little water and start to paint.

The technique goes back to pre-history. Ancient Egyptians, Chinese and Japanese masters, Arab and Indian artisans, all used water-based paints, derived from natural pigments such as yellow, red and brown clay, black charcoal soot, blue and green copper sediments.

In Europe, the forerunner of watercolor painting was fresco painting: wall and ceiling paintings using watercolor on wet plaster, such as Michelangelo's masterpiece in the Sistine Chapel. Both Michelangelo and Leonardo da Vinci used watercolors on paper, but only as preliminary designs for oil paintings and other works. Over the next two or three centuries this habit continued: Rubens and Van Dyck also used watercolor on paper for developing ideas.

The relatively modern technique, known today as watercolor painting, was developed in England in the eighteenth and nineteenth centuries by artists like Joseph Mallord William Turner. They discovered how to use watercolor as a transparent layer that covered, but did not entirely block out, the whiteness of the paper beneath, and this created a 'glowing' or transparent effect, which could be increased or decreased depending on how much paint the artist used.

A great deal depended on the availability of high quality paper – you need a smooth surface that does not absorb too much paint – and this was simply not available in Europe before Turner's time, which explains why it did not develop as an art until then. I mention this because, as you will soon see, we are going to run into problems with the quality of our own paper.

This period also saw the invention of new synthetic colors, giving a wide range of brilliant shades – a product of the industrial revolution. The first such color was Prussian Blue, made by a Berlin chemist from iron oxides. The next was Scheele's Green, named after the Swedish chemist who invented it and derived from arsenic and copper sulphate.

At first, watercolor artists prepared their own paints by grinding their pigments into the gum, which was a tedious and time-consuming process. Then, following the law of supply and demand, some bright English businessman invented ready-made, portable cakes. Next came the metal tube, which still reins supreme.

This I mention because Rowney, a famous English manufacturer of watercolor tube paints, developed a company here in India during the days of the British Empire, or Raj. This company still exists, making standard-sized watercolor boxes with twelve small paint tubes of excellent quality, so I can buy large quantities for my trainings at local rates – it would be far too expensive to import them. So you see, the Raj had its good side, at least for me.

Next, I explain to the group the classic watercolor technique, which is very traditional in England and follows a fixed format. Whenever I open a 'how to' book about watercolor the author introduces painting in this way, whether it's a landscape, flowers, still life or people.

The first thing is definition of form. You have to decide where comes the tree, where comes the mountain, the water, the house. So you begin by outlining the scene with a pencil, so that nothing goes wrong. The form is already fixed and you know where to put which color.

Then you make a soft, thin cover of water over the whole surface of the paper. It's called a wash. You wash the surface so that the color will spread nicely – it's good to use for graduation from one color to another. Then you start coloring. So that's the basic sequence, done in any watercolor. Whatever you do, there is always a certain feeling of order and technique.

But for me, unless I can give a new vision, I'm not satisfied. Even if I can make a better watercolor painting using technique, this is not my interest. My interest is in inviting something unique, something new, to come out of the individuals in my training.

I don't want people to get fixed from the beginning, but rather to stay with their joy, with a feeling of freedom and easiness, so that the experience is more like letting go into nature, rather than trying to copy it. And for this, watercolor has lots of possibilities, because it has some kind of secret rapport with nature. They go together well. Whenever you start painting with watercolor, your connection to nature becomes deeper and more harmonious. It's a magnificent feeling – you understand more, you see more, feel more and sense more.

By the way, when I say these things about tradition, I'm not condemning people like Turner. He was a genius. During my grand tour of Europe, in spite of my attraction to artists whose paintings expressed emotional turmoil and trauma, like Edvard Munch, I went especially to London to see the Turner collection at the Tate Gallery. His landscapes have a disappearing quality – disappearing into the vastness of nature – as well as a feeling of inner radiance and light that wants to burst out of every scene.

He was very prolific, painting in oils and watercolor, as well as making thousands of sketches. One very special quality that I love in some of his paintings is speed. For example, he presents – just in black and white – a steam train coming over a bridge towards you, with clouds and rain billowing in the background, so that the train seems to be coming out of the clouds.

It's called 'Rain, Steam and Speed.' You can almost hear the sound of the train as it comes at you, from out of the clouds and fog. It's a combination of speed, nature and a sense of vastness. Turner is called a Romantic, that's the name given to that particular style and period of art history, but for me it's not romanticism that he captures. It's more like a feeling of mystery, or mysticism – in my view, he was almost like an artistic godfather to the Impressionists.

Like Tohaku, with his black and white paintings of pine trees, Turner gives you a feeling of something transcendental, just behind and beyond the subject that he paints. It's this kind of quality that I try to capture in my own way of painting, and in training others to paint.

I was surprised to learn that although Turner was very successful – enjoying recognition and support throughout his life, unlike many painters, such as Van Gogh and Pissarro, who had to struggle to survive – he was not a happy man. He hated to sell any of his paintings, refused to let anyone watch him while he painted and always traveled alone. He allowed no-one close to him, except his father. Just before his death, he disappeared from his London address and was found months later by his housekeeper, hiding in another house in Chelsea. He died the next day.

Art can be a strange game. Those who can paint luminous beauty like Turner are not necessarily benefiting from a parallel inner experience.

Now it is time to introduce people to the watercolors – our main medium for working with nature – and so I ask people to gather round for a painting demonstration.

I have already asked Fulwari, my main helper, to put out a watercolor set and a sheet of paper for me to use in the demo, but she misunderstood and has prepared two sets. This, I see as a beneficial error, because both Nirvikalpa and I can do the demo together, and this will reduce the risk of people copying what I do.

So now, I am sitting on the floor, next to Nirvikalpa, and we are painting with watercolor, squeezing paint from our tubes onto our palettes. The palette has a certain structure, divided into eight big components – for the main colors that you choose to work with – and about two dozen smaller ones.

I see that Nirvikalpa is choosing reds and yellows, so I deliberately choose something else because – as I said before – I don't want the group participants to think there is a certain style and start to copy us. It's like that here: if you wear a black robe, which in this resort signifies a course leader or meditation teacher, then those who want to learn from you tend to follow you. In fact, it's like that everywhere.

Nirvikalpa is painting slowly, carefully, sensitively, so I do the opposite.

"I am a different type of painter," I announce, playfully. "I'm like a child. I jump in and then I don't look back. Sometimes, I find brushes and the right material, but I want to keep going, so when I don't find a brush I take a sponge..."

And off I go, covering the paper in an abstract, formless way, with big, bold dashes of dark colors. Nirvikalpa's painting is also abstract, but much more delicate and aesthetic, so when we have finished I look at her painting and say, plaintively, like a little girl, "Oh! I like your painting better; I wish I could paint like that."

I know, from long experience, that everyone who does a painting training with me will think, or say, this sentence at least once during our six weeks together. Because when you are painting with so many people you can't help but compare, and when you compare you'll always find someone whose creative expression will trigger this feeling in you.

So this is a reminder that everybody is the same; everybody has the same complex; everybody wants to be somebody else. Even a great painter wants to be somebody else, once in a while. It's only human, and I don't want people to feel guilty about it. Today, especially, I want them to connect with more light-hearted and joyful feelings.

Now it's time for the participants to explore for themselves and I explain today's project: taking a watercolor set, with paper, water, brushes and paints, and finding a spot on the white marble pathway that encircles Buddha Hall, the resort's big meditation hall. This beautiful pathway is, in turn, circled by an outer ring of trees, bushes and exotic plants of all descriptions – a perfect place for nature painting.

Before they go, however, I invite them to join me in a simple and yet powerful partner game that can revolutionize their vision, their way of seeing. It's called "Camera and Photographer."

It is an old therapeutic technique, used in group dynamics for many purposes, such as building trust or intimacy between partners, helping people learn to be more present, more innocent or spontaneous.

In my work I include all of these, but my main motive is something special to a painting training: I want people to experience a basic principle of art.

It works like this: one partner is the photographer and the other is the camera. The one who is the camera has closed eyes and is guided around the room by the photographer, who leads him by the hand or by a light touch on the shoulder. The photographer positions the camera in a place where he feels he would like to take a picture. It could be something close-up, like a rose flower, or a paintbrush, or somebody's face, or it could be something distant like a tree, a wall, the sky outside.

Just to give people a hint, I act the part of the photographer and choose my assistant, Nirvikalpa, as the camera. For my first snapshot, I guide her over to the big black door at the entrance of the room and position her face in front of a doornail, very close. One doesn't imagine that you are going to look at things like that, and I like to go for the unexpected.

Then, as the photographer, I simply say "click," and Nirvikalpa opens her eyes. Then, almost immediately, after only a split second, I say "click" again and she closes her

84

eyes. In this way, she gets a very quick visual impression. Her mind has no time to anticipate what it is going to see, nor to analyze the impression, label it and form an opinion... 'this is a door, this is a paint brush, that is the man I'm attracted to...' etc.

"I was introduced to this exercise about twenty years ago," I tell the group. "For me, it was so fresh to receive images in this way, because I felt they were going straight into my heart. They were pure, unspoiled, virgin.

"As a painter I'd been studying nature for a long time and, up to that point, it always seemed as if I was going out to watch nature, to look at it, to do something with it. Suddenly, when I was the camera, I felt as if the whole of nature was coming into me.

"I also discovered that understanding what I am seeing doesn't take time, or require thinking. In a split-second, you receive the image, and then a totally new and different kind of understanding happens.

"And one more thing: you know that normally you see everything around you in color, you take it for granted, you don't even think about it. But in this exercise the basic impression is not only of color. It is also of light and dark. It is also of contrast. Essentially, it is an impression of black and white."

Most people never think in this way, but anyone who wants to paint nature has to accept it – knowingly or unknowingly makes no difference. In order to represent a landscape, a tree, a flower, a seascape, you have to use contrast between light and dark, and this contrast is essentially a play of black and white.

In the camera exercise, when you open your eyes for only a split-second, you will get some impression of color, but the primary impression you receive is black and white. Check it out for yourself and see. That's also why I emphasize black and white painting in my training: it helps people understand the fundamental role of contrast.

For the next few minutes, I guide people through the camera exercise, giving both partners an opportunity to be the camera. Then the helpers give each participant a set of watercolor paints and a sheet of paper, and we are ready to go to Buddha Hall.

I suggest that they use the camera technique. "In the beginning, don't even think about painting," I advise. "Just sit, maybe for half an hour, with a white sheet of paper in front of you and imagine you are the camera.

"Close your eyes. When you are ready, open them for a second, receive an impression of nature – a tree trunk, a leaf, a bamboo, whatever is in front of you. Close your eyes again. Turn your head in another direction, open your eyes, take another picture, and so on. Get drunk with these impressions, this feeling of freshness.

"Then you can begin to transfer these impressions onto paper. Open your eyes, take a picture, paint your impression, without any idea of making it perfect, or even looking like nature. Don't be worried whether your leaves look like leaves, your trees like trees. There is no need to discriminate. With the camera, you don't have time to bring in the mind, and with an empty mind everything is simply as it is."

"You're seeing, feeling and welcoming an impression – the sunshine dancing on the bushes – without any commentary or interpretation. And you're seeing yourself painting these things without trying to copy, without any feeling of a right way or a wrong way. This is the way I would like you to paint."

Today, we have a unique situation, because it is Saturday. Every Saturday morning in Buddha Hall there is an event called 'sannyas initiation celebration.' It is a ceremony for those visitors who wish to 'take sannyas,' which in the old days – when Osho was alive – meant that you wanted to become his disciple.

Nowadays, it means something slightly different. The emphasis is no longer on discipleship, because Osho isn't here as a physical person, so it's more like a statement by you, from you, to you, that you want to commit yourself to your inner quest, to discover your inner reality through meditation. But anyway this is what Osho meant by 'taking sannyas' and becoming his disciple, so really, nothing has changed.

Maybe this is a good moment to explain the names, because for sure you will have noticed that many of the people I mention in this book have unusual names. Receiving a new name is an option when you 'take sannyas.' Most of the names are from the ancient Indian language, Sanskrit. They help to create distance from your former identity, signifying a new beginning, and since most of the people in my training are already sannyasins – they don't have to be, but that's just the way it is in Pune – they call themselves by these names.

Back in the mid-Seventies, when I took sannyas, Osho gave me the name Meera, which was the name of a very famous, enlightened female mystic who lived in Rajasthan about five hundred years ago. She was born into a royal family but became a passionate devotee of Krishna, singing and dancing ecstatically in the streets, much to the horror of her husband, the Raja of Udaipur.

Today, there is a big statue of Meera, standing in the middle of the city of Udaipur, devoted to her memory. I think she would have loved our weekly sannyas ceremony, which is a very beautiful affair with live music, singing, dancing – a heartfelt and happy occasion – and ideally suited to support our first adventure into watercolor.

I want everyone to be in a joyful mood, joining the dance of life around them, because as I see it, everything in this existence is celebrating. The whole of nature is a dance and that's why I don't care how people paint, but whether joy is happening. Is your hand dancing across the paper? This matters more to me.

And that's why, in my watercolor demonstration today, I taught nothing. I just made a mess. Well, for others it's a mess, but for me, of course, I know so much about painting that I can see where even such a messy painting can go, and how it can develop if I had more time. The important thing, for me, is not to allow people to get trapped in a desire for perfection.

"Use the sannyas ceremony to support your painting," I tell the group. "At any moment, you can jump up, run into the hall and join the dancing and singing. Then, at any moment, you can come back, sit down and paint. Back and forth, as often as you like."

It's not that I simply want people to be happy. There is another reason, very practical and down to earth, that is deeply related to learning how to paint. I remember, so many times I have taken people into nature, given them a sheet of white paper and a set of paints, watched them sit down, get started, and then suddenly collapse. It's true: about eighty percent of people get stuck when they try to paint nature for the first time, and from then on it can easily become a permanent block.

Why? Because you are confronting perfection. You are confronting the impossible. Nature is so beautiful, so colorful, so visually stunning. You don't need to add anything. Wherever you look: at the stars, the trees, the sea, rivers, snow, sunlight or moonlight, nature gives you this feeling. Even a single leaf or blade of grass. There is no possibility of improvement and no chance of painting something that can even begin to reflect the beauty that you see around you.

Of course, in such an impossible situation, you get tense. Again you meet this remembrance that "I can't do it," "I'm not going to make it" – all these old feelings start coming up. The more you have these feelings, the more you move your hand on the paper according to your mind, in an effort to at least create something worthwhile, and the more frustrated you get. You look at your painting, you look at nature, comparison sets in and the gap grows wider and wider.

But today, magic happens. In the sharing, after the morning session is over, I ask the group how many people had a good time around Buddha Hall, and all but two of them raise their hands. I am quite surprised. Let's see...

thirty-six people in the group, including helpers and translators, minus two, so thirty-four people experienced joy, which is really remarkable. Normally, in such a situation, the statistics would have been reversed. Two people would have had a good time, the rest would have been overwhelmed by the challenge.

I could see it happening: people were dancing, enjoying the music and the sunshine; people didn't care, didn't compare what they were doing with others or with nature. Some painted form – trees, plants – while others painted abstract. They used the camera technique to receive an impression, felt an inner response to this impression, expressed the feeling on the paper. When the connection was gone, they used the camera to click on something else.

"The whole vibe around the hall had a bouncing quality and this is what I want you all to learn – this jumping quality in your hearts," I say, in the sharing. "What is really important is that nothing is important. To make a perfect painting, which lasts maybe ten years, is this the aim in our life? I don't think so. What's important is to be here, in the present, in this moment; then whatever you do is significant – that's really what interests me."

What am I doing, when I say things like this? Really, I am being a little bit tricky. I am guiding people into approaching artistic creativity from the back door. If you knock on the front door, you feel such a weight of responsibility. Me? Creative? Me? An artist? Me? The next Leonardo da Vinci? Immediately, you want to run away and forget the whole idea.

But if you go to the back door, there is every chance of a breakthrough. If I tell people that I'm not interested in them making a good painting, but only in their spontaneity, their joy and playfulness, there is an excellent chance that, sooner or later, they are going to connect with their creative impulse and allow it to manifest. When this happens 'good paintings' come by themselves – they are a byproduct.

The creative impulse, as I have mentioned before, lies deep inside us, very close to child-like qualities such as innocence, spontaneity, a sense of surprise and delight. So when I lead people into a child-like space, I am helping them to knock on the door of their own creativity without them even knowing it.

Basically, I am deceiving people, and it works!

As for the two people who did not enjoy themselves, I can sense that this is a double punch: one from nature, because it didn't seem to work, and one from the fact that everyone else enjoyed themselves. So, not to drive them any further down into the dungeons of despair, I simply say, "Well, this is very normal. This is how it happens with most people."

They get the point. In the afternoon, after lunch, when I come back to the pathway around Buddha Hall I see everyone fully absorbed in painting, including the two who had difficulties in the morning.

It is a touching moment for me, because from three o'clock onwards, in India, the light changes. Something about the angle, the quality, of the afternoon sun brings out the strength and power of nature, and this, combined with the enthusiasm and dedication of the group – close together but self-absorbed, each person sitting alone, all along the pathway – makes for a beautiful feeling in my heart.

The way I use watercolor, you need plenty of sunlight. You can put color and water on the paper and within ten minutes it dries, so you can do something more on top, allowing the colors to overlay and complement each other. Automatically, the layers are being created and becoming mysterious, because as you put on a fresh layer the colors beneath come through, creating a very mysterious feeling. This approach to watercolor is based on accidents, very feminine accidents, and creates effects and surprises that just aren't possible with oil painting.

I think that's a mistake people make with the traditional approach to watercolor painting: they outline forms and shapes, paint here, paint there, but they are careful not to overlay the colors because they are so afraid to lose the underlying whiteness that creates the quality of transparency. They think that watercolor technique should be transparent, should have a translucent quality.

True, it can create wonderful paintings. I'm not denying it, because I also paint this way sometimes, but they are missing something. If you stick only with the technique you miss the mystery that is coming out of the earth, the surprise coming out of the darkness, as certain forms, shapes and colors come through the new layer to the surface.

But this sense of mystery does not depend only on using watercolors in an innovative way. It is a by-product of the artist connecting with his or her inner depth.

I will try to describe this process of going deeper into oneself in more detail later on, but for now it's enough to know that, as each day of the training passes, the participants are also moving inwards, meeting themselves in new, deeper and different ways. Sometimes, this is not a comfortable experience.

For example, after a few of days exploring watercolors – in spite of my efforts to emphasize a playful, non-serious attitude – I can sense that some participants are finding it heavy going.

One afternoon, we gather on Krishna House roof for a group sharing, after returning from the Buddha Hall pathway. I can sense that something is in the air, so I ask, "Who is not having a good time?"

Silence.

"Who is not having a good time?" I gently persist.

"I'm not," says Sukhi. "I'm so angry."

Sukhi is an unusual-looking woman: quite small, with close-cropped hair, dark skin and huge brown eyes. She is from Israel, must be about 25, and she looks like she's sitting on a volcano, her whole body trembling with energy, not knowing whether to scream or cry – and very serious, like maybe only Israelis and Germans can get.

"I did Dynamic Meditation in Buddha Hall this morning, very loudly, but still I'm angry," she manages to say.

I'll talk about Dynamic in the next chapter. Suffice it to say, for now, that it's a way of cleaning out strong emotions, like anger. Only in Sukhi's case, it didn't solve the problem.

"I feel pushed," she says. "When I was sitting outside Buddha Hall, facing a sheet of white paper, I didn't like it. I felt pushed, forced, like I'm supposed to do something."

I have a pretty good idea what this is about. I'm sure the exercise reminded Sukhi of many similar situations in her childhood when her teachers or her parents said, "Now you've got to do this. You have to do this because you are my child, my student. You have to be creative, you have to be the best."

Also, in the Israeli conditioning, children are pushed a lot, because the whole country is living under such tension: "You have to be strong, you have to be tough..." It's like a mantra for the whole country. And especially, of course, when all the teenagers are compelled to join the armed forces – usually, the army – and forced to follow orders.

When they become adults, especially when they have just left the army, they don't want anybody to push them around. So anything that reminds them of such feelings makes them go into this kind of reaction very easily.

I think this is common to all conditionings, all countries – all children are forced in this way – but the Israelis have it the most strongly.

I bring a piece of white paper from behind Sukhi and put it in front of her.

"No, I don't want it," she says, pushing it away.

She is still wavering between anger and tears and I feel the need to support her tears, because now there is no need to fight. It isn't anything to do with me or the group. After all, she freely chose to sign up for the group and she also paid a lot of money for the opportunity.

I ask her if she is willing to explore the situation and she nods.

"I want to give you a sentence to say to everyone here, including me," I tell her, indicating all the participants who have gathered around, sitting on the mats in an intimate

92

circle. "The sentence is: 'I don't want you to expect anything from me.' Make eye contact with people as you say it. Tell the group how you feel."

Immediately, even before saying it herself, Sukhi starts crying, feeling the release from internal pressure that this statement gives her. Several other people are moist-eyed, too.

Slowly, she looks around at the people, saying softly, "I don't want you to expect anything from me."

After she has said it many times, I ask if I can give her another sentence. She nods.

"I'm just a child and I want to play."

She repeats the sentence very softly.

"A little louder, please Sukhi."

I want her to declare that she is a child, because I feel she is somehow hiding herself, afraid that if she exposes her truth, her reality, she will be punished or hurt.

"When you were a child, remember how the adults pushed aside your feelings," I tell her. "Remember how the other kids were taking away your toys because you didn't speak up loud enough. That's how they crushed you. So you have to speak up loud, 'I'm just a child and I want to play!' so they don't take away your toys."

She says it three or four times, really loudly, and each time I can feel her becoming stronger. Something is shifting inside her. This is a new kind of strength, an inner strength, without the protective, sullen, fighting attitude.

Then I take her hand, look into her eyes and say, "Sukhi, there's nobody here who's judging you, or pushing you, or expecting anything from you. Can you feel that?"

Then, to the whole group, I say, "All those who feel the same as Sukhi, who had the same or similar experiences, come close to her..."

What a surprise! At least two-thirds of the group surrounds Sukhi with love, holding her hands, stroking her hair, looking into her eyes, showing her more powerfully than any words can do that she's not alone with this feeling.

It's so common. When you are a child, you can't argue; you don't have the words, you can't explain to adults what you are feeling and maybe you end up thinking you are all alone in the world.

I know these people are not coming to Sukhi because they want to console her. They are coming for themselves, to heal themselves. She can feel the togetherness, the common bond – that it's okay to feel this way.

So many problems start happening when you isolate yourself, when you think you are the only one who is miserable. But if you relax and look around, you can see, very easily, that, "Hey, everybody is more or less the same." It relaxes you, the isolation is finished and half the problem is gone.

Now it's time to return to the watercolors. This morning I show everyone how to stretch their paintings on a thin wooden board. This is classic watercolor technique, because whether you follow the tradition or develop something new, you need to have a flat, smooth piece of paper to work with.

The only difference is that normally you stretch a fresh sheet of white paper before you start painting on it, whereas I am asking everyone to stretch the nature painting they did yesterday.

I didn't want people to do it beforehand, because there's more dynamism when the paper is free, when the water moves here and there, accidentally mixing the colors and forming spontaneous patterns. As I said before, one of the joys of painting is how to deal with such accidents, because they open you to a new way of looking at things.

But on the other hand, I want people to experience a silent space, which is a 'must' for nature painting, because you need to tune into the silence of nature. Your paper needs to be like a still and silent lake, with a mirror-smooth surface, reflecting nature. Also, when you want to make really fine movements with the brushes, you need a smooth surface. When the paper is wobbly, curvy, you can't keep an equal width with your brush strokes.

So I try to give everyone a taste of both. First, a spontaneous play of color with a loose, unfixed piece of paper, then, introducing the traditional technique.

Basically, you wet the back of the paper with a sponge, lay it down on the board, flatten it as much as possible, then fasten it down by pasting gum paper around the four edges. When the gum and the paper dries, the paper is left smooth and flat, firmly fixed in place without wrinkles. Now it won't warp or curl when you start to paint.

"Who would like to learn some techniques?" I ask, when everyone has stretched the painting on the board.

Immediately, the whole group comes to me, and I am surprised because a moment before everyone seemed so eager to just pick up their boards and paint sets and run off to Buddha Hall.

Now what shall I do? I can teach straight technique, but this doesn't help my aim to support people's growth.

Which technique do they need? Everybody is different. If you learn one way, then everybody is painting the same, and in this I'm not interested.

So, I decide to show several techniques at once, to give a little variety and choice.

First, a problem is already arising with the paper. We discover that, with this whole batch that we have bought for the training, the surface breaks up easily and becomes too absorbent – one of the hazards of purchasing materials in India. In this country, it's like Russian roulette: sometimes the quality is excellent, like the handmade paper we use for the acrylics, like the Rowney watercolor sets, but sometimes it's…well… just lousy.

So my first demonstration is how to paint in the gouache style, which means using thicker paint on the paper, with not so much water, almost like an oil painting. Those who have broken the surface of their paper can use this style effectively.

Next, I ask Nirvikalpa to demonstrate how to make a transparent painting. Her paintings have this quality, because she likes to use a thin wash of color, and she is very careful, taking good care of her paper so that the surface doesn't break up and you can see through to the white sheen beneath.

Another thing I show is a simple technique for drawing tree trunks and branches. If you look at any branch, you will see it has a light side and a dark side, because sunlight hits the round form and creates this effect. So, very simply, you can dip a brush in white paint and move it across the paper, then, right alongside it, with one edge touching, you can make a similar stroke with black paint.

In this way, you create the effect of a tree branch, dark on one side, light on the other, while in the middle the two colors mix and merge, creating a graduation from dark to light.

Then I show a painting by Teerth, a 42 year-old sannyasin from Spain, whose passion for painting caught fire in my training last year and since then, giving up all other pursuits, he has devoted his time to painting.

He can paint very fast and has the ability to jump, without thinking, from foreground to background, from horizontal forms to vertical ones, from light to dark. He is free to move into the jungle, into nature, and this is the quality that I want others to see and be inspired by.

Last, I come to Sukhi's painting, which eloquently reflects the emotion she was feeling yesterday. It is very dark, heavy, with big movements and one very substantial tree trunk standing alone, taking up almost the whole paper. Clearly, she didn't care about the outcome. She just went with the anger, the emotion.

"Sukhi, how do you feel about your painting?"

"Okay," she replies, now more relaxed and at ease.

"You want to learn about transparency? Can I use your painting to show that?"

"Yes, sure."

By the way, when I talk about 'transparency' in this particular context, I'm not referring to the underlying whiteness of the paper. In Sukhi's painting, that has gone. I'm talking about the transparency between layers of color.

But now I find myself in a dilemma. I asked the question to see if Sukhi is open, flexible, ready to move. She is, but when I look at her painting, I can't bring myself to change it, because if I do anything, a very precious quality will be gone.

"Do you have any idea what this quality is?" I ask, pointing to her painting and sharing my dilemma with the group. I want them to think about it.

Someone says 'strength,' others add 'energy'… 'anger'… 'freedom.'

"This painting has an organic, innocent quality," I explain. "Sukhi was angry when she was doing it. When you are angry it means you are burning with energy, so you are not somewhere else, daydreaming, you are here, you are totally here, in the present, pouring your emotional energy into your work, and this is reflected in her painting – in the strength of her expression."

An idea comes into my head and I ask Deepak, a gentle-looking Greek man in his late forties, to show his watercolor. He did the training with me last year, accompanied by his longtime girlfriend, Aloka. They are both passionate artists and also Reiki teachers, living in Athens.

Deepak's painting is more like a proper painting. He has natural talent, much more experience than Sukhi, and he paints nature in a decorative way.

"Okay Sukhi, today you paint on Deepak's painting, and Deepak will paint on yours."

Sukhi is shocked. She says, "Deepak can paint on mine if he likes, but I cannot paint on his painting. It's too beautiful!"

But Deepak is enthusiastic about the change, saying, "Yes, I like my new painting."

This is an important step for him. Normally, his painting style is very pretty, very organized and contains a loving feeling, but in my eyes something is missing. He can describe this and that, he knows how to depict certain elements, but for him nature is still outside. It's not coming

97

from his guts. He has a tendency to paint fantasy, which is not a bad quality, but what I'm teaching here is to take existence into your belly without any filter.

"Sukhi's painting offers what Deepak's is missing and he can see it, that's why he is happy to work on it," I say to the group. "And Deepak's painting has the lightness, the beauty that Sukhi can't feel or express right now."

Having made the point, though, I end up giving the paintings back to their real owners. I don't want Sukhi to jump over herself. I want her painting to grow at the same pace as her own understanding. But I'm happy at the way both Deepak and Sukhi were ready to let go of their work.

We have overstayed our time in the group room and I can see that some people are already thinking about a break for morning tea and coffee, so I send everyone out to the Buddha Hall pathway, with a quick stop at the resort's cafeteria on the way.

Now we have to set up the room for tonight's special multi-media event, which is my favorite past time – combining painting with music and dance, to create an effect of overflowing creativity and abundance.

Many artists have this longing to combine music and painting, and I am no exception. I remember, once I was painting in an abstract way outside a Jewish synagogue in Toledo, when a member of the Tolmo group – a Spanish painter called Beato – came up behind me, looked at my painting for a while and commented, "Why are you trying to paint music? Why don't you just play a musical instrument?"

I was surprised, because I hadn't really thought about it until that moment, and I could see he had a point.

Wassily Kandinsky, a Russian-born painter who lived in Munich during the first half of the twentieth century, was fascinated by the connection between color and musical harmony. A musician as well as a painter, he once said, "Color is the keyboard, the eyes are the harmonies, the soul is the piano with many strings. The artist is the hand that plays, touching one key or another, to cause vibrations in the soul."

Kandinsky tried to link specific colors to each musical note, saying he even saw colors when he heard music. By the way, he is one of my favorite painters, considered to be the father of abstract art, and also founded the "Blue Rider" group of artists in Munich. I'll say more about him later in the book.

The pyramid room in Naropa is a beautiful setting for what I have in mind. In one corner, we set up for a live band, led by Yoko, a gifted Japanese flute player who studied at Kunitachi, one of the best music universities in Tokyo, and was a concert flautist until, like me, she gave up conventional art and became a sannyasin.

We cover half of the floor with plastic and create between sixty and seventy places for painting, because I have asked all the participants to invite a friend tonight, to paint with them. We shall be sitting in pairs, each with his or her own guest, painting small white cards of handmade paper, like birthday or greeting cards, using acrylic paints. One candle in a brass holder is placed next to each pair of cushions.

When the evening comes, I welcome everyone and demonstrate a dual painting style with Nirvikalpa. I want to show what happens with the colors when two people meet through the heart, sharing their creativity in a playful way.

I make two strokes of color on a plain white card, then hand it to Nirvikalpa who accepts it, continues to paint on it for a while, then gives it back. She also gives me her card, and so it continues. Through the evening, each person will create a little pile of hand-painted cards that can be given to friends or kept as mementos.

I introduce the musicians, the band begins to play, we all dance together for a few minutes, then everyone settles down and we begin to paint. After a while, the helpers light the candles and turn off the lights. With Yoko's flute as background, the atmosphere is magical. This is probably when I feel most fulfilled, both as an artist and a group

99

leader, helping to create this kind of organic, merging, group feeling of creative expression in a relaxed, joyful and artistic atmosphere.

Also, I have to admit, I'm being a bit strategic here, because this free evening for invited guests is a great way to introduce newcomers to my work, and make them think about doing a group or training.

For me, the highest point of the evening comes when I give a freestyle dance performance, using a variety of white materials – big rolls of paper, large pieces of silk and cotton, nylon mosquito netting – in front of a screen on which my paintings are being projected. The screen is white, the materials that I hold up in front of it are also white, so you get this very mobile, waving effect of colorful paintings projected on a series of different, moving surfaces.

I don't have a fixed routine, but I'm not worried. The musicians are playing, people are enjoying and I am spontaneously exploring how to dance with the different fabrics in front of the screen.

To me, it's not just entertainment. It's a way to share my vision of painting as three-dimensional ongoing movement. As I dance, I feel like a seed of creativity, exploding into different shapes, forms and colors.

If there is a message to be conveyed, I guess this is it: just be a seed, just let it open and explode into flowers that shower their fragrance upon all of us, on this life, on this world, before dissolving back into the vast existence. And I think everybody got it, not through the intellect, but through the body, heart and guts.

Now it's really time for me to invite you, the reader, to explore beyond creativity, beyond painting, deeper than the child-like spaces that we have been talking about, because here lies the key to everything that I have been trying to express. The trouble is, it's almost impossible to talk about. Still, I have to try. Without it, nothing makes sense.

But first, I'd better keep my promise and talk about the man-woman, male-female dimensions of painting. It's good to deal with non-essentials before coming to the essential.

Chapter 5

Man Meets Woman,
East Meets West

I don't know much about Indian philosophy, but I am told that in the Vedic scriptures there is a beautiful story of how the world came to be created. One day, God was feeling lonely – which I immediately like, because naturally, if you are sitting by yourself for eternity this is going to happen. Such a human quality! Anyway, God became lonely and so he created a woman as a companion, not for a human being called Adam, but just for himself to enjoy, which seems more logical than the biblical idea of what happened in the Garden of Eden.

The woman was very beautiful and so the God became excited and started falling in love with her. Seeing his intentions, the woman became afraid and – being a woman – started hiding from him. He started searching for her, pursing her, so she hid in the form of a cow and ran away. He became a bull and chased after her.

And that's how the whole saga of creativity begins, with a cosmic game of hide-and-seek, because she kept changing forms, from one type of animal to another, and he kept changing forms in order to follow her. Gradually, all the different species of animals were created.

It's just a story, a myth, invented thousands of years ago as a symbolic way of explaining how pure energy can manifest as millions of forms. And it's chauvinistic – like most religious myths, it makes God male. But still I like it, because it has an element of truth in it. Energy flows between opposites, life dances between polarities, men chase after women, and creativity requires this kind of dynamic movement.

Moreover, this little story indicates that the attraction between men and women is not a serious phenomenon. It is a game, a play, a leela, part of an ongoing, eternal, cosmic dance.

This morning, as we enter the Naropa pyramid, I am in the mood for this kind of game, and I know it will lead to a deeper understanding of an important dimension of the creative process.

"Find a partner, preferably of the opposite sex," I announce through the microphone. "I know there are more women than men here, but if you can't find a man don't worry. Soon you will be meeting your own inner man and he's probably a very handsome guy, so for now – if all the men are taken – just pair up with another woman."

I begin by leading them into a 'stop-go' dance: I touch you and you start to move, dancing around me, while I watch, then you stop, touch me and it's my turn to move, dancing around you, while you watch, until I touch you again… and so on.

"Now you are going to chase your partner around the room," I announce, after a few minutes. "This is a good opportunity to experience what it is like to be the one who is being chased, and the one who is chasing, taking it in turns to be active and passive. Of course, this happens all the time in our love affairs, but most of the time we don't even know what we're doing, so here is a chance to experience both sides consciously, with awareness."

People like this game very much and the energy immediately takes off. The room is a sea of moving figures and an ocean of laughter. I see one beautiful Russian woman, Lena, chasing some English guy and he is very clearly not trying to escape very fast. He really wants to be caught by her. It's not often men have the experience of being chased in such an obvious way, because women have learned over the centuries to be very subtle about it – in case

102

the man gets scared. They have to make it look like the guy is chasing them, while all the time it is the other way around.

'Who enjoyed being chased?" I ask at the end of the exercise, and almost everyone raises a hand.

"And who enjoyed chasing?" Again, almost everyone. So this is a good sign that both the men and the women are willing to move from one role to the other, from active to passive, from the male energy to the female energy, and back again.

Next, we play statues: you are the passive one, and I mold you, or shape you, into a certain position – arms up or down, face turned this way or that, legs apart or together, and so on. Again, after a few minutes, we change roles. Now you mold me.

As another warm-up exercise, I invite people to maintain eye contact with the partner while 'dancing' without music, with nobody leading and nobody following, just being spontaneous in their movements and mirroring each other.

Meanwhile, the helpers have laid out fresh sheets of paper, placed length-wise between two cushions and two sets of paints. I ask everyone to sit down with their partners, with one vertical sheet of paper between them.

"Now you can start painting together with the same feeling that you have just had in these exercises," I tell the group. "All these exercises are connected. You responded to each other while dancing; you can also respond to each other's movements with brush strokes on the paper."

Naturally, most people begin by painting at their own end of the paper, filling in from the bottom, so it takes a little while before the two partners reach a point where their efforts start to overlap and intrude upon each other. This is where it gets interesting, because now two paintings are becoming one, now two painters must somehow meet, merge and find harmony together.

This is a delicate moment. I watch Lena and her partner. They are keeping to their own halves, colors touching here and there at the half-way line, filling in cautiously. But then

103

the man dips a big brush in a pot of white paint and makes a long, bold, curving stroke up through his own territory and all the way into Lena's half.

It changes the painting totally and irrevocably. She pauses, looks thoughtfully at this new and surprising addition, and then responds beautifully, taking white paint and making graceful circles on either side of the long stroke done by her partner. The man smiles, she has accepted his gesture, and a bond of trust is flowering between them. A moment before, it was two paintings, now it has become an organic unity. Now they are painting together.

"Whatever movements and colors come from your partner, you are ready to watch and respond," I say, encouragingly. "You can go in any direction. You are not going to limit yourself to your usual way, sticking to known territory, because if you do, you close your door to learning. Open yourself to learn from someone else, from surprises, because you never know what the other is going to do on the paper."

As I mentioned before, one way to deepen your approach to painting is to allow the quality of the unknown, the quality of surprise, to enter in, and it is one of my challenges as a teacher to create situations where people can have a taste of it. Painting with a partner is a good way to do it. If the other person does something you don't expect, then how will you respond in this moment? In some old familiar way, from your past? From memory? Or in a totally new and different way that is more in synchronicity with your partner?

This quality of surprise works especially well when you paint with a member of the opposite sex. Man's way and woman's way are so different.

I have noticed that male energy, translated into visual expression, includes the qualities of construction, composition, direction and generally giving the painting a feeling of backbone and strength. Female energy finds expression as sensitivity, mystery, sensuousness, poignancy and a sense of merging and melting.

But the real magic happens when men and women discover energies, the masculine and the feminine, within themselves.

This is my goal for the morning, so after the painting session and group sharing, I explain to the participants that we are going to do an exercise that will help everyone experience their male and female energies, both of which are absolutely basic to create a piece of art.

I take them down to the underground, sound-proof chambers and introduce them to an exercise that I learned while training in a method called Star Sapphire Energy Work. It offers a unique way to look at our inner male and female dynamics – after all, we are made up of both our mother and our father. For its approach, Star Sapphire uses the information stored in our legs, because they are far from the head and therefore innocent.

After my introduction, I ask the participants to stand separately, by themselves, eyes closed.

"Stand with your feet slightly apart. Feel your bare feet on the floor and, when you are ready, slowly shift the weight of your body into your left leg, into your left side. Put your whole awareness into the left side of your body. This side represents your female side, which is connected with the right hemisphere of your brain.

"What sensation comes to you when your left leg feels the weight? Is your female side willing to receive it?

"Just feeling the quality, the energy, in your left leg, ask yourself, 'Where is my inner woman standing?' Is she standing on sand, on carpet, marble or wood? Feel the texture beneath your foot, so your woman can connect with her environment."

Of course, the practical reality is that we are all standing on a linoleum floor. But I have done this exercise many times myself, and I know that, with just a little sensitivity, tuning into one's own inner world, it is possible to discover an entirely different reality that belongs to the feminine aspect of one's being.

From this beginning point, I invite the participants to slowly expand their awareness and imagine the whole scene: the surrounding, the environment, whether it is a room, a field, a forest or a beach.

Then, I ask them to shift their awareness to their left hand. "Feel the fingers of your left hand," I invite the group. "See how this hand wants to move. What type of movement does this woman like to make? Is it a slow and graceful movement, is it a big movement, or is it more like an expanding movement?"

In this guided meditation it is important to keep people connected with the body, feeling the inner woman through the left leg and hand, because here lies the unspoiled information we are trying to access. It's another of those hidden secrets of the body that I've been investigating over the years.

"Slowly, you are exploring your inner woman;" I tell the group, "Don't be in a hurry. Pay close attention to detail. This hand is attached to an arm, and this arm to a shoulder. What kind of body is this? Is it old or young? What does she feel like?

"Begin to visualize this woman: what kind of character does she have? What does she need? What kind of activities does she enjoy? How is she dressed? How does she look? Is she a beautiful person? Is she happy? What kind of mood is she in?"

Even in women, the feminine half of the psyche is the side that is suppressed the most. It's a man's world, with a man's values, and so even today women have a strong tendency to let the male side of their nature become the dominant energy. And when one part is always dominating, the other is forgotten, so the inner woman does not usually get enough space to be herself.

The first time I did this exercise it was a shock for me, because the encounter with my inner woman was so real, so clear. I met a totally different person, not at all like my public image. People know me as a vital, active, outgoing person, but my female is a shy, elegant, inward-going

106

person who has no worldly ambition. She simply enjoys the small things of life: cooking, gardening, shopping... and so on.

I became strongly aware how much I was ignoring my female side, how much my inner woman didn't have the space to do the things she really likes to do.

So these days I make a point of asking my woman, "Do you like to paint now, or not?"

Sometimes the answer is very surprising. Even though I am certain that I am in a creative mood, my inner woman doesn't want to do anything, except sit quietly, maybe with a cup of tea, and enjoy doing nothing. She may not be interested in the fact that I have given myself a deadline to achieve some goal – like to complete a painting for an exhibition or a demonstration. She has a totally different set of values.

So I really get to see how much this woman needs to take her own space, and through this exercise I have become much more sensitive towards myself. I get really excited about these two people – my inner woman and my inner man.

"Cover your right eye with your right hand and look out at the world only through your left eye," I tell the group. "See if this woman likes to look around and explore, meeting other people, or if she prefers to be alone, maybe even keeping her eyes closed."

A few people start to walk around the room, but not many want to connect. The general mood is that these 'women' are staying within themselves. Devi, I notice, has turned her face to the wall and hides herself behind her long dark hair. To simply experience her female side alone in this moment is more than enough.

"Let this woman choose where she likes to belong in the room," I continue. "This is a simple exercise but it's important, because when you locate yourself in a particular space you find out more about your woman. Whether she wants to stand in the middle of the room, enjoying the attention... because to be a woman doesn't mean escaping from everything. Some women want to be noticed and admired, while others prefer to be by themselves, or even hide."

This they do.

"Ask yourself: are you the one who made the decision to come to this group? Are you the meditator, the seeker? Do you consider yourself a spiritual being?"

After we have thoroughly explored all these different dimensions of the inner woman, I ask them to close both eyes, say goodbye to the woman and shake their bodies vigorously, letting go of the whole experience.

Now we begin again, this time slowly shifting the weight of the body into the right leg, bringing awareness to the right side of the body, the male side, which is connected with the left hemisphere of the brain.

"Now we are going to meet our inner man," I tell the group. "Does he enjoy taking the weight of the whole body? Is he strong enough?"

The questions I ask are basically the same for both sides, but I shift the emphasis slightly in accordance with male values, because, while you can certainly ask a guy how he is feeling, you will tend to get a better response from a man if you ask him what he does.

"What type of man is he? Does he have a job? Does he support himself financially? Take a look and see."

I repeat the process of connecting with the hand – this time on the right side – and invite people to make gestures, seeing what the man wants to do and how he wants to move.

Now there is a lot more activity in the room. People are striding around, looking outward more than inward, taking notice of the environment and others. The quality of the movements are also changing, becoming more crisp and definite, more strong.

After we have explored the dimensions of the inner man, I invite everyone to find a partner and share their experiences of both energies – male and female – with each other.

When they have been talking for a while, I pose what to me is a very interesting and important question. "Stop for a moment and consider: is your inner man supported by your inner woman? Can they live under the same roof? Can they live in harmony?"

Some people start laughing. Quite clearly, they don't think it's possible for these two characters to get along, even though they co-exist in the same body.

I'm not surprised at this reaction. You may think that, because your inner man and woman are both aspects of you, two halves of one psyche, they already know each other and cooperate in the way you live your life. But very often, this is not the case.

For example, my inner woman was not recognized for her value, she was not seen. My male side was not aware of her presence. In my life, the man ran the show, doing everything from painting to making money, and the woman was lost somewhere in inner space.

It took a real effort on my part to bring them to a point where they could actually meet and where they could see and understand the different contributions they can make, complimenting each other and enriching my life.

Another important aspect of this exploration is to see how outer conflict with members of the opposite sex tends to reflect inner conflict between your own energies. For example, if your find yourself frequently arguing with your partner, struggling for domination, the chances are high that your inner man and woman are doing the same.

Or, if you are a man and you find yourself compulsively and repeatedly attracted to unavailable women, the chances are high that, in your own inner world, your inner woman is also unavailable. Coming in touch with your inner woman can radically alter this frustrating behavior pattern.

In fact, I remember Osho saying in discourse that unless your inner man can meet your inner woman and live in peace and harmony, there's no way to meet the outer partner in a harmonious way.

I continue to guide the exploration with more questions: "Does your inner woman feel supported by your inner man? Which one likes to meditate? Which one likes to paint?" Pretty soon, it becomes clear which of the two is more interested in spiritual growth and art.

One important aspect of these male and female inner dynamics is the movement between being active and passive. It's not that our female side is always passive and the male side active. It can be the other way round, too.

Either way, the exploration of these two sides in us provokes a deeper understanding of when we like to be active, when we enjoy being passive, and, after completing the Star Sapphire exercise, I decide to guide the group in this direction.

We make our way upstairs to Krishna House roof and I lead everyone into a kind of 'let go' dance with a partner.

It goes like this: you are the passive partner, just standing still, loose and relaxed, and then I touch you in a certain way – giving you a gentle push – and you allow your body to move with the energy. Then I touch you in another way and you respond according to this new impulse, and in this way you discover a hidden dance inside that you may never have experienced before.

It's a simple exercise, but significant, because our general attitude towards being receptive, accepting from someone else without giving in return, is to collapse into stagnation or lethargy. This is the disease that has affected India for centuries, this idea that 'God is pulling all the strings so there's nothing I can do.' It is all fate, destiny, karma. It is already determined, already written by the hand of God.

It's not really acceptance. It's more like resignation: 'Okay, this is the way things are, and there's nothing to do about it.' There's no celebration inside the experience of receiving, no quality of aliveness in the acceptance.

So this exercise is designed to give people an experience of 'active receptivity.' Somebody initiates an energy by giving you a little push and you respond and move with it. You are not collapsing, you are not fighting or staying in control, but you are ready to be open, to receive help from others in order to explore your own bodily expression, which sounds easy but in fact is not.

Even with a simple exercise like this, some people resist. They become stiff, like a statue, responding reluctantly or sluggishly to the touch, or they unnecessarily exaggerate the response. Either way, resisting or exaggerating, it is the same phenomenon, which is to remain in control. But with a little encouragement from me, most people get the point and enjoy the exercise.

Then I invite the group to take this same experience to painting, working with the partner that they chose earlier in the day. They sit together on the floor, one behind the other, in front of a blank sheet of paper. Brushes, paints, sponges… everything is available.

The one who sits in front is the receptive partner, whom I call 'Cherry Blossom.' The active partner sits close behind, and I call this one 'Blue Mountain.'

Reaching forwards, Blue Mountain holds Cherry Blossom's hands with his own. Cherry Blossom, with eyes closed, simply allows this to happen.

"Before you start to guide your partner, take a moment to connect with your own energy first," I tell Blue Mountain. "Just close your eyes for the moment, allow a gap, a pause, and drop inside yourself. Then, when there is a readiness, you can start. Take her hand, guide her to pick up a brush, or sponge, dip it in the colors, and begin to paint for her, guiding her hand so that the brush moves over the paper.

"And Cherry Blossom, let your partner take your hand, let this hand move however it wants to move. Now you can really see your own response: Which movement is easy? Which movement is difficult? What is it like to let go into the hands of this energy?"

I let this continue for quite a long time, so that both partners can fully absorb the qualities their roles require, then I tell them, "Stop. Take a moment to feel: how is it for you to be guided, or to guide?

111

"Now change over. Go to the other end of the paper, which has not yet been painted, and sit there. Now the one who was receptive becomes active, and the one who was guiding is now being guided."

In the sharing that follows the exercise, several people say that they took more care and were more aware when guiding their partners than if they had been painting by themselves. They also noticed more strength and directedness in their approach.

Two Japanese women said they felt resistance to being controlled – some kind of rebellion was coming up in them and they enjoyed guiding more than being guided. This, to me, was significant, because these women come from a society in which, even today, women are educated to obey and follow the man, so their resistance indicates that a certain independence is arising.

The sharing is lively and almost everyone has a point of view to express: how they reacted to their partners, what they discovered to be their weakness or strength, in which moments they opened and also when they closed up. Many report difficulty in allowing themselves to be guided.

Through the sharing, almost everybody speaks up, which is good news as far as group dynamics are concerned, because it means that people are no longer feeling shy and hiding themselves.

One of the most important things in my group is sharing time, when people really start exposing themselves. Through this, there's a big chance that we can all grow together – not just following a structured series of exercises and learning how to paint, but deepening our understanding and awareness through sharing.

Just as I am ready to bring this sharing session to an end and break for tea, a conflict reveals itself between Barbara, a good-looking German businesswoman around forty years old, and Manartha, an English landscape gardener who has been visiting Pune for several years.

Barbara begins by saying that, for her, to be receptive is difficult. I ask her about her daily life and of course, as she is a businesswoman, she needs to be very masculine, independent, making her own way in life – and she is not married.

"I don't feel that I need a man," she says, defiantly.

For her it was annoying to work with Manartha, who is a feminine type of man, especially in the way he paints.

"He never drew a clear boundary line for his territory," complains Barbara, referring to the exercise we did earlier in the morning. "And he seems to be the kind of person who enjoys making little details, making the paper wet, dripping and resting, dripping and resting.

"This really touched my nerves. I got upset, so I took a brush and made big strokes all over the paper, just to show him. It's like I'm saying, 'Hey, don't just sit there and be so goddamned patient. Move your energy!'"

Since I'm pretty sure Barbara's attitude toward this kind of man is not confined to my painting training, I ask her, "Does this remind you of the way you relate with men?'

Sure enough, Barbara nods, and then confesses that she had several affairs with 'weak' men and one long relationship with a feminine type of man, the memory of which came up strongly while painting with Manartha.

"Is the relationship still going on?" I ask.

Barbara shakes her head.

"How did it end?"

"I destroyed him," she says, bluntly.

Then it is Manartha's turn to share.

"It was very strong for me, too," he confesses. "I could feel Barbara's disapproval and then it's the same old thing: as soon as a woman judges me, I immediately start judging myself as well – that I am too feminine, I don't take enough initiative, I'm too passive, stagnant…"

Sensing a woman's disapproval, he's already crushing himself down, and this, too, is something that he finds reflected in his relationships.

"What we condemn in others is exactly the part in our own psyche which we are avoiding," I comment, when both

113

of them have finished. "Because that's the part that was not given a chance to develop.

"You can see it clearly: Barbara has a pattern of seeking out weak men and dominating them, because her inner man is not giving her feminine side a chance to express itself. Manartha lets women take the initiative in his relationships and withdraws within himself, but what he really wants is to expand his masculine energy."

This encounter has been important for both of them – a real opportunity to look inside themselves – and I remind them of the exercise that we did, a few days earlier, about liking and disliking what someone has done to your painting. "You can reject the contribution of your partner, or you can see it as a valuable gift, bringing something that has been missing in your life and your creativity – it's up to you," I explain.

This reminds me of my meeting with Govind, which was one of the most important events of my life – both as a woman, and as an artist. So if you will excuse me I will make a small detour here and tell you how it happened.

You will recall that I was in Toledo, enjoying a passionate affair with Aroldo, working with the Tolmo group of artists and learning all I could about art. Then, after three years in Spain, I went back to my village on the northern coast of Japan. I had a sudden urge to see my family and to enjoy an important annual festival – held for two days in July – called the Wild Fire Festival, or in Japanese "Kiriko Matsuri."

On the first day of this festival, I was standing in front of my house, when a foreigner came walking by. It was an unusual sight because in those days, before I got into the habit of taking my European friends home to see my parents, you never saw a foreigner in my village.

He was good-looking in a dignified sort of way, older than me, with blond, wavy hair, piercing blue eyes and a kind of serene, knowing air about him. Later, I wasn't surprised to learn that he was a professor and a scholar – he

114

had the vibe of someone who knows a lot, not just through books but also through personal experience.

He stopped, not far away, took out his camera and started taking pictures of part of the village. Naturally, my curiosity was aroused, so I went up to him and said, in English, "What are doing you here?"

He looked at me for some time, smiled and said, "I came here to find you."

Now, that is quite a line! Something from a movie script. The kind of thing a woman hears once in a lifetime.

I was intrigued, thinking, "Hmm, who is this guy, coming into my life?"

I invited him home for tea, and after that, slowly, slowly, we became friends and, later on, lovers. In those days his name was not Govind, but that is how I think of him, so that is what I'll call him in this book.

He was German by birth, but spent his time travelling between Japan and the USA, where he taught an unusual course, combining anthropology and architecture, at the Massachusetts Institute of Technology in Boston, and also at Harvard.

Talking with him, I soon understood that Govind had a deep love for Japan and lived in Kyoto, one of the most beautiful and ancient Japanese cities. His academic course, which on the face of it was simply a series of lectures about Asian architecture, was – I gradually discovered – quite mysterious and deep. He was looking at the origins of architecture and their connection with the human psyche. Very soon, I learned that there was a lot more to Govind than meets the eye.

But the real revelation came when I visited his house in Kyoto. It was pure Zen. It was so beautiful, and this beauty came not so much from the objects he had put in his house, but from what he left out. In other words, it was the space itself that created the whole atmosphere.

The Japanese have forgotten about the beauty of space and emptiness, which was once regarded as an essential feature of architecture and design, and a link to the inner

115

space that is experienced through meditation. Now they fill their houses with junk, just like any family of western consumers.

But Govind had penetrated the beauty of ancient Japan and – with an enthusiasm that only a foreigner can have, coming fresh to an alien culture and falling in love with it – had even intensified it. For example, in one room he had not put any furniture, just a painting in one corner and, nearby, an ancient musical instrument. And then, in another corner, just single flower, emerging from a small vase.

There was a little Japanese style veranda connecting the house with the garden. In fact, I soon realized that the house was designed as part of the garden, not the other way round, so even when you were inside, the architecture served as a continuous reminder to look out at the beauty of nature.

In another part of the house, a bamboo partition was hanging, with just enough space between thin strips of bamboo to see through to the nature outside. The whole effect was abstract and somehow very cooling, bringing me into a space of silence and stillness inside myself.

This became a turning point for me. It was like a spiritual and aesthetic homecoming, because all the beauty of Japan that I had rejected, turned my back on, choosing instead the chaos and wildness of western modern art, was coming home to me through the eyes of a foreigner.

I was an Eastern woman, gone to the West to find her freedom of expression. He was a Western man, coming to the East to fill his soul with silence and beauty. And then we met and were able to give each other the part that had been missing in ourselves.

I will tell you more about Govind later, because he was the man who brought me to India, thereby opening an even deeper dimension of art for me. But right now I want to talk about Pere Tanguy, a very unusual man who lived in Paris in the second half of the nineteenth century.

The reason for suddenly introducing Monsieur Tanguy is this: the merging of East and West that I experienced through meeting Govind in Kyoto is not new; it has been going on for a long time, ever since Japan was forced to open its borders to foreigners in the mid-nineteenth century.

As some of you may know, the Tokugawa Shoguns who ruled Japan from 1603 onwards – in the name of a puppet emperor – had closed the country to foreigners and all external influences. Then, more than two hundred years later, in the 1850s, an American naval commander called Commodore Perry arrived with a fleet of warships and forced the country to open its doors again.

Naturally, when world trade opened up, many works of art from Japan began finding their way to Europe, and soon Japanese woodblock prints became fashionable in Paris. At this point, I need to give a short discourse on the Japanese tradition of making woodblock prints. You will see why in a moment.

In the Japanese language, the technical term for woodblock prints is *moku-hanga*. *Moku* means wood. *Han* means 'a printing block,' and *ga* is 'picture.' But in common usage, nobody uses the term *moku-hanga*. Instead, the art of making woodblock prints is almost always referred to as *ukiyoe*.

It was something new for the West, not only in the subjects portrayed, but in the way this technique made it possible for thousands of people to own one painting.

In the *ukiyoe* tradition, an artist and an engraver work very closely together, almost as one person. The artist creates a painting and gives it to the engraver who carefully carves out printing boards – one for each color to be used – following exactly the shapes created by the artist in each of the colors. The original art is destroyed in the process.

When each board is daubed with its specific color and pressed on a blank sheet of paper, an exact replica of the painting can be produced – providing, of course, that all the boards are exactly aligned. In this way, the printers have the capacity to hand-print copy after copy, as many as they need, mass marketing the painting to the public.

Woodblock prints recorded Japan's natural beauty, as well as city and village life, together with portraits of the public's favorite kabuki actors and sumo wrestlers. A special sub-category provided ordinary people with a taste of the exotic life behind the walls of the 'water world,' including portraits of the lovely geishas and women of pleasure – rather like modern-day pin-up posters.

The three great masters of woodblock prints in Japan are Hiroshige, Hokusai and Utamaro. Many people in the West are familiar with Hokusai's thirty-six paintings of Mount Fuji, especially "The Great Wave Off Kanagawa," where the mountain is seen far away in the distance, from the ocean. In the foreground, a towering blue wave with a white crest seems certain to destroy the long, narrow boats – filled with people – that ride the smaller waves in front of it.

Hiroshige became even more famous in Japan than Hokusai, whose works had inspired him to be an artist. He began by making traditional paintings of theater actors and courtesans, but attained the peak of his success as a landscape artist, turning well-known, everyday scenes into lyrical vistas.

Interestingly, Hiroshige always included people in his landscapes – traveling, fishing, cultivating fields, drinking tea – as a way of connecting human beings with their natural environment.

Utamaro became famous for his portraits of beautiful women. Like Toulouse-Lautrec, who drew inspiration from Utamaro's work, he loved to portray women sensuously combing their hair, washing their bodies, changing their clothes...

He was also renowned for his depiction of tragic lovers – those who had broken the strict rules of Japanese society for passion and love, and who suffered death or suicide because of it. Such stories, loosely based on fact, were extremely popular with the Japanese public, both as plays and as paintings.

The lives of these three masters covered the second half of the eighteenth century and the first half of the nineteenth; in other words, the period just before Japan opened its doors to the West.

The style of woodblock prints, with its emphasis on flat planes, strong linear outlines, simplicity and vibrant colors, made a deep impact on many French painters, including Gaugin, Toulouse-Lautrec, Degas and Van Gogh. And here we come to the relevance of Pere Tanguy – why I suddenly thought of him in connection with the merging of East and West.

Monsieur Tanguy was, as I have said, an interesting man, a kind of unsung hero of the Impressionist era. He was a Paris communard, a socialist, and made a living by selling art supplies to painters in Paris, first by walking around on foot, and later by setting up an art supply shop in Montmartre. He sympathized with the poor artists who needed his supplies and – much to the disapproval of his wife – often accepted their works as payment for his painting materials.

In this way, Pere Tanguy slowly became an art collector and dealer, while his shop became a meeting place for avant-garde artists such as Guillaumin, Pissaro, Renoir, Gauguin, Cezanne and others. In the winter of 1886, Van Gogh became friendly with Pere Tanguy and, at about this time, made at least two portraits of him, one of which contains the reason for my affection for this little man.

Van Gogh painted him sitting in his shop, wearing a big planter's hat and a double-breasted coat, capturing the man's general mood of contentedness, stoicism and good humor. Behind Tanguy, on the wall of his shop, van Gogh depicted an array of Japanese woodblock prints, including a rural snow scene, a tree in blossom by a river, an actor and a picture of Mount Fuji right behind his head. So Tanguy not only knew about the prints coming from Japan, he was also collecting and selling them.

To me, this portrait of Tanguy is a magical and historical time capsule. It shows how the art of Japan came to the Europe and influenced the birth of modern Western art, including the artistic genius who was painting this portrait.

My feeling is that, for people like Van Gogh, Japanese art helped to create a revolution in understanding. It offered a return to a more innocent approach to painting, where the first impression is most important – not depth, three dimensions or correct sense of proportion, which are the usual concerns of western art, based on logic and reason.

For example, Sharaku, another ukiyoe artist, sometimes paints the human hand very small and the face very big, which simply doesn't happen proportionally. But if you look at it innocently, you can see that the artist is more intrigued by the expression of the face – that is his primary focus – so naturally other parts of the body are left behind.

When a child looks at the world, it also happens in this way. A child doesn't think that the hand should be the same size as the face, this part should be proportionate to that part... and so on.

The Impressionists and their successors in the modern movement caught hold of the same basic idea: it's not the faithful reproduction of reality that's important in a painting. It's the impression that the outer world makes on your spirit, on your heart, that matters most, and the expression you give to this inner feeling on canvas.

It means that each artist's way of looking at the world is going to be unique, because each has a different personal experience. And this is what makes the Impressionist era the dividing line from the traditional way of painting and the beginning of a new era.

This is the reason why I love Van Gogh's portrait of Tanguy. For me, it creates half of a circle: the East going to the West and influencing the birth of modern art. My own story, how I fell in love with modern art in the West, and then returned to an appreciation of Japanese art through the eyes of Govind, creates the other half.

I sometimes think that if I had a time machine I would love to go back to that little shop in Montmartre, where I could purchase Pere Tanguy's whole collection of paintings – Cezannes, Van Goghs, Pissaros – for a few hundred dollars. Then I would tell him, "Monsieur Tanguy, one day, about a hundred years from now, what you have hanging in your shop will be worth not only millions of dollars, but hundreds of millions of dollars."

I think he would laugh and enjoy the joke, because in those days, almost alone, he had a vision, a deep insight, that these poor, struggling artists were bringing something great into the world and were therefore worth supporting. That's why he ignored the complaints of his wife, accepting paintings no one else would buy.

And I think he would also like the fact that this news was coming from a Japanese woman, who could have stepped out of one of his prints on the wall – of course, a little differently dressed, since I much prefer jeans and t-shirts to kimonos. A Japanese woman who, more than a century later, may be helping to bring another revolution to the world of art.

Okay, enough of my fantasies about time travel. We need to go back to the group room, otherwise I will not have enough space left in this chapter to include what I want to say.

As I said before, I'm not keeping track of the exact progression of exercises in the training – that we do this on the fourth day, and this on the twelfth, and so on. I can't possibly tell you everything we do in six weeks, so I'm just describing the most important parts to give you the general idea. If you can understand my basic approach to art, that is enough. You don't need to follow a specific sequence of events.

We are still exploring the dynamic between male and female, so one morning I ask the men to gather together in one group and the women in another. Immediately, I can see that there are too many women to make a single group, so, without thinking too much, I divide them into three:

1, A group of sensitive artists like Fulwari and Nirvikalpa – people who love painting and who have done several trainings with me.

2, A group of women who possess soft, feminine qualities.

3, A group of women who are more outgoing types.

121

"Take a few moments to connect with the people in your group," I tell them, after the sorting process has finished. "Look at each other, hold hands, or put your arms around each other's shoulders... feel the energy of this group.

"You may notice that your group has a certain quality, a certain direction in which your collective energy would like to be expressed. Now I am inviting you to express it, either in the form of theater, talking or dance – or maybe through not doing anything. It's up to you. Whatever comes out of your group, let me know and we will do it the way you want."

After a few minutes, it becomes apparent that all of the groups are choosing dance as the medium of expression, and it is really remarkable because within two minutes they have choreographed their presentations and are ready to begin. It's amazing what you can do when you are not given any time – something arises spontaneously that surprises everyone, including yourself.

I act as the DJ, looking quickly through my collection of CDs and my two ipods, trying to find the kind of music that each group wants.

One of the women's groups – the outgoing types – goes first, choosing sensuous music with a good beat, with the flavor of South American salsa, that allows them to be energetic and yet at the same time to be graceful and feminine.

The men have requested wild, rhythmic, high energy music, like a mix between African and techno, and they immediately create – easily and naturally – a sense of male bonding and tribal energy. I can see how much the women are enjoying the way the men dance in front of them and this, in turn, encourages the men to show more of their power. This is something you don't often see in the normal course of social life: men coming into their energy and power in a relaxed and playful way.

The group of experienced painters creates something totally different. They choose soft, watery music, blended with silence, and they dance together like a flower opening

122

its many petals, expressing a quality that, to those watching it, takes you inward, inside yourself.

The last group, comprising soft, feminine women, has not really created a cohesive dance. You can't see much happening, in an organized way, but the feeling they exude is harmonious and uniform. It's more of a quality, less of a choreography.

Next, I ask the groups to go to four very large pieces of paper – each one is made of eight sheets glued together – and give expression to the energy that they have experienced in the dance. Everyone sits down, picks up the brushes and sponges, and begins to paint.

Watching the men, I notice something I've seen before: men have an ability to quickly connect and work as a team without discussing much. Around the big sheet, each man takes a lot of space for himself, but at the same time there's a quality of playfulness and freedom that allows them to work together in harmony. I notice other qualities, too, that men bring to art: no fear of losing anything, just splashing color in this moment, making bold and big strokes with strong colors like black and white.

When all four groups have had time to explore and experiment, I ask the women to come and watch the men as they paint.

"What do you see in the men's painting?" I ask, when they have gathered around.

Their responses are perceptive: "Its one energy… it's organized… there's lots of movement and direction… Yes, and they are not afraid to make mistakes…"

The presence of the women soon results in an element of performance coming into the men's creativity. They get even more wild, throwing colors here and there, lifting the whole sheet of paper together, making a big rip down the middle as they do so.

They we go to the painting done by the outgoing woman and watch them. Their painting is beautiful, but when the men arrive something new happens. The women also get more wild and crazy – they start walking on the paper with bare feet, throwing colors at random, lifting the painting here and there, until it is just a big brown mess.

"What do you see?" I ask the men.

Mostly, the men come up with the same qualities the women said about their own work, but then one man, hesitatingly, offers a controversial point.

"It feels like they got lost," he says. "It's like... they picked up on our energy, but it's not really their own quality."

I agree and ask the women to stop for a moment.

"What I see here is that there's a feeling of competition with men in the way you are painting now," I tell them. "To me, this is significant, because you can see the same thing happening all over the West now, especially in countries like America.

"The women's liberation movement, which first gave us the awareness that we've been denied the freedom men have given to themselves, has gotten lost into competition. It's still a man's world. Male values dominate. But now women are competing to excel in those values, in business, in politics, in sport, running after soccer balls and even – my god, can you believe it – taking part in ugly events like boxing matches.

"And of course, some of them do well, beating men at their own game, but that's not the point. We have not yet given ourselves permission to really be women, to explore the feminine values in a climate of freedom.

"That's why this painting has become a mess," I continue. "You were following men into their energy and wildness, and lost the sensitivity and beauty of your own work."

One woman is offended. "We're not imitating the men," she protests. "I really like to be wild!"

"I'm not saying women shouldn't be wild," reply. "Not at all. I myself am a very wild woman. I'm just pointing out a tendency to imitate instead of being true to yourself."

It's a difficult thing for them to digest, but some get the point.

"Yes, I felt I was becoming more aggressive and this is not my way," says one of them. "Before, when we were on our own, there was space to go at my own speed, and I felt something was growing between us, but now I can't 'feel' the painting any more."

One of the men speaks up, saying he felt something similar when the women came to watch his group – how he got lost in performing for them.

"Nothing is wrong," I say. "I don't want you to feel bad. It's just something to watch: how easily we lose the connection with ourselves."

Now we go to the painting created by the feminine women. Here, watching them work, I see that they have confined themselves to separate areas of the paper, making little compartments of the painting in an unspoken agreement not to overlap each other.

"You can see that they are not connecting with each other," I tell the group, after a while. "In a way, this is a beautiful quality. It means each one is staying with herself, not being aggressive or violent with the others. But this also means the painting has no dynamism, no movement. The risk is that it will become stagnant."

Lastly, we go to the group of experienced painters.

"What do you see here?" I ask members of the two other groups.

"There's a lot of harmony and joy in the way they are painting," says one of the women.

A man adds, "They are like us, high energy, but sensitive at the same time."

Others say, "There's so much silence... They're not discussing anything, just responding to each moment together.... It's beautiful to watch."

I nod my agreement. "That's right. Nobody is interfering with each other, but still the whole painting is happening in an organic way. Nobody is disturbing each other, but each painter's work is a continuation of the next.

"This is what I see: if you totally give your love to what you are doing, you can also take other people with you, as part of it, and you can grow together."

Then I put on some lively music and we all dance together, slipping out of the intensity of the exercise and into a more celebrative mood. I'm happy at the way this exercise has turned out, because it has been a good learning. The participants understand that energy can take a different turn at any moment and it is easy to lose the connection with it, going into some idea or trip.

But this is not forever. Just a little awareness, you stop, connect inside, and the energy comes flooding back.

Which provokes a very important question: from where does this energy come? What really goes on inside us? The answer will, I hope, be found in the following chapter. I say 'hope' because we are entering a dimension of human experience that is difficult to talk about. It is almost like trying to say the unsayable, express the inexpressible – which, come to think of it, is what true art is all about.

Chapter 6

The 'M' Word

"Who likes Dynamic Meditation?"

My question kick-starts a new day for the painting training in Naropa Pyramid and in response about forty percent of the participants raise their hands.

"And who doesn't like Dynamic Meditation? Don't be shy, I'm not going to report you to the head teacher."

About thirty percent raise their hands.

"And the rest of you are in between, undecided, right?" Without waiting for an answer, I continue, "Okay, now we are going to make some theater around Dynamic, so I want you to form into two groups. Those who like Dynamic in a group over here, on this side please, and this includes people who don't necessarily go to Dynamic every day, but who like it a lot. And then people who don't go, who don't like it, over there. All of you, who are undecided, please go to one or the other – just see which way you are leaning and go to that side."

When the two groups are formed, I invite those who don't like Dynamic to sit down and become an audience.

"All of you who like Dynamic, this is your chance to show it. Go to the people who don't like it, and convince them how good it is how much you like it, what a great meditation it is."

There is laughter in the room because people know I am not being serious. This is a game, not a mission. Nobody can take me seriously for long because I am just not that kind of person. There is always some kind of bubbly, playful energy coming out of me. Of course, there are times when I am down, sad, worried... caused by the usual things like uncooperative boyfriends, upset plans, bad news, and so on. But it doesn't last long. I enjoy my life so much I can't stay miserable for more than five minutes – fifteen at the most.

Still, there is a purpose to this drama. I personally consider that the whole of Osho's work is condensed in his original meditation technique, Dynamic Meditation, and I want everyone to get a deeper understanding of it.

Dynamic Meditation is certainly a challenge. To do it, you have to put out a lot of energy, make a really big effort – in fact, a total effort. And the first part of this effort is to manage to get out of bed at the right time, because at the meditation resort in Pune, Dynamic begins at six o'clock in the morning, every morning, 365 days a year.

This means, if you're like me, you need to set the alarm clock for 5:30 and then resist the temptation to switch it off, roll over and snuggle back under the sheets, thinking "Mmm, this is so cozy, I'll do Dynamic tomorrow."

No, instead you need to drag yourself out of bed, throw on a maroon robe, stagger out of the apartment, jump astride your scooter and roar off down the road, through the dark and deserted streets of Koregaon Park. You need to park as close as possible to the ashram's back gate, walk through the winding paths to Buddha Hall, kick off your shoes, enter the hall, find a space and be ready as the meditation leader picks up the microphone and says "Good morning, welcome to Dynamic Meditation."

This is just the beginning. Now comes the really hard part, or the really good part, depending on how you feel about it – because for some people it is challenging, while for others it is the best work-out in the world.

Even Osho has described Dynamic as "a very cruel method." In one of his discourses, he says, "A chaotic, a dynamic meditation, is a very cruel method. It is not like sweet prayer, it is bitter, but it can cleanse much dust off your being. It can bring great awakening to you. It can become your first satori. Just a hundred-percent commitment is needed."

This is the important part: the commitment. All the energy that you have, you have to put out. Naturally, some people tend to avoid going because when you have to get up early… and then, when you're not even fully awake, start deep chaotic breathing… then shouting and screaming like a madwoman… then jumping up and down… well, it's not easy.

So the mind tends to make up reasons to avoid the whole experience. Also, so much emphasis is given to it – everyone who is participating in groups, or working in the commune, *should* go to Dynamic every morning – you can easily persuade yourself that "Hey, is this a kind of military service, boot camp? I am not in the army. Why should I bother?"

In my groups I don't like to push people. I want them to understand how important Dynamic is for one's growth, but still, I want it to be *their* understanding, not something like a school rule, or the ten commandments of sannyas. Hence, I devise this little theater game.

"Okay, now really go for it," I say encouragingly, to the group who like Dynamic. "Sell Dynamic to these people. Let them know how good Dynamic is for your body, your mind, your energy… You have to really persuade them to do Dynamic."

With a lot of enthusiasm, noise and theatrical gestures, the people who like Dynamic walk over to their audience and try to convince them. Watching from the sidelines, I can see an energetic difference between the two groups – not great, but it is visible. Those who like Dynamic look younger, fresher, brighter – generally more alive.

They do their best and many people from the other group seem to be listening attentively and are clearly enjoying the show but not enough to immediately jump up and join the other group. I let the theater run for a few minutes and then it is time to switch roles.

"Okay, very good. Thank you. Please come back and sit down. Now those who don't like Dynamic; it's your turn. Try and persuade these meditators that you are right."

This is also amusing to watch, because some of those who don't like Dynamic pick up their pillows, stroll sleepily across the room towards their audience, rest their heads comfortably on the pillows and say things like, "Mmm, this is so good. We can always meditate later – there are so many meditations to choose from every day. It's so cold this morning... so nice and warm in bed... let's just sleep a little longer..."

Looking around, I notice Alexandra sitting beside me, not participating in either group.

"You're not taking part?" I say to her.

She shakes her head. "No.

"Why?"

"I can't decide once and forever. I can only decide each moment."

The way she says it impresses me. I don't feel she is just making an excuse to stay aloof. It's her truth, her authenticity, and it gives me an idea. So, when the second part of the drama is over and everyone has sat down, I invite people to watch Alexandra and myself. I set up the situation as another theater piece – you can maybe tell, by now, that I love drama.

"Now, I am a group participant, very new to Pune, who doesn't know what to do," I tell the group. "I feel insecure – whether to go to Dynamic or not? I want people's opinions and Alexandra is my first group leader, so of course I want to ask her."

I sit down next to Alexandra, very respectful and shy. "Excuse me, you know I've just arrived, this is my first group, and I'm not sure if I should go to Dynamic or not. What do you think?"

Alexandra, not at all intimidated by her role as a therapist, replies, "For me, this morning was a very good morning for Dynamic, because I woke up early, I wanted to get out of bed, and I felt a 'yes' in my heart to go and meditate. It's like that, for me: if I feel to go, I go. Otherwise I don't go. I can't fake it. So I can't say you 'should' go to Dynamic every morning, because then I would be a hypocrite. I can only tell you this: for myself, I decide moment to moment."

Afterwards, a couple of my assistants tell me they were worried about this dialogue with Alexandra. And even inside my own mind, there was a little voice saying, "Meera, what are you doing? You are the group leader, you are supposed to make sure everyone does Dynamic, and here you are giving energy and importance to someone – just arrived off a plane from Greece – who is saying something entirely different."

But I trust my intuition. I want to give people the option, the freedom to choose, because if they are pushed to meditate it doesn't work, especially with Dynamic. You really need to decide for yourself, so that your total energy is connected with your inner decision. So I prefer to take people in this direction, into freedom of choice, rather than into "How many times did you go this week?"

One more thing about Dynamic, before I explain the stages of the meditation: it presents people with an opportunity to experience the feeling of being total, and this in itself is a big key to unlocking the secrets of life. If you can be total in the way you live, moment to moment, you don't need therapy. And what is the way to go through life with totality? Dynamic will teach you that.

"So… does everyone know the stages of Dynamic?" I ask when Alexandra and I have finished talking. "What is the first stage?"

Before anyone else can speak, a clear, loud, male voice announces, "Deep, fast, chaotic breathing, through the nose, emphasizing the exhale."

Everyone turns to look at Rishiraj, a 42 year-old German sannyasin who has done the training three times and is one of my helpers. He speaks in such a tone of school-masterly certainty that even I am surprised – those words come right out of the resort's meditation manual.

By way of explanation, Rishiraj smiles and says "I used to lead Dynamic every day at a meditation center in Germany."

"Great!" I reply. "Then you can demonstrate it for us."

"No problem."

Rishiraj gets up and stands in the middle of an open space created by his seated audience. "Normally, when you want to take a really deep breath, you focus only on the inhale," he explains. "You don't bother about the exhale, you let it take care of itself. But in Dynamic you do the reverse. You emphasize the exhale, breathing all the way out, and then let the inhale happen by itself. Like this..."

He breathes strongly out, through his nose, hunching his chest inward in an effort to expel all the air. Holding his hands like loose fists in front of him, he brings his arms sharply in towards his chest at the same time, so his whole upper body is involved in expelling the air. The inhalation that follows – as he says – happens by itself.

Then, making noisy exhales – rather like an old steam train puffing slowly out of a station – he continues to breathe in this way, with strong exhales and relaxed inhales, gradually building up speed. His arms are flapping like a bird opening and closing its wings. Then, just as he has built up a good rhythm, he breaks it, varying the exhales – some short, some long – bring in an element of chaos.

I should add that Osho has created some truly amazing music that accompanies this meditation. He directed its composition, working with a German musician, Georg Deuter, who is quite well known in the world of 'New Age' music.

I didn't realize how important the music was until I went to a techno party a few years ago and noticed that a friend, who accompanied me, was watching a clock on the wall for a long time while people were dancing.

When I asked what he was doing, he said, "These are exactly the beats used in the first stage of Dynamic."

Osho invented Dynamic thirty or forty years ago and at that time, of course, there was no techno music. But I guess

132

he knew that the modern mind needs this kind of support for going into the body, into chaotic breathing, and that's why he chose it.

Breathing chaotically like this for ten minutes – that's how long the first stage lasts – also provokes a chaos in your body, especially in feelings that are somehow locked up in the body armor and muscle tissues. It provokes a lot of emotions that would otherwise remain dormant or suppressed. Pressure builds up, getting more and more ready to burst and then…

"Second stage!" I call out to Rishiraj. He hasn't been breathing for ten minutes but this is just a demo.

Instead of stopping to explain the second stage, Rishiraj just explodes into it.

"I hate this group! I hate painting!" he shouts, loudly and angrily, but there is humor in it, too, and the whole group roars with laughter at this turn of events. They know the second stage of Dynamic is catharsis, spontaneous emotional expression, but no one – including me – has anticipated this particular avenue of expression.

Rishiraj stamps his feet, shouts, screams, throws his body around wildly in an impressive demonstration of the second stage and then, after a few minutes, with all the skill of a professional actor he suddenly stops, smiles calmly and bows, inviting – and receiving – enthusiastic applause for his performance. His emotion was real, but somehow he was behind it, or outside it, watching it, which is really something that only a good actor or a meditator can do.

"Third stage," I announce, and Rishiraj reverts to his role as instructor. "Jump up and down, with arms raised above your head, landing on the flat of your feet. It's important that your heels hit the ground, sending a shock wave of energy up the back of your legs to the sex center. And all the time you are saying loudly, 'Hoo! Hoo! Hoo!'"

This, as you can imagine, is a very strenuous activity. There are certain African tribes that jump like this for hours, until they faint and fall unconscious on the earth, just to have a taste of the transcendental. For city-dwellers like ourselves, a few minutes can seem like a lifetime.

Each of the first three stages lasts ten minutes, making a total of thirty minutes of extremely intense physical activity and emotional catharsis. The key to the whole thing is the chaotic breathing in the first stage. If you put your total energy into the breathing, then the catharsis explodes by itself, and then, after releasing so much emotion in catharsis, the jumping is easy – well, easier than it would be otherwise.

"Stop!" I call out, and Rishiraj freezes, not moving a muscle, his arms held in the air. He is breathing strongly from the effort but otherwise completely still, his eyes closed. Gradually, his breathing calms down, becoming normal and quiet. This is the fourth stage, silence and stillness, when meditation can happen.

You may wonder about this phrase 'when meditation can happen,' because the whole hour-long experience is described as a meditation. In fact there are dozens of different meditations offered in the resort – Dynamic, Kundalini, Nataraj, Nadabhrama, Gourishankar, Whirling, Chakra Sounds, Zazen, Vipassana, Gibberish – and there are thousands of different meditations available worldwide.

An important distinction needs to be made between these meditation techniques and the state of meditation itself. They are two separate things. You can do a technique. You can't do meditation. Nobody can do it – that's why it remains such an elusive and mysterious thing. It can happen to you, but you can't force it. So all of these techniques have one common purpose: to help bring you to a state of relaxation and receptivity where the state of meditation can happen, flowering spontaneously inside you with all its silence, grace and beauty.

The sudden stop at the end of Dynamic's three active stages is designed specifically for this purpose. You have just spent thirty minutes exhausting all your physical, mental and emotional energy. Then you don't do anything – can't do anything, anyway, even if you want to, because everything that you have inside you has just been put out. Now the energy that was exploding outwards turns suddenly inwards.

You simply remain aware and alert, watching your breathing as it slows down, watching the body sweating and cooling off, watching the thoughts passing through your mind. Then there is an opportunity for a gap, for real silence, for a state of 'No Mind' to happen.

No doubt as you read this you are thinking to yourself, "My god, do I really have to go through thirty minutes of sheer torture, just to experience a little glimpse of meditation?"

And the answer, most probably, is "yes." Because the modern mind is so busy, the modern body so tense, the modern emotional state so uptight, that unless we get rid of all the crap inside with an extreme method like Dynamic, there is very little chance of creating enough inner space to make room for meditation. At least, that's my experience, working with thousands of people during the past fifteen years – and on myself, too.

I'm not saying you have to do Dynamic every morning for years. I haven't done that myself, so I'm certainly not recommending it for others. I'm just trying to show the importance of a method like Dynamic, because – as I said in the beginning – it reflects and condenses Osho's whole approach to spiritual growth.

It's like a scientific formula, written by a meditative Einstein: energy plus catharsis plus awareness equals 'a state where meditation can happen.'

This doesn't mean that meditation *will* happen. There is no guarantee. It means that it is more likely to happen than if, for example, you just sit down, close your eyes and expect to be transported into a state of twenty-four-carat gold enlightenment.

A lot of the group programs, or therapies, offered by the meditation resort in Pune contain variations on this basic formula. They clean out all the rubbish inside and help to energize people in such a way that meditation happens more easily.

The fourth stage of Dynamic lasts fifteen minutes, making a total so far of forty-five minutes, and the last section of this hour-long technique – which Rishiraj is now demonstrating for the group – is dance and celebration, accompanied by light, joyful music that supports a general mood of happiness.

This stage looks like an afterthought, something nice to round off the hour, but in reality it's crucially important. Osho's approach, as I have mentioned before, is intense but not serious, and the element of dance helps to maintain a playful quality. I think Osho knows very well that a serious attitude towards meditation is sure to create a saintly, spiritual ego in the seeker and so he tries to avoid it at all costs.

Dynamic seems like a really big challenge, especially when you do it for the first few times. Immediately, the mind wants to protest: "I can't breath like that! I can't shout and scream for no reason! I can't jump up and down like that like for ten minutes – are you crazy? Are you kidding me? I'd probably have a heart attack or injure myself. I just don't have that kind of energy."

But energy is a strange thing. The more you use it, the more you have of it. And this reminds me of a story concerning Georges Gurdjieff, who himself was a very strange man.

Gurdjieff was born in the Caucasus – in Armenia or Georgia, as I recall – and led a bizarre life. His parents died when he was young, so he traveled with nomads, crossing deserts and mountain ranges, developing a thirst for spiritual growth, learning from secret spiritual schools and exploring different meditation techniques. He wandered through the turbulent region of the Middle East and Southern Russia, gathering disciples and trying to avoid the ravages of the First World War and the Russian Revolution.

An Englishman called John G. Bennett met Gurdjieff in 1921, in a refugee camp in Istanbul. Bennett recognized him as a spiritual teacher of great value, and two years later went to stay with him in France, by which time Gurdjieff had created his Institute for the Harmonious Development of Man in Fontainebleau-Avon.

One of the first things Gurdjieff asked Bennett to do – oddly enough – was dig a large ditch in his garden. Here I need to return to my group in Naropa Pyramid because, continuing my love of theater, I have impulsively decided to act out the whole scene with the help of Rishiraj.

I have appointed Rishiraj as Gurdjieff, which of course he thoroughly enjoys – all men who are meditators want to be spiritual masters – and myself as Bennett, which is also typical because in my amateur theatricals I tend to choose the more innocent role, the beginner, the new and ignorant disciple. I guess there's a message in it for me, too.

'Yes, Mr. Bennett, come this way, I have some urgent and important work for you," booms Rishiraj, puffing out his chest and assuming an air of great dignity and authority.

"I need a long ditch, from here to here, and it must be this deep… like so… and this much wide… like so. You understand, of course. I would like you to dig it as one continuous effort, without taking any breaks, hmm? Very good."

And off he goes, leaving me to dig this imaginary ditch across the pyramid room. Bennett was 26 years old at the time, while I am 54, so it's a good thing that I can work with an imaginary shovel instead of a real one.

It's a big job, the sun is hot and the work is tiring. The first layer of my physical energy – what I normally think I can do without rest and refreshment – is quickly exhausted. But to my surprise, I discover that when I push myself and keep digging, I suddenly break through to a second layer of energy that keeps me going until – after many hours of continuous work – I have succeeded in digging the ditch.

Proud of myself, I go and fetch Mr. Gurdjieff, and Rishiraj comes to survey my handiwork. "My dear Mr. Bennett," he says, clapping me on the shoulder and taking liberties with history – because neither of us can remember

137

exactly what was said between these two men. "I must apologize to you profusely. Actually, I had no intention of creating a ditch here. I do not know what I was thinking about. Now please fill it in, immediately, without breaks, under the same conditions as before."

I want to protest, loudly. This is absurd! But Mr. Gurdjieff has already turned his back, is walking away, and I remind myself that I came here, to his institute, with the avowed intention of learning as much as possible from him. So, rolling up me sleeves, I start to fill in the ditch. The day has passed, evening has come and night is falling. The second layer of energy into which I tapped some hours ago is now completely exhausted, but, just as I think I must surely collapse, I suddenly break through into a third layer, deeper than the first two.

To my astonishment, I am filled with vigor, with life. Late in the night I fling the last shovels of soil into the ditch and my work is done, but I cannot sleep. I am so awake, so alive. I have never felt this much energy before.

"The story is true and I use it to show people how tricky the mind can be," I explain to the group. "Dynamic looks like an exhausting meditation, so in the beginning you can easily persuade yourself that you can't do it. But that's because you haven't tested yourself. You haven't explored your full potential. You haven't tapped into the deeper layers of your energy."

This is something not many people understand. Meditation doesn't happen just by sitting down and closing your eyes. That's why nearly all of the techniques offered in Pune are designed with active stages in the beginning – to stir up your sources of energy. Meditation needs energy. Meditation needs intensity and totality. So does painting. Look at this description by Vincent Van Gogh of how he works:

"I bring every ounce of blood with me when I paint, for my mind vibrates with the wind and my hands strike the canvases with lightning. My ears hear my brush pressing on the colors while my feelings become the painting. I watch my thoughts float onto the canvas while my hands move to the rhythms where nothing else has purpose. It's one continuous movement over another, flowing forth with a tip of madness that's tucked inside burnt-sea-mist of ocean browns, deep-green-gold of emerald dawns that nestle with the twilight-almonds for ending the day."

This man is not painting from his intellect. His whole being is on fire. He is painting from his guts, with his heart and soul. And this is how the spiritual seeker needs to approach the inner quest as well. Which brings me to the question I asked at the end of the last chapter: where does all this energy come from?

Actually, nobody knows. It is a mystery. It is beyond the reach of the mind to put a name to it. But what we do know is that it becomes available by penetrating deeper and deeper into ourselves.

As for me, I did not know anything about the dynamic approach to meditation, nor of its intimate relationship with art and creativity, until I came to India in 1974 – so now I'd like to leave the group room and tell you something more about my personal life.

I was back in Toledo when I received a very beautiful letter from Govind, my new companion, teacher and lover, saying that he wanted to take me on a tour of India, showing me the country's ancient architecture and culture.

In the letter, there was a sentence that made me shiver, where Govind had written, "There is only one thing I have to do there, apart from traveling: I have to meet a sage."

I didn't understand my reaction, why these words made me shiver, so I looked up the word 'sage' in the dictionary. It said, 'one who knows the truth, one who reaches the heights of the human possibility' – something like that.

I was puzzled. Things like this I'd never heard about. I had been so much into art that I'd never even considered there were more significant things to experience in life.

Govind had heard about Osho from students at MIT who had become sannyasins, so when we arrived in India our first stop was Pune. I don't have much recollection about the

139

ashram from those days, except that it was much more like you would expect an Indian ashram to be – it didn't have the 'resort' flavor – and also was smaller than it is now.

I first saw Osho one morning in his daily discourse, which he was giving on a large balcony in the house where he lived.

I was a little late for the discourse, but – India being India – you were allowed to go in even if you were not on time. So I crept softly up the stairs and sat at the back of the room, close to the top of the staircase.

Osho was talking on a famous Zen story concerning Chiyono, a high rank courtesan in ancient Japan. She became interested in Zen Buddhism and wanted to become a nun, but was so beautiful that no monastery or teacher would accept her – fearing her presence would disturb the other monks and nuns. So she burned and disfigured her face in order to be admitted.

Chiyono meditated for forty years and then, one full moon night, she was carrying water from the well in two buckets, hanging from a bamboo pole on her shoulders. Suddenly the bamboo broke, the buckets fell, the water rushed out and, in the sudden, unexpected shock of that moment, she became enlightened.

Listening to Osho tell the story, I felt deeply moved. Something completely new, unknown and yet strangely familiar stirred in my heart – some remembrance, or longing, for that mysterious state that Chiyono had searched for and attained. To my surprise, I found my cheeks were wet with tears. I was experiencing for the first time how tears can be shed without sorrow.

As the discourse ended and Osho stood up, everyone on the balcony shouted a traditional Indian greeting in praise of holy men, "Bhagwan Shree Rajneesh ki jai!" It was really a scene – something I'd never encountered before.

He responded with a namaste greeting, hands pressed together in front of his chest, and then started to leave, walking straight towards me, because his private quarters were downstairs and he needed to use the staircase.

He had to walk past me, no more than fifty centimeters away, and as he approached I found myself returning his namaste greeting. I looked into his eyes, he looked into my eyes and we had a big smile together. That was a wonderful feeling. And then a sentence came to me, 'I can really trust this uncle,' because with his long beard, black and gray mixed with white, he looked like an uncle to me. So that was the first impression I got of Osho, and it was a beautiful meeting – eye to eye.

A little later in the morning we were in the ashram office, in an adjoining building, when a Greek woman named Mukta came walking through, holding a pencil and a piece of paper, saying, "Who wants to see Bhagwan tonight?" As I said before, in those days he was called Bhagwan Shree Rajneesh. Now he is Osho, so that's what I call him.

Of course, Govind said, "Yes, we want to see him," and so that was the second time I met him, in what is known as 'darshan' – personal talks with the Master – on a large and elegant car porch at the back of his house. There were no cars there, just a gravel pathway to some white marble steps that led up to a small patio, also made of white marble, where he would sit in his chair every evening and talk with people.

On that occasion, there were about a dozen of us, as I recall. We sat around him in a semi-circle on the floor. He wore the same simple style of white robe that he used in discourse, lightweight and synthetic, with a turtle neck – I don't think he wore anything else at that time.

There were all kinds of Indian night sounds behind us in the garden – frogs and crickets and night birds – and I immediately noticed a very large frog, or toad, sitting close beside me on the floor. He stayed there for the whole hour, not moving, just sitting like the rest of us, and I remembered stories I'd heard of animals being attracted to holy men, or mystics, like Ikkyu in Japan, or St. Francis in Italy. Anyway, he was a really cute frog.

When my turn came, Osho called me forward to sit in front of him and said "I have a present for you."

I thought, "Wow!"

He smiled and said, "Don't be shy, come closer."

I scooted forward, cross-legged, until my knees were almost touching his feet.

"Close your eyes."

I did.

Then he put a mala of wooden beads around my neck, with a locket hanging from it, containing his picture, and touched me lightly on the head.

"Good," he said, "Come back."

I opened my eyes, he leaned forward and gave me a sheet of paper on which he'd written something and also signed his name, with the date.

"This will be your new name," he explained, "Ma Anand Meera. 'Ma' means 'mother.' 'Anand' means 'bliss.' And 'Meera' means…" he paused, waving a finger at me playfully… "I don't tell you. Everybody will know. You ask them, or go to the bookshop and find out for yourself, hmm?"

Then it was Govind's turn. He came forward and received the name Swami Anand Govind. I found out later that among Osho's sannyasins every male disciple is called 'swami' and every female disciple is 'ma.' The prefix 'anand,' which we both received, is very common.

Osho was explaining that 'Govind' means 'cowherd' and is a very respected name in India, also used in the devotional songs that I heard the Indian sannyasins frequently singing. But my English was not so good and so instead of 'cowherd' I heard Osho say 'cow head.'

The image of a cow's face sitting on Govind's shoulders suddenly flashed into my mind and I burst into loud laughter. Osho looked at me in surprise, with big amused eyes, like "Did I say something funny?" It was an incredible moment, because he wasn't at all disturbed by my outburst, just curious, and that was typical of the way we would meet in the years to come – with lots of laughter and playfulness. I always really enjoyed it.

Next day, I asked people about my name and that's when I discovered that Meera had been a famous Indian mystic, who lived about five hundred years ago and who became a devotee of Krishna.

As I mentioned earlier, Meera was so ecstatic in her love for Krishna that she danced and sang in the streets, much to the outrage of her husband, the Rajah of Udaipur, and his family. Her songs and devotional poems are still widely sung throughout the country, and it is said that, while she was alive, the great emperor Akbar disguised himself – he was a Muslim – and entered her temple to see her dance.

Over the next few days, I was introduced to the active meditations that were held daily in the ashram, especially Dynamic Meditation, but I didn't have long to experiment with them because soon after meeting Osho, Govind and I left on our tour of India. With Govind, I really got to see the best architecture and temples – Konark, Puri, Khajuraho, Kashi – because he was passionately interested in all of it, taking lots of pictures and making notes. By this time, I was falling in love with him and, through his passion for this strange country, with India as well.

While in Pune, I'd heard Osho saying that India is more than just a geographical region. It represents the inner world, the search for the hidden and the mysterious – that's the real meaning of India – and in this way India belongs to all human beings. That's also what India came to represent for me, helping me to recall a natural and organic space inside that had somehow been overlooked or forgotten until now.

I was intrigued by the bazaars and the busy quarters of the towns, the sounds and the smells of the countryside, and especially by the contrast of dark and light, because inside the older shops they always painted their walls blue. This created a dramatic effect: dark, windowless rooms filled with dark brown figures, contrasting with brilliant white sunshine outside. It touched me, tickled me somewhere in my own depths and reminded me why I had become a painter – at least, from the visual aspect.

I loved sketching people bathing and praying in the Ganges, the holy river of the Hindus, especially women. They move so gracefully, walking deeper into the water, still clothed in their saris, hands clasped together in a namaste, whispering their prayers. When they had totally immersed themselves, they turned around and came back, their saris sticking to their bodies and I could see the beauty of their forms. It was erotic, artistic and yet still a prayer.

During that first trip to India, I started having a different image about painting, less connected with emotion and intellect, more connected with the human longing for religion – religion in the real sense, not as a formal ritual or organized church. I saw that the human heart has a capacity to go higher in spirit and was intrigued by the challenge to capture this quality, especially by drawing and painting women in the water.

Another thing that fascinated me was the geometric patterns made by ripples spreading out through the water as bodies moved in the river. I'd always felt drawn to geometric patterns in nature – in water, trees or flowers – and searched for the most simple, basic patterns; sometimes a triangle, sometimes a square, sometimes an octagon.

For example, the hidden symmetries in the way a flower grows petals are simply amazing. It's been almost like a scientific exploration to me, an invitation to look deeper, towards the core, the essential.

That's why, later on, I was never interested in copying the nature that I painted, like a photograph, but tried instead to express its hidden message. Traveling through India, my love of hidden symmetry merged with a spiritual quality of longing and gave a new dimension to my art.

It was a magical tour, but then, all too soon, it was time to say goodbye to Govind – at least for the time being – as he needed to return to Japan and I was heading back to Spain.

Arriving back in Toledo was a shock. I was dressed in the

bright orange clothes worn by Osho's sannyasins and also wearing the mala around my neck with his picture. In India, it was accepted as just another form of religious expression, but in Europe I was a walking advertisement for some strange Indian guru – I think that's why Osho did it, both to advertise himself and to test the commitment of his disciples. The whole town made fun of me.

It was heavy going, with everyone laughing at me, and even the local gas company could enjoy the joke because their employees, the ones who delivered propane bottles to my house, were dressed in a bright orange uniform. So whenever they saw me they would smile and call out "You like this color, eh? Next time I bring you one of my costumes!"

Some sannyasins wore pants and shirts in orange, adopting a more western style, but I wore the same robes I'd used in India, and this had the effect of making me look like a Catholic nun. So I soon got the name "the Japanese nun."

Aroldo, my longtime boyfriend, was annoyed, not because I'd had a love affair with another man, but because I'd been initiated as a sannyasin, which he took to be a form of sheep-like devotion.

"You didn't have enough of fascism with the Franco regime?" he yelled at me. "So now you have to become a blind follower of some stupid guru? You have to choose – either me or Osho."

It was difficult to defend myself. First of all, my English was not that good. Second, I did not have a rational explanation for what had happened to me in India with Osho, because it was more like love than logic. But I did have a sense that I had found something deeper and more significant than my passion for art – a higher kind of creativity, something that could revolutionize my life.

Later on, I became more articulate about it and could find ways to help people understand. For example, everyone knows that in Europe, in the fifteenth and sixteenth centuries, there was a great upsurge in culture and creativity known as the Renaissance. The cradle of this movement was Florence, a wealthy Italian city of traders and bankers whose patronage allowed art and architecture to grow in exciting new directions.

The Renaissance was rooted in the rediscovery and revival of the classical values of Greece and Ancient Rome, but it also offered a new and daring vision of human beings as capable of progress and growth.

It began with a new generation of artists like Sandro Botticelli and reached its height with Leonardo da Vinci, Michelangelo, Titian and Raphael, who, among other things, introduced accurate anatomical representation and expressions of human emotion. In other words, they turned away from the stiff stylization of earlier times and were the first to paint in a way that made people look real.

By the way – and this is just an historical aside – at around this time, in the early fifteenth century, far to the north, in the Netherlands, there lived a Dutch painter called Jan van Eyck. He was busy exploring the possibilities of mixing color pigment with certain oils that would evaporate at a consistent rate – like linseed and nut oils.

In this way, van Eyck succeeded in perfecting the technique of oil painting, giving artists the ability to paint in a far more refined way, capturing minute detail, delicate textures and subtle effects of light.

At the same time, in India, there was also tremendous flowering of creativity, but in a very different direction. Since the times of Gautama Buddha and even earlier, India has been giving birth to enlightened mystics, but in the fifteenth and sixteenth centuries there was a tremendous burst of spiritual awakening, producing many mystics of the highest quality.

They included Meera, my namesake, and her spiritual teacher Raidas, who by trade was a low-caste leather worker – one more reason why Meera's royal relatives were horrified by her behavior. It also included Kabir, a weaver, whose incredibly beautiful songs and poems are still sung today, and Chaitanya, a Brahmin scholar who threw away his books and danced and sang in the streets. Nanak, the mystic who founded the religion of turban-wearing warrior Sikhs, was alive at this time, and also Farid, a Sufi mystic.

These are just the ones that we know. There were probably many more enlightened mystics moving around the country during the same period, but India has never been very interested in keeping historical records, so we will never know the full extent of this spiritual explosion

So what is the difference between these two great movements? The answer is simple and profound. In Italy, the energy of creativity moved outwards, into artistic expression. In India, it moved inwards, into the flowering of human consciousness.

This does not mean it is an 'either-or' situation, that you can have art, or you can have enlightenment, but you can't have both. Not at all. In fact, one of Osho's biggest insights – and his message to his sannyasins – is that a whole and healthy human being is one who can enjoy the best of both worlds, the inner and outer together.

But throughout history there has been an unfortunate tendency to divide human experience in two halves, into the spiritual and the material, and to set these halves against each other.

By the fifteenth century India had already chosen the inner against the outer, embracing the teachings of men like Adi Shankara who taught that the material world is an illusion, something to be rejected and renounced.

And Europe was forced to choose the outer against the inner – giving birth to modern Western materialism – because the early Christian Church had blocked the inward path, teaching that salvation is attained only by believing in a single savior, not through self-inquiry and meditation.

It's not really my field of interest, but, just to complete the story: the philosophy of Western materialism reached its height with René Descartes, who is famous for declaring, "I think, therefore I am," thereby making the thinking process and the mind the basis of human identity, and doubt the primary method of scientific investigation. Materialism came to its logical conclusion with Karl Marx, who finished the job by saying there is no soul, that consciousness is only a byproduct of matter.

For me, this kind of broad understanding came much later. As you can imagine, returning fresh from India, not even knowing what had happened to me, I had no words to tell Aroldo about the significance of my personal discovery, that I had not become a blind follower, but was for the first time looking for my true inner self.

Osho was not a guru for me, but an inspiration. I could see in him my own potential, rather like looking at the paintings of a great artist and, in response, feeling a longing to discover and express my own source of creativity.

So, even though I loved Aroldo, I could not agree to his ultimatum to drop Osho. I knew there was no going back, so, regretfully, with tears and heart pangs, I watched Aroldo depart. But I stayed on in Toledo, developing my work as a painter and also – after about a year – opening a small meditation center where I practiced the active meditations and offered them to others. Pretty soon, I had a small and dedicated band of meditators to keep me company.

I now traveled between three widely-spaced countries, living mainly in Spain, visiting India whenever I could, staying a few months in Pune – usually with Govind for company – and also making trips to Japan to see my family.

My approach to painting slowly underwent a profound change and I think I can best explain it by returning to the Naropa group room and the training process I've been describing through these chapters.

I haven't said much about the instructors' training, which every year in Pune I run parallel to the painting course. This year, there are five trainee instructors and we meet every morning, half-an-hour before the regular course begins, to review the events of the day before and deal with any issues or questions that have arisen.

One morning, when the course participants had a day off, I met with the instructors in the group room, gave a set of watercolors to each one, and then invited them to choose a spot in the room and begin painting. I didn't say 'you have to paint nature,' or 'you need to look outside,' but when the instructors chose their places I noticed that almost all of them were facing the windows.

The room is on the second floor, so it looks out into a sea of leaves and branches – some bamboo, some trees. It's really a very beautiful outlook, especially when the sun is striking the leaves in the early morning and late afternoon.

Watching the instructors, I realized that their attention was going out to catch hold of the natural beauty, to grasp what is outside and bring it onto the paper. So after about an hour – when everyone had made a good start, covering most of the paper – I called them together and asked them to display their work.

"I see beautiful paintings here, but it seems that your experiences in the training have been left behind," I said, when we had looked at all the papers. "I see nice trees and plants, but I don't feel *you*. Even though we have spent many days diving into the depths, you can see the tendency. It's the same for almost everyone: to get pulled by the outside.

"We forget immediately, because beauty is like addiction, beauty is like a trap – you get caught with beauty – and this is natural. You have to keep reminding yourself about the real purpose of painting. You are not trying to depict something, like a photograph, because in this way you miss; you get hooked with the form, or with beautiful colors.

"Rather, go into your own depth. Your depth has so many layers and no form. All the shapes and colors disappear when you close your eyes. Through this course, your aim is to discover the essence of beauty, which is in you. It's beyond any framework of beauty, beyond any idea of beauty. This is what I would like to teach you."

In my own work and through teaching others, I have seen, over and over again, the tendency of the human mind to become addicted, to get caught and fixed, hooked on a certain feeling, attitude or approach. It just seems to be part of the mechanism of our bio-computers. And it is not only to beauty that we artists become addicted.

As I told you before, my personal addiction was to the artistic expression of suffering. I was a devotee of artists like Honore Daumier, a nineteenth century Parisian artist who during his life was hailed as a brilliant caricaturist and satirist, but who later gained recognition for his paintings of the poor and the downtrodden.

In paintings like 'Third-Class Carriage' and 'The Burden (The Laundress)' he portrays ordinary scenes of how the poor live, travel and work. He does it with simplicity, honesty and compassion; showing the tiredness, the weariness, capturing a universal quality of human suffering.

I used to think "Yes! This is it! This is what art is really all about." But it was an addiction, a narrowing of my vision. I'm not saying painters should avoid such scenes. I'm just showing how we tend to get caught in a particular way of looking at the world and give it exaggerated importance and significance.

The cure for my own addiction came in an unexpected way. It came through meeting Osho, but it was not, as one might expect, as a result of understanding how meditation takes you beyond the mind and its attitudes. It was through discovering the quality of playfulness.

During one of my early visits to Pune, someone asked Osho a question about creativity, saying that, as an ashram cleaner, she didn't have time to do anything creative in her life.

Osho replied by saying that his work, too, as a Master, is a kind of cleaning, every day trying to empty people's minds of all the rubbish that gets in the way of meditation.

Then he went on to say that creativity has nothing to do with any particular kind of work. It has everything to do with the quality of your own consciousness – the way you do your work.

This impressed me very much, striking a chord of truth in my heart. And what he said next I have never forgotten, because somehow it took a weight of seriousness off my shoulders and put art in a totally new perspective:

"Painting is just as ordinary as cleaning the floor. You will be throwing colors on a canvas. Here you go on washing the floor, cleaning the floor. What is the difference? Talking to somebody, a friend, and you feel time is being wasted. You would like to write a great book; then you will be creative. But a friend has come: a little gossiping is perfectly beautiful. Be creative. All the great scriptures are nothing but gossips of people who were creative."

I loved the image that his words provoked in my mind. I can either throw colors on a canvas for painting, or I can throw water on the floor for cleaning – both can be equally creative. From this perspective, there is no division between the artistic and the mundane; all human activity is equally significant.

And he said one more thing, which really tickled me: "If you clean the floor with love, you have done an invisible painting."

The idea intrigued me. Instead of putting paint on a clean and empty canvas, you are taking dirt off the floor to make it clean and empty, reversing the process, and look.... an invisible painting!

In a way, it was a severe blow to my ego as an artist, but it came as such a revelation and with such a feeling of liberation that I did not receive it as an insult, or feel at all wounded.

So this was the beginning of my transformation as an artist, laying the ground work for the development of my training. I was not only discovering meditation, the art of going inside myself, I was also beginning to understand how a playful, non-serious attitude can help this inner quest – in fact, not only the inner quest, but also the outer expression of art.

And if I have to point my finger at one stroke of genius in Osho's approach to meditation – and also the least understood by others – it is the way he combines meditation and playfulness.

Just think about it for a moment. The human quality of playfulness has never been regarded as a worthwhile value by adults, and certainly not by 'serious' artists. It is something for children. Why? Because you cannot build an impressive social personality on a foundation of playfulness; you cannot puff yourself up and pretend to be a very important person.

But this is exactly its value. On the spiritual path, the ego is the barrier that prevents you from diving deep within yourself. It is an attachment, something that keeps you clinging to the surface – you don't want to let go of your superficial identity, because you have so much investment in it. You worked hard to build up a respectable image as a professor, a writer, a musician, a businessman.

A playful, non-serious attitude helps to loosen the grip of self-importance.

In my own experience, playfulness acts in the same way in terms of creativity. You don't get stuck with a particular style, value or vision. You are always ready to let go, explore something new, open yourself to the unexpected and unknown.

Of course, playfulness alone is not enough. It can be just childish. So meditation is needed to bring depth, while playfulness keeps you flexible and light. Together, these two qualities can light a flame in your heart, connecting you with your own source of creativity. Then any technique that you learn will serve your inner core of expression – not the other way round.

Connecting to this creative core is the single most important endeavor for any artist, and one way to do this is to learn how to paint your own self-portrait – naturally, because when you paint your own picture you are bound to look deeply into yourself. And this is what I am going to describe in the following chapter.

Chapter 7

Self Portrait

I have said that the three pillars of modern painting are Vincent van Gogh, Pablo Picasso and Jackson Pollock. This is only part of the truth. And the truth is that modern art is such a complex phenomenon that you can hardly turn a page in any art history book without reading: "this fellow is the father of a particular movement... that fellow is the founder of another branch... this radical group pioneered a certain style..."

It's an endless labyrinth, all inter-connected and cross-fertilized. For example, Wassily Kandinsky is said to be the father of abstract art, but he was heading for a career as a lawyer in Moscow until a painting of a haystack by Claude Monet at an Impressionist exhibition stopped him in his tracks. Does that make Monet the grandfather of abstraction? Pablo Picasso is the founder of Cubism but his breakthrough painting, Les Demoiselles d'Avignon, is basically a fusion of Paul Cézanne and African sculpture. Are these, therefore, the original sources of Cubism?

In such a fertile and confusing flood of creativity, you can find your heroes according to your personal taste. But, like almost everyone who knows anything about modern art, I have to pay homage to one man who, perhaps more than anyone else, can rightfully claim to be the father of modern painting. It is, of course, the man I just mentioned, Paul Cézanne, and before explaining why I want to introduce him at this point in my book, I would like to say a little bit about him.

Cézanne was born in Aix-en-Provence in the South of France in 1839. Like so many other artists before and since, he fought against his family's wishes in order to be a painter, moved to Paris and by 1874 was exhibiting with the Impressionists during their long and bruising campaign for public recognition. But within a few years he had withdrawn his allegiance from the movement, choosing instead to pursue a solitary path.

His aim was not to convey an impression, or sensation, conjured on canvas by the skilful use of brush strokes and the subtle interplay of colors. He wanted to build something more durable and solid, something more like architecture, and the surprising thing is that he succeeded, although his achievement – as usual with genius – did not find widespread recognition in his lifetime. Perhaps only Camille Pissarro, one of his few friends and painting companions, fully understood the implications of what he was trying to do.

Cézanne considered human perception to be basically confused and unreliable, and, as a way of overcoming this difficulty, discovered that any element of nature can be translated into certain fundamental shapes, like cylinders, cones and spheres. His primary concern was structure, including not only shapes and forms, but the patient building of small, mosaic-like areas of color to create a completely integrated painting.

Strangely enough, he gained the title of the father of modern art for reasons that he himself would have considered improper. His aim was to create an art form that corresponded to nature that reproduced on canvas an accurate reflection of nature. But the method he developed took on a life of its own and opened the door to Cubism and abstraction, leaving nature further and further behind.

You see the point? It's a bit like my fascination with ripples on water I mentioned in the previous chapter, and the enjoyment I found in getting closer to nature by looking for its basic patterns. When you find them, as a painter, you have a choice: you can use these patterns to reflect nature more deeply, or you can make an art form out of the patterns themselves – abstracting them from their natural context.

This is what happened to Cézanne, and such is the fate of great pioneers, because they never know who is coming after them and what will be done with their discoveries. Which brings me to my own particular use of Cézanne's methods and why I began this chapter with him, so let us return to the group room in the Naropa Pyramid.

We are about half-way through the training and so far we have been focusing on two main themes: primal painting and nature painting. Today, I will introduce a third element, one that many of the participants will find the most challenging – self portrait.

For this, we are using a type of paper called 'Kent.' As the name suggests, they make it in England. Usually, architects and designers use this paper, which has a non-porous surface so you can freely use brushes and sponges without fear of breaking the surface and making it absorbent – although some people in my training will succeed anyway in doing exactly that. In a big group like this, with so many first-time painters, you can't prevent these kinds of accidents.

The size of the paper is 40x50 cm. And, like the preparations for watercolor painting, we begin by wetting the paper on one side, then sealing it down around all four edges with brown gummed tape on a board, so that it is flat, stable and fixed.

The brown tape, itself made of paper, shrinks and becomes taut as it dries, thus stretching the painting surface and making it flat – something I should have mentioned earlier while introducing watercolor.

Everybody is given a small plastic container and I ask them to squeeze large tubes of black and white gouache or tempera paint into the container and mix a nice thick grey color.

"But if you mix straight black and white the effect looks a bit like a cemetery, kind of flat and dull, rather boring to look at and work with, so mix in a little bit of Persian blue or red, and this will give it vibrance and depth," I advise. "Red creates a warm grey; blue creates a cool grey, so you can choose according to your own feeling."

It was Aroldo, my Swiss artist lover, the man who contributed so much to my life as an artist, who educated me in the use of grey as a medium for painting. The advantage is that you can use it as a middle tone, and from there go either towards darkness or light. Once you wash it, it becomes white again and if you want specific dark parts – let's say, in the case of self-portrait, the eyeballs – you can put a darker grey or even black. So it's a very convenient material, especially since we have been emphasizing the importance of contrast and working so much with black and white in the group.

Individual mirrors have been set up around the walls of the room, just below window level, with sheets of protective plastic spread on the ground in front of them and a cushion for each person to sit on. Each person has his own space, his own mirror. Each person will sit or kneel on the cushion, his board in his lap, facing the mirror.

There is a reason why I don't want them to put the board on the floor, which has been my standard method with painting so far. It's a question of distance. When you look in the mirror and then down to the floor, you have time to forget what you saw. If you have the board on your knees, in your lap, you can see the mirror and the paper at the same time – in terms of horizontal planes, the board begins where the mirror ends and the distance your head moves is minimal.

When everyone is sitting down, boards in their laps, I invite them to begin by closing their eyes and touching the surface of the paper. This, as I have explained before, brings them into the kinesthetic sense, into feeling, and more easily into a child-like, innocent state. Then, after a few minutes, with eyes still closed, I ask them to begin touching their faces in the same way. Fingers are very sensitive, rather like the antennae of insects, and can capture all the details of the face.

"Feel the sockets of the eyes, feel the nose coming out; trace your fingers around your mouth, your chin... exploring with eyes closed," I continue. "Imagine this is the very first time you are touching yourself. Take in the back of your head, feel the skull, the crown and all around your ears..."

This approach helps to take away the fear of what is going to happen, because I know through experience that almost everyone in the room is tense with expectations and self-doubts: "My god, I am going to do a self-portrait and I don't even know how to paint! Maybe I can paint a few leaves, a few branches; maybe I can do something abstract, but to paint my own face...? Impossible!"

Then slowly I invite them to catch hold of the entire head with both hands.

Now here comes Cézanne:

"Find out approximately... while you are touching your whole head, taking the whole thing in your hands... what are you?" I ask the group. "Are you an egg? A banana? Or more like a potato, tomato or apple?"

The group starts laughing, which is exactly what I want because it relieves the tension, eases the self-doubt, and at the same time gives people the foundation, the starting point, from where to begin a self-portrait: the basic structure and shape of your own head.

This is why I always think of Cézanne at this point in the training – as an inspiration to eliminate all nonessential material and get down to basics. He was more interested in cones, spheres and cylinders, but my eggs and apples serve the same purpose. Such an approach may seem simple – too simple – but it is of crucial importance in capturing a solid, existential impression of what you are about to paint.

Once you get the foundation right; once you really catch hold of the entire three-dimensional shape of your own head and translate it on paper, then you have passed the first and biggest obstacle in self-portrait. Then everything else – eyes, nose, ears, all these little things – are just decorations.

157

It is for this reason that I love Constantin Brancusi's sculpture, 'The Sleeping Muse.' It is so simple and yet so beautiful – just a head lying on a flat platform of stone. You don't see exactly the nose or eyes; just a trace, a suggestion. The entire 'isness' of the head is expressed through the basic shape, which in this case is egg-like by nature, with a bare minimum of detail.

Brancusi was a Romanian who was associated with the Cubist movement in the early part of the twentieth century. He wasn't really a Cubist, since he was not interested in breaking down the unity of his subject into its component parts and then reconstructing them. On the contrary, his passion was to capture the essential form and bring it out, manifest it, so in this way he was a direct descendant of Cézanne.

The genius of a man like Brancusi is that through so little he can convey so much: the feeling of a sleeping being who is nevertheless filled with creative potential and possibilities.

My purpose in the group is the same: how to let people touch their own physical existence, stripped down to its essence. From this point, you can elaborate, creating not only a physical likeness but something that conveys much more than mere physical existence, but this has to be the base, the starting point.

"Now, when you feel ready, open your eyes, pick up a brush, dip it in your container. Hold the brush close to the paper but don't start painting yet. Then, close your eyes again and press your free hand against your face, feeling its contours. Start moving the brush across the paper, translating onto the paper what you are feeling with your other hand.

"You are going to paint with the same feeling as touch. Can you do that with the brush? Can you paint with this feeling?

"If you lose it, you can stop, put down the brush, close

158

your eyes, take your head again in both hands and again remember the feeling. Do it as many times as you like."

When I see everyone working like this, gently touching their faces and painting blindly, with as much care and sensitivity as they can manage, it reminds me of the famous story of Helen Keller.

Born in the United States in 1880, she caught the disease meningitis at a very early age and became totally blind and deaf. She had to learn everything through touch. The breakthrough moment came when her tutor, Anne Sullivan, held one of her hands in water and then spelled the word 'water' with her other hand. The feeling had turned into a word. Here, in my class, the feeling turns into a picture.

After exploring this way of painting for a while, I invite the participants to open their eyes and look into the mirror in front of them.

"When you open your eyes, two people are meeting," I guide them. "Somebody who is in the mirror is watching you, and you are watching somebody who is in the mirror."

This is similar to the exercise where I asked people to stand in front of their own painting and let it talk to them. It's an effective way to neutralize self-judgment. Otherwise, when you look in a mirror, immediately you start projecting all kinds of opinions onto yourself that you have gathered through years of self-familiarity: 'I don't like my nose... my lips are too thin...' and so on. Then it becomes difficult.

"By introducing the idea of a person in the mirror who is separate from you, you can observe more accurately, so I would like you to continue to paint with this in mind – you are painting the person in the mirror, not you."

Moving around the room, I see a number of problems to take care of. The first thing is that, even though I have instructed them to paint only the head and to make it larger than life size, using the whole of the paper, many people start painting a small head.

"I don't know why people do this, but it's a common tendency – it happens in all my groups – and my feeling is this reveals something very psychological," I say over the microphone, after making people aware of the problem.

"Maybe it reflects a deep belief about ourselves: we shouldn't exist, we shouldn't take so much space; we don't have the right to assert ourselves so boldly.

"Otherwise, what is the problem? You know that on this paper nobody else will be represented; only yourself. Only you are standing on the stage, so why don't you take the space? Be bold, courageous, and make your painting one-and-a-half or two times bigger than your actual face."

Another thing that happens is that people tend to move too quickly past the foundation work of painting the shape of the head and start making line drawings of the eyes, nose and ears. So again I need the mike.

"Here, the problem is that after about ten minutes you can't move further because once you define the lines you don't know what to do anymore, right?"

Those who have fallen into this trap nod their agreement.

"So then you start making a little bit shading here, a little bit of shading there… chippy, chippy, chippy…"

I mime a painter making small, hesitant movements with his brush.

"So this becomes an imitation of how you think you ought to be painting. The purpose here is not that. It's about touching and sculpting. Please remember how you painted in total darkness and you had no problem. You were allowing your hands to feel what needed to be done and you trusted them. So remember this sensuous feeling, this organic feeling, and why you have lost it in this moment – just remember that."

Now people's hand movements get a little better, but still I see how easily people lose contact with themselves. When the brush touches the paper it is not in one bold, strong line, allowing energy to take over. No. It's like fear lines: cautious, filled with hesitation, not wanting to make a wrong move.

"No, we are not doing that," I say, gently to one participant, who has made a line drawing and has now stopped, not knowing what to do next.

"Just relax, take a sponge, dip it in the paint. Okay, now, hold your head with your left hand, close your eyes and with your right hand move the sponge on the paper. Let your right hand express what your left hand is feeling."

Immediately, he gets scared. "But if I do that I'm going to lose my face," he objects.

I smile and give him a reassuring squeeze, my hands on his shoulders.

"So what? What are you afraid of? When you close your eyes and look inside yourself there is no face. Let go!"

He laughs but still, I notice, as he follows my suggestion, he peeks with one eye at the paper, as if to say, "Okay, I'll do it the way Meera says, but I'm going to save at least this much of my nose…"

Actually, the session is going well. Gradually, with my encouragement, even the beginners are moving through the basic errors and gaining self-assurance, finding the trust and confidence that whatever they do will come out good.

By the way, I have forgotten to mention an important detail. In this self-portrait, we are painting only the head – nothing else, but if an artist is sensitive, an impression of the neck and the rest of the body will be conveyed simply by the way the head is being painted.

In a way, you are painting 'behind' the object, including that which the eye doesn't see. For example, in a frontal self-portrait you can't see the back of the head, but still the feeling of it should be there – like the invisible person in Professor Fujii's empty chair; like Brancusi's head, where you can feel the whole sleeping form.

To conclude this first session, I suggest to everyone to cover the entire paper with grey, including the space outside the shape of the head.

"Look in the mirror… your face is not separated from the space around it," I tell them. "If you really look at your face, together with the space, the brightest part is probably your eyes. So if you want to bring out your shining eyes then you have to make the space around your head darker, otherwise that will take over and dominate."

They know what I am talking about, because by now they are no longer newcomers. They have been painting the spaces in between trees, using the same understanding. For example, you can approach a tree indirectly, painting the space behind and around it so that the tree is revealed, standing naturally – without even painting it – like a hidden tree, created by everything else, by its own absence.

I watch as everybody transforms the white paper into a uniform grey mass – some with enthusiasm and trust, others with more hesitancy and doubt. I can see them thinking "My god, it's all grey, what shall I do now?"

"Don't worry," I assure them. "Even though you cover the paper, it's not just one solid grey, like wall paint. You can still see an impression, the basic shape of the head is not lost and that is the only important thing right now. You have been moving over the surface with your brushes, with your sponge, so a kind of molding has happened, like sculpting with clay.

"In fact, there is no need to think of this as a painting right now. Think of it as clay. You are like a sculptor molding the clay; and you have established the basic shape. You don't need to define the details yet."

After this first session, we create a new routine. From now on, every morning for an hour-and-a-half, from 8:00 until 9:30, we will work with the self-portrait on a different section of Krishna House roof that is open to the sky, shaded by two large, over-hanging trees.

This part of the roof is surfaced with small pieces of white ceramic tiles – typical of India's architecture and by chance an excellent medium for reflecting the early morning light.

Here, we set up the mirrors and sitting positions, each person choosing his or her place facing the low walls that surround the roof. And here we will work together, every day, before the official group time begins. It is a beautiful space, magical at this time of day, and even though it is outside the usual group hours nobody minds getting up early to make it here on time.

Like me, they all want to squeeze the maximum juice out of this training.

There are many things I have to teach about self-portrait. For example, one basic and very important technique is learning how to measure. This you do by holding the wooden end of a brush at arm's length in front of you, between your eye and your reflection in the mirror.

You mark the top of the object you wish to measure with the wooden tip of your brush and then you run your thumb down from the tip to mark the length of a certain feature – the width of an eyebrow, the length of an ear. Then you can bring the same proportion to your paper and increase it to one-and-a-half times the size, or two times, according to your need.

Another basic element is the position of the eyes. "I see have to correct a belief that your eyes are at the top of your head," I say, on one of those first mornings.

"I'm not kidding! It's a common mistake to paint the eyes much closer to the top of your head than they really are. So just take a moment to feel where your eyes are, in relation to your chin and the crown of your head. You will be surprised. Almost half your head is above your eyes.

"You can feel, too, that your eyes are not just decorative. The sockets in which they rest are part of your skull's basic shape."

Some of the best lessons arise spontaneously, for these make a deep impression, coming as they do out of unexpected situations.

For example, one morning, after working on the self-portraits, we are under the covered section of Krishna House roof – in our main studio – at the beginning of group time and I have asked everyone to bring their black-and-white nature paintings, which we have not looked at for some time.

This they do with some reluctance, conveyed by a few grumbles and moans, because for them this painting has been left far behind. I can understand their feelings. The world of color, in both nature and primal painting, now seems much more appealing, but still, there are lessons to be learned.

"In a way there is a continuation from the self-portrait, which we have just been doing, to these black and white paintings," I explain. "If you totally disconnect with the features of the face – the eyes, nose, mouth – not naming each object but just converting them into light and dark, you start understanding more about structure. You see that the way the light is hitting the face – why it makes a shadow here, a highlight there – is because of its structure."

Although people are listening politely, I can see that I am not making much of an impression this morning, and I can understand why. We have been over this territory before – or so it seems. Yet still, I feel there is something essential here to grasp.

"Forget that it's a face," I persist. "This is not easy. One of the crucial skills of a painter is to be able to paint what he actually sees, rather than what he thinks he is seeing, or what he's been told he is seeing.

"Beginners, especially, tend to paint from preconceived ideas, from memory. You look at your face in a mirror every day – as you dress, as you clean your teeth, pluck your eyebrows – and, as you do so, a parallel self-image arises in your mind. The two go together, whether you are aware of it or not.

"It's a real meditation to drop the past and trust this moment, painting only what you see. What you actually see is a translation of light and dark, and in this way you can paint nature, your own portrait, anything.

"This is not just something that I teach," I say, trying to stress the point. "It's basic teaching at any school. That's why I spent two years only drawing – to see how I can give

164

a two-dimensional piece of paper the illusion of three dimensions, using only the contrast created by pencil or charcoal on white paper."

This also does not create the spark I am looking for, and then suddenly I look up and see Halima, a beautiful Japanese woman, standing behind the group that is seated around me in a semi-circle. She has been busy looking for her painting and, having found it in a pile at the other end of the room, arrives now at the perfect moment, for in her face I see the inspiration I am looking for.

"Halima, don't move! Don't sit down. Yes, just stand there, exactly as you are. Now, everybody, look at her face. You see how the morning light is hitting her face, strongly on the left cheek, a little less on her right cheek..."

There is no direct sunlight, it doesn't reach here now – the sun is already too high, above the roof. But there are two different strengths of light coming in through the open sides of the group room, from different angles, criss-crossing on her face.

"Look, it's a symphony of light and dark. You can see how her whole face is revealed – the whole structure of her face – through the contrast that is being created."

It is an inspiring sight, the face of a beautiful woman, caught in a natural dance of light and dark, and everybody gets the point. Now we are no longer in a classroom, talking theory and technique, now we are in a living painting, experiencing the mystery of nature and art together, and now I am happy. The lesson is conveyed.

Looking at Halima, I am reminded of Georges de la Tour, a French painter who was captivated by the play of light and dark. He was a seventeenth century artist who, though greatly admired during his lifetime, was completely forgotten after his death in 1652 and did not re-emerge from obscurity until the early twentieth century.

It was in 1915, after patient detective work by art historians, that his 'Newborn,' or 'Nativity,' was presented to the public – it had been attributed to another artist – and slowly other works were tracked down, restored and added to his credit. I remember him now because he worked in an unusual way, placing lighted candles below the faces that he was painting, thereby creating a soft, warm, mystical effect. Much later, Hollywood used similar below-the-face lighting techniques to create scary monsters in horror movies. German film director Fritz Lang used it to convey deep, brooding feelings, like those expressed by the leading characters in his classic film 'Metropolis,' while Soviet film director Sergei Eisenstein employed similar techniques in epic movies like *Battleship Potemkin.*

But centuries earlier, Georges de la Tour had used the same technique to produce an entirely opposite effect, making people beautiful and radiant, as if touched by some kind of spiritual magic – just like Halima, caught in this natural cross-play of light.

"Now you are going to get to know yourself in a new and deeper way, through self portrait," I tell the group. "As you work on this portrait, many feelings, many ideas about yourself will come up, and I don't want you to suppress them or dismiss them. Let them be there as long as they want.

"But keep bringing your attention back to this essential discipline, seeing your face as a play of light and dark.

"Really, it's a paradox. I'm asking you to *not* look at yourself as yourself, or even as a person. But if you explore what I am saying, you are going to discover yourself in a way you have never known before. You are going to confront yourself, accept yourself, welcome yourself, and at the same time you will learn the most difficult thing that there is to learn in the world of painting."

Here we come to the essential function of this training, or perhaps I should make that plural – functions – because it is a multi-dimensional experience. As advertised in the resort's group program, I am showing people how to discover their creativity. That is the first function.

But, as I think must be obvious by now, you can't help people do that unless you help them to discover themselves, peeling off layers of superficial identity and penetrating into

166

their depths. The two go together in the training and when working with self-portrait they are simply inseparable. It is one and the same process.

And now, if you excuse me, I will make one of my excursions out of the group room, because I must talk about my sister Taeko. There is no direct connection between self-portrait and what I am going to say about my sister, but on an indirect level you can see it clearly. Self-portrait is part of a search for a deeper identity and in this same search Taeko helped me tremendously. That's why her memory comes up so strongly for me now. She opened a door that changed my self-image as an artist and also my approach to painting.

Taeko, you may remember, was younger than me. She was also very different in temperament. I was the rebel, the bohemian artist, wearing t-shirts and jeans, saying anything outrageous that came into my head, wandering like a hippie around the world.

Taeko was more refined and delicate. She enjoyed beautiful clothes, liked elegant surroundings and was attracted by richness, eventually marrying a wealthy Japanese doctor. But even though we were so different, she loved me and my work. When she knew I was poor in some far-off land, she'd stuff a bunch of money in an envelope and mail it to me – not even noticing that you could see the bank notes through the white envelope.

On one occasion – this was a few years later – when I was living in America and feeling very poor, because nobody was buying my paintings, she invited me home and organized an exhibition for me near Tokyo, in the Guma prefecture, and it was a great success.

I was very touched. She went around knocking on the doors of all her friends in order to persuade them to come to the exhibition and in five days helped me sell about forty thousand dollars worth of paintings.

It was amazing, mind-blowing, because in America it had been such a struggle. I couldn't pay the rent, I couldn't eat, nobody seemed to like my work and then suddenly I brought the same paintings to Japan and, with a little help from my sister, they were appreciated as valuable art.

One day, while preparing for that exhibition, my sister found a box of paintings that I was keeping back and exclaimed, "Why don't you exhibit these paintings? They are so beautiful!"

I shook my head and replied, "No, I don't want to. I don't want to sell them."

Taeko kneeled down and touched her forehead on the floor – that's the Japanese way to ask something – and pleaded, "Please show them. You don't need to sell them, but I really want you to share these beautiful paintings with the public."

This was the first time I understood that it was not just sisterly love that motivated Taeko to help me. She also loved my paintings, and this realization came at a time when I really needed support, not only in material terms but in the form of artistic encouragement.

Whenever I was in Japan and we were staying together for more than a few days, Taeko would ask me to paint cherry blossoms for her, but somehow I always resisted her request. It seemed so trite, so mundane, so kitsch. Cherry blossoms? What am I? Some chocolate box decorator? I did not say so, but I considered it beneath my dignity as a contemporary artist to stoop to such popular trivia.

Later, I understood where my resistance was coming from. The artistic ego always wants a challenge. It needs complexity, difficulty, impossibility; whereas to recognize beauty as beauty is a very simple thing. There is nothing to figure out – natural beauty is just how it is – while my drive as an artist had been fuelled by a desire to be deep, intense, dark and even a little bit tortured.

And you know how it is with artists, especially modern artists. We are terrified of being dismissed as unoriginal, decorative or conventional. Nobody wants to be mistaken for some kind of Sunday painter, like a dentist who drills teeth during the working week, then drives off into the countryside to paint pretty landscapes at the weekend.

I think that's ninety percent of the problem these days – why art has become so utterly bizarre and stupid. Over the years, the general public has become familiar with modern art, with Picasso, Kandinsky, Pollock, and this makes it seem safe and conventional. So new generations of modern artists feel forced to shock the public to prove to themselves that they are still progressing.

A negative public reaction becomes the criterion: if people hate it, or don't understand it, then it must be art. What these artists don't seem to realize is that they are still making themselves dependent on the public for their sense of accomplishment and self-worth. Instead of looking for approval, they look for outcry and protest, but it's the same search for acknowledgement, only standing on its head, yoga- style.

As for me, in spite of my experiences in India, I still carried the feeling that to depict suffering and struggle was more valid than portraying beauty and nature's dance. As far as I could see, beauty had no need of my personal signature; it was self-evident, anonymous and a little bit banal.

There was one exception. When Taeko's first son, Taketo, was born, I was so struck by his beauty and his Buddha-like face – especially when he was sleeping – that I could not stop drawing him. He reminded me of Brancusi's head... a real sleeping beauty. Still, drawing Taketo was my only concession to orthodox art.

Then Taeko became sick and soon it became apparent that it was very serious. She had cancer. After giving birth to her third child, the placenta stayed inside her womb and developed carcinoma, which quickly spread through her body. She went through many operations but nothing helped for long. Soon, I knew she was dying.

"Dear Sister, paint cherry blossoms for me."

How could I refuse? I would have done anything to give her happiness as the flame of her life started to flicker and grow dim. Already, I had dropped all my painting projects,

169

my traveling, my plans, staying constantly by her side, studying everything I could about cancer, arguing and discussing with countless doctors in a desperate and futile effort to find a way to stop the deadly disease that was eating her inside.

So I strapped her little daughter Keiko on my back and walked up into the hills behind her house to see the cherry blossoms in the evening light. It was a magical moment. The whole hillside was covered with cherry trees and the evening sun beams, cutting sideways through the branches, made all the blossoms translucent.

"Ooh! Ooh!" cried Keiko, repeatedly, pointing with her little fingers to the pink, shimmering wonderland above our heads. Her innocent eyes helped me see the beauty I had so determinedly ignored.

Returning to the house, I took up my paints and brushes and poured my love into those blossoms – blossoms that are such a common and universal symbol in Japan that they decorate almost everything, from gift wrapping paper to breakfast plates. Blossoms that I had taken for granted as part of a culture that no longer interested me.

And then the magic happened. Without effort, without struggle, a beauty that I had never tried to express until this moment poured out of me onto the paper. The blossoms danced into being at the end of my brush, as if happy to have been finally allowed out from my heart, delighting in their own appearance.

It was so easy, so natural, almost as if it had nothing to do with me. The paper was filled with vitality and life, expressed through delicate colors and light, and I was in awe, for unexpectedly I had stumbled on a realization: not only could I see beauty; I had a natural gift to manifest it, reproduce it in the form of painting.

But it was more than mere reproduction. As the painting took shape, I sensed a mystical quality inter-mingling with the blossoms, almost like a 'thank you,' a gratitude from them to me. I understood, then, that nature needs a seer. It

170

needs someone to appreciate and honor its colors, its flowers, its shapes and patterns.

Later, this became one of the most important elements of my training: inviting and encouraging people to develop a sense of communion with nature, so they can feel it is a two-way affair. It's not just that they want to paint nature. Nature also wants to be painted; it wants its mysteries to be made manifest in a sympathetic, poetic and psychedelic way.

Taeko loved my cherry blossoms and in her smile of appreciation I saw a hint, a suggestion, that for a long time she'd known something about me that I myself had been unable to see: my own simplicity and my rapport with nature. How strange that, in doing a simple favor for my dying sister, I found instead that she'd given me one of the greatest gifts of my life.

That beautiful smile of hers came back once more, in the last days of her life, and I need to mention it here because – although it has nothing to do with art or creativity – it has everything to do with meditation. And it is something for everyone, because sooner or later we are all going to face the same thing.

One of my deepest concerns was that, even though I showered Taeko with love and care, I felt a sense of failure because I could not get her to face death. She simply refused to accept that she was dying and was not interested in meditation, so my desire that somehow she should be using this opportunity to meditate and die consciously was constantly frustrated.

She suffered a lot as the cancer grew worse and as the end came closer she appeared to be slipping into a coma, but still she was dancing – her lifelong passion – by making slow movements in the air with her left hand. I felt sad. I'd lost contact with my sister. Soon, she would breathe her last and be gone.

Then, in the last few days, a smile appeared on Taeko's face, growing slowly bigger and bigger until it bathed her whole face in radiance and joy. I could not believe it. I was puzzled. The very thing that I had wanted to give her, through meditation, was happening on its own. In her final moments, I was so absorbed by her smile that it was some minutes before I realized she had stopped breathing – she had gone.

Later, when I returned to Pune, I asked Osho a discourse question about it, and he said:

"Meera, the question you have asked raises a very fundamental thing, and that is: if by chance somebody dies in great suffering like cancer, the suffering of the cancer does not allow the person to fall into unconsciousness. So just before death when the body separates from the soul, a tremendous experience happens which happens only to the mystics, to the meditators..."

He explained that, ordinarily, people die unconsciously so they never know they are separate from the body, then added:

"But the meditator goes many times into the same position consciously, where he stands out, away from his own body. In other words the meditator experiences death many times consciously, so that when death comes it is not a new experience. The meditator has always died with laughter.

"You were trying to teach your sister meditation. But it is difficult, because when one is in such suffering all your talk seems to be nonsense. But when she really died, just a moment before, as the separation happened, she must have realized, "My God, I was thinking I am the body and that was my suffering. My identification was my suffering." Now the separation, the thread is cut – and she smiled.

"Certainly you must have been puzzled about what happened, because she was fighting with death, fighting with suffering, was not listening to you or making any effort to learn meditation. Still she died in a very meditative state. This happened accidentally."

Taeko gave me so much, and this was her parting gift, her final offering: a smile that I accepted as encouragement to move deeper and deeper into meditation, to find the point at which I, too, can know that I am not the body – and therefore not touched by death.

There are many ways to approach meditation, hundreds of methods have been developed over thousands of years, but since I am an artist I have developed a few techniques of my own. Self-portrait is one of them.

Now I think it will be helpful if I invite a couple of the participants to speak about their experiences with self-portrait, to give you an idea of how it affects people. We can start with Naveena, a beautiful 30 year-old woman from Israel, who works as a massage therapist and body worker, and who has joined my training for the first time.

Naveena:

Even before we started the self-portrait I was aware that one of my basic issues was the desire to look good, not just in terms of my physical appearance but in what I can produce and show others.

I remember one session when Meera asked us to bring one of our nature paintings to show to the group, and her comment about mine went straight to the point. I don't recall her exact words but she said something like: "You're too attached to wanting to make it beautiful… paint a nice tree, make a photocopy and then send home to mom."

It was really a shock because I could feel it was true. She could see right through me – just from the painting – without even talking to me or knowing my background. And that realization stayed with me; the understanding that my painting and my energy wasn't clean, but somehow polluted with hidden motivations that were surfacing only now.

Then we did a night session in the pyramid courtyard, working by candlelight, painting on the ground, under a huge tree that was floodlit. Meera's invitation was to tune into the tree and start painting. There was soft flute music playing and it was a very beautiful scene, with candles flickering, people silently working, the tree spreading out above us and a bright moon shining through the leaves and branches.

173

In a way, it was a big invitation for me to go into my pattern and try and look good by again painting something really beautiful. But I didn't. I didn't paint the tree at all. I just tuned into myself, into how I was feeling inside, and let the brushes move according to my inner feeling. It was an energy painting, abstract and free-flowing, and for the first time I felt really clean, with no attempt to step back, judge and evaluate what I was doing. I'd dropped the greed to produce something that others would look at and say, "Wow, Naveena, that is really beautiful!"

When we came to start the self-portrait, the same theme continued and went deeper, because I could immediately feel the desire to make myself look as beautiful as possible. I didn't follow it, I didn't allow it to capture me, but still, I knew it was there.

My first attempt at self-portrait was not successful, because I was working with a sponge, became impatient, pressed down on the paper too hard too many times and broke the surface layer. This made my face look very strange and one person commented, "Oh no, you peeled off your skin!"

That comment hurt. So I started again with a fresh sheet and went more slowly and carefully.

I'd been working for a few days and the portrait was taking shape when, one morning, Meera came to look and remarked, "Now you're going to the other extreme, from beauty to ugliness. What are all these wrinkles doing on your face? You're a lot younger than this, you don't need all these lines. Can't you take them off?"

I tried, but when I took them off one part of my face they soon re-appeared somewhere else, so I had to recognize the fact that these wrinkles were somehow reflecting the way I was feeling about myself.

It was a hard feeling to accept: yes, that's how I am inside, behind the pretty looks, that's who I am... kind of old, unhappy, worried, stressed. It was a difficult thing to deal with every day, sitting with it on my lap for an hour and a half, but at that moment it felt more real than the face I could see in the mirror.

It also brought up old memories, attitudes I'd absorbed from my upbringing, especially from my mother. I could hear her saying, "You can't be happy. Somebody will always come and put you down, bring you back to the ground."

The reality was that, in the Pune commune, during the past couple of years since my first visit, I have been flying. There's been a shift in my underlying mood, from feeling basically down and miserable to one of happiness. It's a very new way of life and it's taking time for me to accept it, to let it trickle down into my heart and into my blood.

So there were many things going on at once during the training: the superficial, 'make everything beautiful' layer that Meera saw in my first paintings; the deeper layer of my old attitudes, and the new and fresh quality that was growing in my heart.

My self-portrait reflected a lot of the 'me' I'd been before. The wrinkles stayed and that's how it ended. I can't say I was happy with the painting, but I was happy to experience the process, because at that moment it was a true reflection of the things I was feeling.

Another participant who had a deep experience with self-portrait was Urmila, a 31 year-old graphic designer from Geneva. She'd done part of my training the previous year and already, in the early part of this year's training, had experienced some deep emotions connected to her parents and the way they had suppressed her creativity as a child.

Urmila:
Painting the self-portrait was a powerful experience for me. Immediately, with the very first session in the Naropa pyramid, I was shocked by my own reaction, because as soon as I sat down in front of the mirror, with my board on my knees, I began to cry.

175

I didn't want to look at myself in the mirror. I didn't want to see 'me' reflected there. I wanted to escape. My first thought was "I've got to go outside and have a cigarette," but I stayed sitting there, tears running down my face, knowing "I have to go through this and not run away from it."

I wanted to smash the mirror, break it into pieces, so I didn't even try and paint. I sat there, watching my violence, my anger, my sadness, not even knowing why I couldn't face myself. Most of the time I kept my head down.

During the second session, again, I was crying the whole time. I did a little painting, just with a sponge, mechanically following what Meera was saying.

In the third session, I stopped crying and began to paint more, trying to look at myself, trying to see what was happening inside at what was being stirred up by this process: why I hated myself.

And the answer was clear enough. I didn't like the face in the mirror because in it I saw my father, my mother. I didn't see myself at all – only them. There was no space for me.

This continued for several sessions and I stayed with it, looking and painting, looking and painting. Then I started doing one of Osho's meditations: you look in the mirror, you look at 'you,' but, as you do so, you imagine that you don't have a head. You're looking at yourself from the heart, your eyes are filled with energy from your heart.

This helped me to change my vision and to meet myself. I started doing the meditation for a few minutes at the beginning of every self-portrait session, and soon I felt something changing inside. I went very slowly – not much painting but a lot of meditation.

At home, I also started to chant the Sufi zikr: "La Il Allah, Il Allah Hu," which is another powerful heart meditation. Every morning, after coming back from Dynamic, I would take a shower, sit down and do the zikr for a long time, then come to the resort for the self-portrait session. Often, I was late and felt guilty about it, but I had to respect and trust my own sense of what was good for me.

The change continued until at last I felt I was painting with a new, sweet kind of energy. I was accepting myself, meeting myself. Still, I continued to paint very slowly, because I knew that if I speeded up I would lose contact with this new and precious feeling.

At the end, when the self-portrait was finished, I felt very surprised that it had been me who had painted it. It was me, my self-portrait, with no sign of my father and mother, both of whom had been there so strongly at the beginning. Now, instead of shutting me out, they had completely disappeared.

The whole experience felt like a big present, because it gave me the opportunity to face myself and, in a very deep way, to change the way I felt about myself.

As you can see, we have come a long way, starting with Cézanne, starting with people closing their eyes and putting their hands on their heads to comprehend the basic structure, and then going deeper, journeying through all kinds of attitudes and emotions to the final expression of self-portrait.

The end product is simply stunning. When we put thirty of these self-portraits together for an exhibition at the end of the training, it creates such an impact that people walking through the resort – passing by our portrait display outside the book store – have to stop and stare.

You find yourself looking at thirty naked faces on one huge paper wall. There has been no attempt to create an outer image, which is the primary concern of ninety-nine percent of all portrait painting. There is no façade. So when you look at them, something hits you in your guts; it somehow makes you remember your own naked face, behind the mask of personality.

And here you can also see the dramatic effect of the use of grey, because it strips away the softening effect of color. There is no distraction. No cosmetic filter. It's pure and raw and intensely beautiful.

Having talked so much about self-portrait, I can sense the structure of the next chapter taking shape in the back of my mind. Because we have opened the door to the inner world, to what lies behind the social mask that is our normal face. Now I have to take you through the door and describe the inner landscape – and its impact on art.

Chapter 8

The Inner Landscape

I'm a bit hesitant about trying to describe the geography of the inner world, because I'm not used to writing about it. This is not my way of dealing with the inner world – in the systematic and linear way that's necessary for a book like this.

My approach is more intuitive and impulsive. Something comes up in training about a person's inner process and I dive into it, feeling my way as I go, following the energy like a dog on a trail of scent. Only afterwards do I get a conceptual sense of what happened.

But if I want to convey the significance of the revolution in art that I'm proposing, an attempt to describe the inner world has to be made, even if it feels a little awkward for me to express it. And so, with this personal disclaimer waving in my hand, I will begin.

I want to start with a brief look at modern painting as it developed after Cézanne and the Cubists. As you will see, this also provides a rough guide to the inner landscape – as far as western artistic minds have understood it.

I'd like to kick off with this bold statement:

"A clean sweep should be made of all stale and threadbare subject matter in order to express the vortex of modern life – a life of steel, fever, pride and headlong speed."

Thus declared a group of revolutionary young artists in 1910 as they wrote the Manifesto of Futurism, a short-lived but influential movement that sought to free art from the past, from all conventions, and harness it to the emerging values of the present and the future.

The Futurists certainly had good reasons to feel they were justified in trying to make "a clean sweep." By 1910, industry and technology were transforming the face of society. Motor cars, trains and planes were accelerating the pace of daily life beyond all expectation, and the paintings produced by this group tried to reflect this change by portraying dynamism and energetic movement.

Strangely enough, the very values worshipped by the Futurists killed off their movement, especially the exploding popularity of the new motion picture industry. Movies, as their name suggests, are so much better at expressing speed and other feverish elements of modern life than static paintings, and in a few years Futurism simply became irrelevant.

However, the impetus for change given by the Futurists was eagerly taken up by others in a restless, almost frantic search for artistic innovation and exploration. And, for those painters who were searching, it became ever more clear that naturalism and pictorial representation needed to be left further and further behind – abandoned to the photographers and movie-makers. This, in turn, inevitably drove them in the direction of unhindered imagination.

Dada, the next wave, used the irrational and the absurd to underline the point. Born in Zurich in 1915 as protest against the First World War – and against the bourgeois values that supposedly were responsible for it – the movement was deliberately anti-aesthetic, anti-traditional and anti-intellectual.

As part of this protest, Marcel Duchamp, the enigmatic French artist, achieved notoriety for his painting of the Mona Lisa with a moustache, for his 'Fountain' pissoir – nothing more than a signed porcelain urinal – and for his painting of an ordinary kitchen instrument: a hand-operated, chocolate-grinding machine.

Duchamp's influence, by the way, spread far beyond Dadaism. His small but controversial output spanned

Cubism, Fauvism, the Futurists and Surrealism, and he also pioneered two major innovations: kinetic art and ready-made art. His most famous painting is 'Nude Descending A Staircase,' an attempt to portray continuous movement, Futurist style, through a series of overlapping cubistic figures.

Members of the Zurich Dada group came from many countries, including Romania, Germany and France, and by the time the war was over branches of Dada were springing up in Paris, Berlin, Barcelona, Basle, New York and other cosmopolitan cities. But by the mid-twenties the movement had burned itself out, being essentially a protest against convention, without its own intrinsic driving spirit.

Meanwhile, something else was going on in Europe that was to forever change the way we human beings look at ourselves, and therefore – inevitably enough – at the way we approach art. Sigmund Freud had opened the doors to the subconscious and unconscious regions of the mind, showing how they influence our so-called conscious or waking states, and at the same time he developed the radical new profession of psychoanalysis as a cure for neurosis and hysteria.

Two aspects of Freud's work became significant for artists. First, he gave tremendous significance to dreams and fantasies – observing that they more truly represent the way we are than our superficial behavior and attitudes. Second, he developed the technique of 'free association' as a way of tapping into deeper layers of the mind.

If you don't know this technique, it's very simple: you observe and record – by writing down, or speaking aloud – the continuous stream of thoughts that are passing through your mind, without any attempt to control, censor or influence them. You will see how one thought leads to another, not as a logical progression, but through association, creating a long chain of linked ideas. Like the analysis of dreams, this process can reveal underlying feelings and offer insights that would otherwise remain concealed.

Both of these developments inspired a French writer called André Breton to abandon Dada in favor of something more positive and deeply fascinating. He wanted to use Freud's methods as tools to dive into his own mind, discover what he called "the real process of thought" and then give it expression.

In communion with other like-minded artists who wanted to go in this direction, Breton called this new approach Surrealism. Breton was a writer, but many painters followed in his pioneering footsteps. One of the first and best was Joan Miró, a talented young Spanish painter who, while not confining himself to the new movement, was able to give Surrealism a visual dimension, using elements of dream and irrationality, plus a flavor of playfulness and humor.

The Surrealists freed painting from any rational or logical link to the 'normal' way of seeing things, but at the same time used recognizable forms and images – bizarrely and randomly connected with each other – as a way to offer us dream-like, sometimes nightmarish revelations about our own minds and lives.

A couple of decades later, Jackson Pollock and the abstract expressionists completed the task, giving direct expression to feelings emerging from the unconscious part of the mind, expressing them without form, not even themselves knowing what was arising and manifesting until they saw it taking shape on the canvas.

Now, let's go back, for a moment, to Picasso's fascination with the way children are able to paint freely and spontaneously, not governed by the dictates of form, convention and style. They can do this effortlessly, for the simple reason that they have not yet been taught any of these things.

Picasso wanted the same freedom of expression, as did many other artists who followed him, but still – unlike children – they wanted this expression to be meaningful. They wanted it to be significant. Even if, like the Dada painters, absurdity and irrationality were chosen as vehicles for expressing freedom and rebellion, nevertheless the very theme of absurdity gave their work a *raison d'être*. They weren't just being absurd for absurdity's sake; they wanted to make a serious point.

So modern art became a two-pronged search for freedom and meaning, and the theories and discoveries of Freud conveniently gave everyone a signpost, a direction in which to travel in order to find both: into the realms of the human mind.

Mind became the treasure box, the unfathomable well of ideas and source of inspiration for artists, even to the degree that art itself became almost irrelevant. Instead, it was ideas about art that took over.

Here, I refer to the next stage in modern art: the progression from abstract to conceptual art, where the idea, or concept, is all that really matters. Some kind of creative expression has to be there, of course, otherwise no-one can appreciate the concept, but it is the concept that is glorified. Artistic expression becomes secondary.

As a logical extension of this trend, Joseph Kosuth, in 1966, created a dictionary definition of the word 'painting,' in the form of white words on a plain black background, mounted it on a square frame and presented it as art.

Conceptual art spawned a great deal of discussion, much of it focused on analyzing and investigating the language of art – inspired by the philosophy of Ludwig Wittgenstein – and on the photographic documentation of artists at work. Both were part of an effort to free art from its traditional forms – most notably, painting and sculpture.

More recently, conceptual art has again favored the creation of actual installations or objects, like British artist Tracey Emin's 'unmade bed,' exhibited in 1998, complete with dirty sheets, blood-stained underwear and used condoms. Furniture made out of toilet rolls or kitchen sponges, dissected animals suspended in formaldehyde, lights coming on and going off... in all cases, it's the idea that holds sway, not the form of expression.

Mind, therefore, reigns supreme. It dominates art. It has a stranglehold around its throat. So, naturally, it is important

183

that we understand the mind and view it from as many angles as possible.

Before doing so, however, I want to share with you something that I learned only after coming to India and listening to Osho talk about the culture of this country, which has been steeped in meditation for thousands of years.

This is one of the things I love about Osho's approach to spirituality. It's not just his own thing. It's not like he says to everyone: 'Okay, do Dynamic, do this and that, and this is my teaching.'

No, he talks a lot about the whole history of spirituality, how it developed in India, how different mystics adopted different approaches, how it went astray, found itself again... and so on.

Osho also talks about the development of modern psychology in Europe and America, and makes the point that Indian culture, which is so much older than Western culture, never showed any interest in studying the mind and its contents. Strange, when you think about it, because this same culture has been very interested – almost obsessed – with meditation, and meditation is the art of going inwards, into your own interior reality.

Naturally, when you go inside, you meet your own mind and its workings. Check it out for yourself: when you sit down and close your eyes for meditation, one of the first things you become aware of is the mind's thinking process – the chatter of thoughts passing through your head.

So why didn't the Indian mystics bother to examine and analyze the mind? Why didn't they take a short pause, not even a coffee break, at this early point on the inward journey and develop any form of psychology?

The answer is revolutionary, radical and for Western culture very disturbing: because they placed no value on it. The very thing that we revere and exalt, they ignored as a minor sideshow to the main event.

To the Eastern mystics, all that is valuable and worthwhile lies beyond the mind.

Peace, silence, love, compassion, bliss, a feeling of wholeness, a sense of oneness, union with cosmic consciousness... all of these precious and higher human qualities lie beyond the mind. So why waste time examining a mere mechanism, a bio-computer, a thinking machine, that offers none of these things?

Of course, the expression of higher qualities can come through the mind. Beautiful poetry, songs, sutras, stories, music, art... almost all of the outpourings of mystical experience will use the mind to find creative expression. But this is a by-product. The first and most important task for the spiritual seeker is to penetrate deep into one's own being and find the real source. Expression will follow naturally and spontaneously, like a stream flowing from a newly-tapped spring.

By now, you can probably see the direction in which I'm heading, but before spelling it out, I want to say one more thing about the mind. Why does the mind have an unconscious region? What exactly is the unconscious?

I'm not a psychologist, but as far as I know, it is the dumping ground for everything we have rejected about ourselves. In terms of human evolution, it is a relatively recent phenomenon. People living in primitive tribes don't have a mind that is split into conscious and unconscious parts – certainly not to the same degree as modern, civilized human beings.

The very process of civilization has created the unconscious, because so much has to be rejected and repressed in order to conform to acceptable social behavior. Our sexuality, our rage, our animal urges, our traumas and wounds from childhood, our tears, our feelings of inferiority, our lack of self-worth, pain of abandonment....

All of this is denied, rejected and repressed. It is buried deep in the basement of the mind and a lid is placed over it, so that we can walk down the streets of civilization looking and behaving like everyone else: well-mannered, polite, smiling and phoney. This basement becomes the unconscious. It is our very own, private and personal garbage dump, where we throw everything we want to hide, everything we cannot face, dare not show to others.

Do you see the implication? This is the place to which modern art's obsession with the mind, and especially with the unconscious, has brought us.

To put it bluntly: for nearly a century we have, as artists, been poking around in a garbage dump, a trash can. Not only that, we have been exalting the garbage, praising those who have given artistic expression to it, and paying millions of dollars for the privilege of hanging it on our walls.

This is why I had to begin my book by declaring that I have to straighten up the whole direction of modern art. Of course, it sounds terribly egoistic, but really I have no choice. Once you have seen what the mind is, once you place it in perspective, once you taste and experience the qualities that lie beyond the mind, you can't help but shake your head in wonder and sorrow at the way we have been worshipping it.

I don't want to deny the usefulness of this machine. I'm not against the mind. It's a wonder of bio-engineering, very helpful in arranging schedules, counting numbers, analyzing, measuring, dissecting and calculating. It's been a blessing – and a curse – in terms of developing science and technology, and creating a comfortable lifestyle for us all. Hot showers, cell-phones, computers, limos, planes, pollution, global warming and nuclear weapons... you name it, we needed the mind to develop it.

But, as we all know, none of these wonders of the modern world have brought us more contentment, peace, happiness. None of them have helped us to be more loving and compassionate. None of them have made us more fulfilled. And this is hardly surprising because the mind just isn't the right tool to produce these qualities. It's not designed to supply them. It's just a bio-computer.

It's the same with art. You can try and create art with the mind, but you will produce only garbage – interesting garbage, perhaps, and cleverly expressed, but garbage nevertheless. Why? Because mind isn't designed to produce

186

art. That's not its function. Or, rather, it can produce an imitative version of art, a kind of plastic substitute, but certainly nothing compared to the art that can flow from beyond the mind.

In saying this, I'm very much aware of my own limitations. I can't prove what I'm saying. I can't express it very well, or convincingly. And I'm talking to people who have lived in a culture and a society that has no understanding of meditation. For thousands of years, western culture has lived without meditation and only very, very recently, in the last few decades, has it opened its doors to eastern spiritual influences.

So for me to say, now, that modern western art can only develop and progress by moving into the dimension of meditation must seem to many people like I'm coming from Mars – an alien arriving from outer space, speaking an unknown language. Still, what can I do? I have to say the truth. That's my only responsibility. What happens after that is really none of my business.

There are many maps of the inner world – talking about chakras, energy centers, astral bodies made of light, different levels of consciousness – and, because it can only be experienced subjectively, it is difficult to figure out which ones are the best and most accurate. Up to now, I have found Osho's maps to be the most practical and effective, so I will try and give you a brief understanding of how they work.

When you sit down to meditate, closing your eyes, focusing your attention inwards, you gradually become aware of several layers.

First, you are likely to notice the sensations in your body: the way you are sitting, how your body feels at this moment, whether you feel comfortable or whether there are any slight aches or pains in your arms, legs, torso.

Then you become aware of thoughts passing through your mind.

By the way, most people never get even this far, because their whole attention is directed outwards, and modern society has designed millions of ways of entertaining and distracting people so that it never even occurs to them to look inwards.

Television, movies, DVDs, websites, video games, radios, sound systems, Walkmans, newspapers, books, magazines, shops, sport, clubs, discos, gymnasiums, theaters... we are surrounded by so much... er... I want to say 'crap' but my Japanese politeness prevents me. Anyway, you get the point. Almost from the day we are born, our whole attention is directed outwards and nobody is educated in the art of looking inside.

This is why, when people begin to meditate, they are often surprised by the intensity of the thinking process inside their own heads. Osho, who has explained this phenomenon to thousands of beginners, especially westerners, says:

"When people start meditating for the first time, they are puzzled – they think that there have never been so many thoughts in their mind as there are now. That's a misunderstanding. Thoughts have always been there, but they were not aware of them.

"When you turn your focus on your thoughts, suddenly you become aware of a great crowd, a continuous crowd moving day and night. There is never any rest: the body sometimes goes into rest but this thought-process continues. And it is always a rush-hour there. The traffic is always jammed, and each thought is trying to compete with another thought. There is great conflict, struggle."

Explaining how to develop the art of watching one's own thoughts, Osho continues:

"Whenever you are sitting, just close your eyes and watch with no judgement, with no evaluation: don't say that this thought is good and this thought is bad. All thoughts are simply thoughts; there is no distinction of good and bad. A thought is a thought is a thought; it has nothing to do with good and bad.

"Once you say 'this is good'. you start clinging to it; once you say 'this is bad', you start pushing it out. Then conflict

188

arises, then you cannot remain detached, you cannot remain distant, you cannot become a witness – you become involved. So no friendship, no enmity, neither for, nor against – just a detached observation of what goes on."

This detached observation is for Osho the key to meditation, because it is through the neutral activity of inner watching that the grip of the mind is loosened and the crowds of thoughts begin to thin out.

He also says that fighting with the mind, trying to force silence on it through some kind of spiritual discipline, is absolutely useless – worse than useless, because it simply represses thoughts and drives them into the unconscious. It's a bit like me trying not to think about miso soup when I'm hungry, or forget a guy that I've just fallen madly in love with. It's just not possible to get rid of thoughts by saying to the mind, 'Okay, now be quiet!'

The art of watching, or 'witnessing' as Osho likes to call it, gradually penetrates deeper and deeper, below the level of thinking and into the world of feelings, emotions and moods. These, too, can be watched, with the same results until finally you penetrate beyond mind itself, into the realm of silence and emptiness:

"Then sometimes gaps of silence will come. Suddenly the road is empty and nobody is walking, neither thought nor feeling. Emptiness passes by, and it will come like a breeze, it will refresh you, it will make you new, it will give you a new birth and a new way of living. That's exactly what sannyas is!"

As I mentioned in chapter six, Osho's development of Dynamic and other methods of active meditation helps this process by awakening physical and emotional energy before moving into a silent or passive stage. Everything gets stirred up, making sure there is plenty to watch.

It also ensures that the meditator is vibrating and pulsating with life – he doesn't want people to mistake the dead silence of a graveyard for the living silence of meditation. The more energy that is available, the more potent and profound the inner experience can be.

189

The courses at the Pune meditation resort are designed to help people move deeper into this process more quickly, especially courses that release energetic and emotional blocks, or resolve childhood issues, including basic traumas like shock, shame and abandonment. It's a fast method to clean out old mental and emotional junk, get the body streaming with energy – breath work is particularly good for this – and help people move into meditation more easily.

Okay, now, if you have been following me through this map so far without too much effort, you may be thinking – as many people do – that the road through the inner landscape looks pretty simple and straightforward. "It doesn't look so difficult; it won't be too long before I'm transported to the realms of infinite silence and bliss," you may be thinking.

In a way, it's true. Meditation, when done sincerely, regularly and totally, begins to produce results within two or three weeks.

In another way, however, there is an unseen difficulty, and this may help to explain why there are not enlightened beings walking down every street in your city, and sitting in every coffee shop – why, in fact, enlightenment is such a rare phenomenon.

The problem is contained in a single three-letter word: ego.

When you become a watcher, a witness to your own thoughts and feelings, you start to dissolve your identification with these thoughts and feelings. But your sense of self, of who you think you are, is made up of these identifications. So you are, in reality, dissolving your familiar sense of self. You are dissolving your own ego.

This is the difficulty. In meditation, all your ideas, attitudes, beliefs and concepts about yourself start to disappear. And you may not want this. You may be attached to, or identified with, dozens of different ideas about yourself.

For example, you may be identified with a certain religion: "I am Christian, Jewish, Muslim, Hindu." Or with a certain country: "I am American, Japanese, German, Italian." Or with certain ideas about yourself: "I am likeable, handsome, capable, compassionate towards others, a leader among men, socially superior..." and so on.

Just think for a moment: if you are English, and a soccer fan, and you are watching Germany defeat England in a match for the European championship, does this make you feel angry, miserable, disappointed...? If so, you are identified with your nationality.

I could go on, but I'm sure you get the point. Ego is made up of a thousand and one identifications and this makes it a very fragile affair. It can be easily punctured from a hundred different directions, and most of our time is spent trying to build it up, polish it, protect it. Not many people become interested in dissolving it. That's why enlightenment is rare.

By the way, I realize there are other definitions of ego, used in certain schools of psychology, but here I'm sticking to Osho's way of using of the term, in the context of spiritual self-inquiry.

One more thing I need to mention: the basic reason why our egos are so fragile is that they are false entities; they don't really exist. Ego is a bit like a patchwork quilt, made up of the opinions of others, which we have been absorbing since we were children. Essentially, it is the self-image we have developed in response to those opinions. Our real, unique individuality, which comes with us into the world, is hidden much deeper inside us.

Now, at last, let us go back to the group room, because I want to get away from theory and give you some down-to-earth, practical examples of how this works in daily life. And as we do so, I want to remind you of what I said at the beginning of this chapter: I'm not a theorist, or academic. I'm giving these explanations just to convey a broader understanding of the context in which my work takes place.

The incident I'm about to describe happened at the end of a five-day painting workshop that I was leading, a couple of weeks prior to the annual training.

At the end of any course, it's beautiful to bring everything to a happy conclusion and round it all off, so everyone leaves with a feeling of completion. It's beautiful, but it doesn't always happen like that and I have to allow incompletion and disharmony when – as in this case – they unexpectedly surface.

This particular workshop has gone well and there is very little time left on the final afternoon, but I want people to be aware of whether or not they had fully participated, especially in the group sharings, so I say:

"This is the last sharing. If something is not completed, if you feel there is something that you wanted to express but did not have enough space, this is the time to do it."

Following an impulse, I add, a little provocatively, "Don't just look at yourself. Look around the group and see if there are other people who you feel didn't express enough."

A young Israeli guy, Santosh, who I have mentioned before, is participating in this group and has touched a soft and loving space inside himself – that's what impels him to sign on for the longer training. He looks around the room and, in a gentle way, addresses his friend Prem, another Israeli in the group.

He says, "I would like to have heard more from you."

His comment is, on the face of it, surprising, because Prem has been talking quite a bit during the five days. But what Santosh means is that this talk has been superficial and Prem has not really shared himself in a deeper way. He hasn't taken any risks, exposing himself to others.

It's a perceptive comment, and looking at Prem, I add, "Can you connect for a moment with what Santosh is saying, and see if there is any truth in it for you?"

Suddenly, Prem is in the hot seat and I can see that it affects him very much. He is surprised, almost shocked, by this unexpected turn of events. My guess is that, in his mind, he was quite satisfied with his 'performance' – the way he'd conducted himself in the group – and now, at the last

192

moment, for one of his best friends to disagree is a major exposure.

I know the feeling myself. It's like you put a mask in front of your face and you think everyone accepts it and likes it, so much so that you begin to think the mask is you. Then suddenly someone says, "Hey, Meera, I'd prefer to see your real face, not that phoney mask."

It's embarrassing, humiliating. It's like being caught with your pants down around your feet. And it's often the case that the reaction, the feeling of humiliation, is far bigger than the incident that provokes it. Ego is so fragile. Just scratch it in the wrong place – or right place, depending on your perspective – and suddenly the mask is shattered.

Something like this is happening to Prem, and a few minutes later when the workshop ends and everyone has hugged their goodbyes, he stays behind to talk with me. Then it all comes pouring out: how he doesn't feel he can trust me any more as a group leader, how he doesn't feel supported by the group…

In fact, the group participants stayed entirely neutral during the brief exchange involving him. Nobody else had spoken, besides Santosh and myself. Most people were in an open, loving mood and had just watched what was happening without comment. But the very fact that no one had spoken up in his defense – "Hey, what are you saying? Prem's a great guy!" – was probably evidence enough that they had all turned against him.

For my part, I simply listen and receive him, very much in the way that I'd suggested for the exercise "I don't like what you did to my painting." You simply make space inside yourself to listen to the other person and, as I said before, when you do this sincerely, the other person – if he or she is at all sensitive – will soon begin to feel recognized and acknowledged.

It is even more important to do this with Prem because, of course, I represent the teacher, the authority and maybe also the mother – my position as a female workshop leader is like that – so he needs to feel received and heard.

At first, he attacks me: 'You're not a good group leader because you didn't bring the group to a happy end...' and so on.

But when I don't defend myself, or shoot back, his attitude gradually softens and after a while he starts to examine his own part in the affair – 'maybe this is an issue I need to look at.'

We stay in the room for about an hour, with Prem doing most of the talking. The helpers are packing up everything around us – sets of paints, water buckets, mattresses, cushions, papers – but I make sure we keep a little corner for ourselves. I have a feeling that if we leave the room Prem will close up and it will be difficult to continue.

What begins to emerge is Prem's deep pain and frustration with his mother, how as a child he was never able to get her to love him even though he tried hard, in so many different ways, to win her approval.

He tells me this has carried over into his adult life because he is a handsome, quite masculine-looking guy, with an independent, rather arrogant vibe. He finds it easy to attract women, to get lovers, but somehow he never manages to feel loved by them. So he tends to isolate himself, feeling separate and alone, and then the world around him becomes a dark and dismal place.

Prem admits that during the group he'd had a big expectation, or hope, that I would approve of him as an artist, a painter – and instead he got unwelcome feedback about not sharing himself.

"Actually, you did get my approval, but you don't remember," I remind him, with a smile.

He is surprised. " I did? When?"

"The first painting you made in the group was very beautiful – a total mystery. You showed your potential for connecting with emotional depth inside yourself. There was a 'not knowing' quality about that painting, rather than just a reflection of mental ideas," I explain.

"When I saw that painting, I said to you: 'You can dive into the feeling of a painting – that's a very important

194

quality.' But you were not looking for my approval then. You were relaxed, at ease in yourself, so my praise didn't matter much. Later, when you were hankering for approval, you didn't get it. That's usually how it goes around here!"

By the way, I should mention that there's nothing wrong with wanting approval. It's a very human quality. But the problem is that it makes you dependent on others, pulling you out of your own center. And then, as a painter, you become disconnected with your own source of expression. You start painting for other people.

Essentially, this is the same problem that I mentioned in chapter two. When an artist starts to gain public approval, the ego gets supported and the desire to continue receiving this support can easily become the priority. Even a genius like Picasso admitted, toward the end of his life, that he had sometimes compromised in order to fulfill the expectations of his admiring public.

Prem and I talk for a long time, but the issue isn't fully resolved. These things don't disappear so easily and by the end of our talk, when I really have to go, he is still saying things like: "I don't get any feeling of support from the group. I'm not accepted as I am, and I don't feel safe to express myself."

We have arranged a tea party for the whole group at my home on the following afternoon, but Prem says he will come only if he can bring a friend with him, Rupa, a woman who has not been part of the group.

I don't mind. In fact, for some time I've been wanting to meet Rupa because I know she is a very good dancer and I am interested in working with her, putting on a multi-media performance in the resort.

But still, I want to know why.

"Rupa really loves me, accepts me and I need her support to appear in front of the group, after what happened this afternoon," he explains.

"Okay, you can bring her," I say. "But I wonder if you can see that you're relying on reciprocation: 'if you support me then I will support you, if you love me then I will love you.' There is no risk involved in this kind of relating – it's a bargain, a contract, everyone stays safe.

"But these people with whom you have been painting during the past five days are all seeking their own authenticity. In a group like this, courage and trust to expose yourself is the very foundation – the key to letting go your defenses, letting go of your ego, moving more deeply into yourself."

I don't think Prem is ready to hear what I'm saying, but anyway we have to break off at this point.

The next afternoon comes around, and all the other group participants have gathered in my living room – passing around the tea and cakes in a festive mood.

Prem is late. For a while, it doesn't seem like he is going to come, so when he finally walks in the door with Rupa, everyone spontaneously cheers and claps in a very friendly way. There is so much love in the room that he simply has to see that all his ideas about the group – how people feel toward him – are his own projections.

Seizing the opportunity, I ask Prem to sit down next to me and, without words, to look around the group, making eye contact with each person.

"Take a look and see whom you can trust," I suggest.

I am holding his hand as he looks into people's faces. I can feel his tension in the way he grips my fingers, but slowly, as he starts naming people, his grip on my hand relaxes more and more.

Even though he doesn't say it, he is becoming aware that he is the one who is preventing love from happening, and this is a very important insight – for him, for anyone -- to have.

I don't want to make a big deal out of Prem's experience, because it's not exceptional – such things happen in almost every course or training. I'm just using it as one example of how tricky it can be to navigate in the unknown seas of your inner world.

One moment, you're feeling calm and centered, thinking you're one of the most conscious and alert beings on the planet, able to walk through life with full awareness and trust. Next moment, someone says something that hits your ego in a delicate spot and suddenly all awareness is lost.

This is why I include exercises in my courses like inviting others to work on your painting. It gives people a little mirror in which to see whether they have some ego investment in what they are doing. It helps to make a distinction between artistic creativity and the claim of the ego that says, 'This is my creativity! This is me! Don't spoil it! Look at how beautifully I can paint!'

Ironically, this claim of the ego is the very thing that is preventing you from creating something really authentic, truly original.

But I don't want to give the impression that 'ego is bad,' or support the idea – so common among traditional religions – that we have to suppress our egos, be humble, put others before ourselves and all that ugly, pseudo spirituality.

It doesn't have to be that serious. We all have an ego. So what? The main thing, as Osho points out in his discourses, is to get in touch with the inner reality that lies beyond the ego.

Then if someone praises you, and you feel your ego inflating like a balloon, you can take it lightly, non-seriously. And if, in the next moment, somebody else comes along and criticizes you, puncturing your balloon so all the air comes rushing out, you can take that lightly, too. You're not afraid, you don't lose your trust. You know that, deep inside, you're not the ego. You are far beyond it.

By now I hope you can see my basic direction in working with people in my courses. Working with the medium of painting, I help them connect with child-like qualities like innocence, spontaneity and playfulness as ways to side-step the difficulties created by ego – all your attitudes and beliefs about yourself, and what you can and cannot do.

It's important to remember that this happens within the overall context of meditation – regularly meditating in the morning and evening – which helps to take everyone deeper inside themselves. And also within the context of group energy dynamics, which makes learning faster.

But ego is a tricky thing. It's not just a question of noticing when the balloon called 'me' starts to inflate and get in the way of creative flow. Some people come to me with the opposite problem: their balloon is already deflated. They have such low self-esteem that it seems almost impossible for them to think they can do anything worthwhile.

Sukhi, the young Israeli woman, is an example of this reverse situation. You may remember, a few chapters back, I was talking about the pressure she felt to perform and the expectations from others that were crushing her. You may also remember that she had painted a big black tree trunk with watercolor and very little else surrounding it on the paper.

As the days of the training pass, her mood remains mostly dark and I do not try and persuade her to come out of it. In fact, I am happy that her paintings are reflecting this mood, because it shows something valuable – she is not pretending that everything is okay by trying to paint pretty pictures. She is not hiding anything from herself; she stays with her mood rather than trying to escape from it.

But then I notice her way of painting begins to develop a mechanical quality. I can see she is moving her brushes across the paper automatically and I feel this is a good time to intervene – maybe some change can happen.

This is part of the job of any instructor, or group leader. You have to be able to 'read' the participants. You have to be able to see the degree to which they are present, here and now, in this moment, and how much they are absent, somewhere else. It's in their body language, in their eyes, in their energy, in the way they paint.

I'm not saying you have to be a policeman, spying on everyone all the time, because my approach is basically to let people do what they want – supporting their freedom and creativity – but it is important to notice when they have lost contact with themselves, as in this case.

I know that, in addition to her beaten-down attitude towards painting, Sukhi is going through a hard time with her boyfriend. In fact, it's quite common that these things go together. There is usually at least one person in every group who faces a problem similar to Sukhi: the painting brings up her lack of self-worth – "I'll never be good enough" – and at the same time she is having a love story with a partner who reinforces this poor self-image.

It's a double dose of misery: failure in the group room and a critical partner at home. But it's not a bad thing, because it can help the one who is suffering to see the pattern and come out of it. And this morning, as I look at Sukhi, I think maybe this is a good moment to start.

I go over to her, sit down beside her, look at the big black tree that dominates the painting, and ask, "Are you enjoying your dark painting?"

She shrugs. "It's okay."

I look inquiringly in her eyes, "Is it true, what you're saying? Are you really enjoying yourself?"

If she'd said 'yes' I'd have left it at that, not wanting to impose myself on her process. But now, returning my frank gaze, she admits, "No. Not really."

"So, okay, why not try using some lighter colors?"

I watch as she chooses a bright, beautiful yellow for a new branch, but after two or three strokes the color fades, absorbed by the darker paint behind it.

"It's no good," says Sukhi. "It's all going into darkness."

"Why do you think it does that?" I ask.

"Yeah, well, the lighter color on the brush starts melting as soon as it touches the dark surface."

"Is there another way to paint?"

Sukhi hesitates, then a mischievous smile starts creeping across her face.

"Well," she says, "I guess I can always throw the paint on the paper."

And with this, she takes a pot of bright yellow and pours a long streak of vivid color down the side of her dark tree. It doesn't disappear – there is too much of it to be absorbed by the colors underneath.

Then she picks up a brush and starts dripping other light colors on her painting, without touching the paper. They also remain, without being absorbed.

Sukhi is really enjoying this sudden turn in events.

"You like it like this?" I ask.

She smiles, "Yes, I like it."

My intuition is right. Sukhi is ready to come out of darkness. It sounds simple, but you really have to know at which moment to give a hand, supporting a person's growth, because many people are not ready to be encountered directly with their issues.

If you say, for example, "You're not doing the right thing. Just stop using black and start using yellow," there is every chance that you will take away a person's creativity, just as it was crushed by similar remarks so many years ago, in childhood.

By the time the morning is over, Sukhi's watercolor painting is full of colors and yet it is not just a chaos. Some expression of the depth of nature is also emerging and I sense she can develop it much further.

In the afternoon, we are gathering downstairs in the Multiversity Plaza for an exercise, when Sukhi appears with her boyfriend. She introduces me to him and he immediately starts putting her down, in a humorous way, half playful, but I can tell immediately that this is his usual way of relating to her – his way of keeping himself safe by making her feel inadequate.

"Maybe she has some potential as a painter, but you will have to hit her hard to get it out of her!" he says, with a laugh, talking about her participation in my group.

"Excuse me, but you are absolutely wrong," I reply, in a polite but firm manner. "She does not need hitting at all. That is entirely the wrong approach. She is growing wonderfully, she is discovering her joy, her uniqueness, and she is really flowering. You are projecting your own mind onto her."

He is shocked by my words. But I can also see that he is an intelligent fellow and, after absorbing what I have said, he apologizes. I am happy I met him directly.

That evening we are scheduled to paint around Buddha Hall. It is a beautiful full moon night but it is so cold and I am feeling so tired that I am thinking of canceling it. To my surprise, everyone disagrees, they all want to paint, so I leave them to take care of themselves and go to bed.

Next day, after the morning session is over, we have a sharing on the roof and Sukhi takes the microphone.

"I got the point last night," she says. "I couldn't really see my painting. I saw only the beauty of nature and the mystery – plants look really mysterious in the moonlight. It's like you are under water and all the jungle is growing under the water. It was so beautiful and I couldn't see my painting, so I just moved my hand with the brush across the paper. It was so easy.

"In the morning, looking at what I'd done, I was surprised at how quickly I can paint and something clicked in my head that 'Wow! If I say 'yes' to my heart, to feeling the beauty and allowing my hand to move, it all happens by itself. I don't need to struggle in order to grow.'"

For someone like Sukhi, this single phrase, 'I don't need to struggle in order to grow,' is worth a hundred sessions on any therapist's couch. It's a major breakthrough in self-understanding, a golden key to transforming her life.

Then she holds up a different painting, in black and white, that she has been working on during this morning's session. She smiles and says, "You all know my black and white painting – it's mostly gray, with just one dark tree standing in the middle. At the time, it was important for me to say 'yes' to the grayness inside me.

"This morning, when I compared my painting to the nature surrounding me, I couldn't see any connection, but then I remembered how easy it was for me to paint last night, so I started anew. I kept the tree, but made the background again, I put branches here, there… they came by themselves... and in one hour my painting had grown in such an incredible way."

She holds it up for everyone to see. I find myself looking more at Sukhi than her painting, seeing the sparkle in her eyes and the confidence and vitality with which she shares her experience. Such a transformation!

A little later on, the group is discussing nature paintings that we have done in color, and I ask, "Who feels stuck with their nature painting?"

Several people raise their hands, including Sukhi, but I laugh and shake my head and say, "No, Sukhi. You are not allowed to raise your hand. You are not stuck. The lesson you learned with black and white will carry over into your color paintings as well."

These two examples of how ego can get in the way of creativity both concern people from Israel, but this is just coincidence. In my experience, working with hundreds of people, these kinds of problems don't belong to any particular nationality or ethnic group. They span the whole width of humanity.

You may have noticed that during this chapter I have focused on things that stand in the way of meditation and spiritual experiences, rather than the experiences themselves. This is intentional and reflects Osho's basic approach. The art of watching or witnessing is directed towards those things that obscure our inner reality, such as thoughts, beliefs, attitudes, emotions, moods, repressed traumas.

As these are brought into the light of awareness, their grip on us dissolves, and we find ourselves more and more rooted in our real, authentic consciousness. This, in turn, is the doorway that opens to the beyond – to silence, peace, love, bliss. It's a bit like removing rocks from a stream. Take away the obstacles and the water flows by itself.

In a way, it's similar to be being a specialist in the discovery and restoration of old paintings: you're cleaning some rather ordinary work of art when suddenly you realize there's a masterpiece hidden underneath. Very patiently, very carefully, you remove all the surface paint until finally the masterpiece is exposed and revealed. There's no need to do anything with it directly. It's already there, waiting to be discovered.

It's the same with your inner world. You just need to get rid of all the crap that's been dumped on you since childhood – I think its called 'education' – and slowly, slowly, you discover the individual that you have always been. And with your individuality comes your natural creativity, the spontaneous expression of who you really are.

In this next chapter, I am going to try and say a little more about this expression and about the inner world in general, because here, for me, lies the whole secret of bringing about a revolution in art.

Chapter 9

The Search for Synthesis

I'd like to start this chapter by talking about Wassily Kandinsky. You may remember that, two chapters ago, we left him at an Impressionist exhibition in Moscow, in 1895, standing in front of Claude Monet's painting of a haystack,. He was 29 years old and enrolled at the University of Moscow to study law and economics.

Looking at Monet's work, Kandinsky was at first offended by the fact that he had to refer to the exhibition catalogue in order to realize the object he was looking at was actually a haystack. But then "I noticed with astonishment and confusion that not only does the picture enthrall one, but also impresses itself indelibly on the memory, always quite unexpectedly appearing down to the last detail before one's eyes."

What impressed him deeply was "the unsuspected power of the palette, a power which had earlier been hidden from me, but which surpassed all my dreams. Painting acquired a fairy-tale strength and a magnificence."

One year later, he had abandoned a promising academic career and was studying art in Munich. But it would be a mistake to suppose that Monet alone was the cause of Kandinsky's radical change in lifestyle. Another major experience was seeing Wagner's "Lohengrin" in Moscow, where the composer's powerful music provoked within his mind wild patterns of psychedelic colors, forming "drawings before my very eyes".

His lifetime work of seeking a relationship between music and color was born at that moment.

Munich in 1896 was a ferment of new ideas about art that separated the Naturalists, those seeking to represent life as it is, from the Symbolists, who were intent to seek and express more depth and meaning in their paintings than the mere reproduction of nature could supply.

Kandinsky, very clearly, already belonged to the Symbolist school, but at first he disciplined himself to study classical drawing, composition and a variety of painting techniques.

In the early years of the new century, his paintings had tended towards the sweetly romantic, including lyrical scenes of his beloved Moscow, but after a few years in Munich he began to develop a more radical style, experimenting with strong patches of unmixed color in juxtaposition to each other.

His paintings became increasingly abstract, with only a minimal suggestion of form, like his dynamic black railway train charging across a bright green landscape in 'Murnau - View with Railway and Castle,' and even more so in 'Picture with Archer,' where recognizable forms have almost disappeared.

Music was never far from his mind when he painted and, commenting on this, he explained, "I applied streaks and blobs of colors onto the canvas with a palette knife and I made them sing with all the intensity I could."

In 1909, Kandinsky was an influential force behind establishing a New Society for Munich Artists, but within two years his evolving love affair with abstract painting had outgrown the society and – facing mounting opposition from within its ranks – he resigned and broke away. Within a year, he had formed the legendary Blue Rider Group, a gathering of avant-garde artists who were determined not to be constricted by any conventional ideas.

At this point, I want to take you into Kandinsky's personal life in order to mention Gabriele Munter, one of the few female artists of that period, who first studied with Kandinsky in Munich and then became his lover.

She joined the Blue Rider Group and bought a small house in Murnau, south of Munich, as a summer home for herself and Kandinsky, which became a kind of commune for radical artists, including Alexei Jawlensky, Marianne von Werefkin and August Macke.

I have visited that little house many times, because in it I see a reflection of my own dream of an artist's commune – a group of painters living, working and growing together. The atmosphere inside is playful and joyful, and many parts of the house have been painted spontaneously, with shapes like plants, or abstract patterns.

I also want to acknowledge Munter's generosity of spirit, because even though Kandinsky left her after a ten-year relationship, she kept his paintings and saved them from the Nazis in the 1930s by hiding them in the cellar of her Murnau home. She lived long, eventually enjoying recognition as Germany's most important woman artist, and died in 1962.

Kandinsky was one of those uncommon painters whose artistic talent was accompanied by a strong need to explain intellectually everything he was trying to do, and in 1911 he published his landmark treatise "Concerning the Spiritual in Art."

In it, he stated that one of the chief responsibilities of any artist was to halt the rush towards materialism that he saw everywhere in early twentieth century society, and lead the way towards a spiritual revolution.

"When religion science and morality are shaken and when the outer supports threaten to fall, man turns his gaze from externals in on himself," Kandinsky wrote.

"Literature, music and art are the first and most sensitive spheres in which this spiritual revolution is felt. They turn away from the soulless life of the present towards those substances and ideas which give free scope to the nonmaterial strivings of the soul."

Reading these words by Kandinsky makes me think, "My god! If Wassily thought the world was soulless and materialist in Germany in 1911, what would his impression be today if he suddenly found himself in a shopping mall in Tokyo?"

One of his main assertions is that true art, at its highest expression, always points towards the spiritual dimension of man's evolving consciousness, and this is where I wholeheartedly agree with him – why I rank him as one of the most significant modern painters.

He spoke of an artist's 'inner need,' by which he meant the painter's deep impulse for spiritual expression. It is this impulse that drives an artist to try and capture something ethereal or mystical, beyond the material world, and give it dimension, form and color.

One aspect of his own 'inner need' was to try and discover a hidden connection between color and form in painting, to see what impact this can have on the human psyche. He was particularly intrigued with the idea of expressing conflict and struggle – in an abstract way – while at the same time including within the painting a promise of eventual resolution and harmony. In this, he was influenced by the work of Rudolph Steiner and the Theosophy movement.

As I have mentioned before, he wanted to establish a system, or code, linking colors with musical notes – creating abstract paintings that would evoke the sounds of music within the person that looked at it. In fact, one of his dreams was to create a synthesis of all kinds of art, embracing music, painting, dance – what might now be called 'multi-media' art – bringing different forms of creative expression into a state of divine harmony.

To be honest, I don't think he succeeded in any of these aims, except perhaps in a general way. Of course, if you paint with dark colors, you are going to trigger an association with heaviness and dark emotions in most of your viewing public. If you paint chaos, or struggle, you are going to provoke some kind of parallel emotional response.

But even if you have developed your own, personal system of coding color with musical notes – as Kandinsky did – it remains subjective. It does not become an objective standard for everyone, just because one sensitive artist defines it that way.

For example, put a hundred people in front of one of Kandinsky's 'musical' paintings, like his "Yellow-Red-Blue,' painted in 1925, and ask them to sing, or hum, the musical notes or tune this provokes in them. I guarantee you that they will all be different. You will get a hundred different tunes.

This, to me, is perfectly okay. I like variety and don't much care for the idea of color being chained to music in a fixed way. When I put on my multi-media shows, using live music and dance with a slide-show of my paintings, I know that it is going to be a different experience every time, and I enjoy the surprise that each new event brings. I welcome the unexpected – this is what makes life interesting and fresh.

But still, I want to bow down to Wassily Kandinsky, not only for being the father of abstract art – which in itself is a major achievement – but for his aim of infusing art with spirituality and consciousness. That's why I want to talk about him. Because to me, art needs to have this dimension in order to be truly significant and meaningful.

I am not against other forms of art – as entertainment, as decoration, as social commentary, as an expression of inner turmoil, and so on. But, for me, the spiritual element gives art its highest flights and its deepest relevance to human evolution and aspiration.

Kandinsky was by no means the first man to give art spiritual significance. Down the ages, many artists have felt the same way. But because of his emphasis on abstraction, he was the first to free art from orthodox religious themes, while at the same time emphasizing its spiritual function.

You see the point? Religion has been such a trap for the human spirit, loading mankind with so much guilt and condemnation, that the art associated with it has never – for me at least – been truly liberating.

Walk into the Sistine Chapel in Rome and look up at the ceiling. You will see the genius of Michelangelo in his portrayal of Jehovah's act of creation, giving life to Adam and Eve. It's beautiful, sensual, magnificent, but you cannot separate it from the oppressive message that goes with it: Adam's disobedience, the original sin, the fall of the whole of humanity into sin, the condemnation of the flesh, the threat of eternal damnation... and so on.

It seems to me that all major religions have contaminated art in this way, thereby perverting man's quest for inner meaning with all kinds of nonsense. So I am grateful to Kandinsky for removing art from convention and giving spiritual expression a new look.

By the way, I can't leave Michelangelo without mentioning that he didn't want to paint the Sistine Chapel ceiling. When you look at it, how beautiful it is, you just can't believe it. But he resisted the request, or command, that came from Pope Julius II, complaining 'painting is not my art,' and even when he finally consented, he was far from enchanted by the project.

Imagine him, in the Sistine Chapel, high up on a wooden scaffold, giving birth to one of the greatest pieces of art in the Christian world. You'd think he would be in a state of reverent awe, but instead – working in the most uncomfortable positions – he wrote this self-mocking poem about his difficulties:

I've already grown a goiter from this toil
As water swells the cats in Lombardy,
Or any other country they might be,
Forcing my belly to hang under my chin.
My beard to heaven, and my memory
I feel above its coffer.
My chest a harp.
And ever above my face, the brush dripping,
Making a rich pavement out of me.
My loins have been shoved into my guts,
My arse serves to counterweigh my rump,
Eyelessly I walk in the void.

Ahead of me, my skin lies outstretched,
And to bend, I must knot my shoulders taut,
Holding myself like a Syrian bow.

Of course, this has nothing to do with Kandinsky, but I want to salute Michelangelo for his irreverence and his raw, earthy sense of humor. It makes me wonder what he would have really painted on the Sistine Chapel ceiling if he had been given a totally free hand.

Now, back to Kandinsky and his revolution. Whether Wassily succeeded in conveying the spiritual element in abstract form is something that has to be decided individually, by each person that views his paintings. For me personally, he stands as a pioneer, a predecessor, because in my training – especially in the 'primal painting' section – I encourage people to search for, and express, the same meeting of abstract art and mysticism.

Certainly, in his own life, Kandinsky seemed contented enough with his achievements and his later pictures – those painted within a few years of his death in 1944 – contain a light-heartedness, innocence and humorous element that to me indicates a feeling of fulfillment.

I would like to expand on Kandinsky's success and make the spiritual dimension more accessible to those artists – and their public – who are looking for it. And by chance I find myself well placed to do so, not through any particular genius on my part but simply because I am an artist who has stumbled upon a rich treasure box containing almost all of the mysticism and meditation of the East.

Through meeting my spiritual master, Osho, I have been introduced to a wide variety of spiritual traditions and have learned to distinguish what is valuable in them from what is mere scripture, dogma and creed.

What it comes down to, essentially, is providing maps and methods for going inwards, for penetrating your own innermost core of consciousness. This, of course, presumes an initial understanding, which I hope most of you have grasped by now, that all that is valuable in human

211

experience – creativity, individuality, ecstasy, joy, silence, bliss – lies within yourself.

It is only a question of how best to go in and get it.

Here, I don't want to set up Osho as another distraction. Having disposed of the exclusive claims of orthodox religions and their founders – the only begotten son of God, the last messenger of God, the perfect incarnation of God – it's not my intention to create a new idol to replace them.

I love Osho precisely because he invites people to discard all belief in saviors, scriptures and other outer religious supports, and to take the responsibility of finding out the truth for themselves, through direct personal experience. He's devised a few methods of his own, like Dynamic, but he doesn't make exclusive claims for them. It's up to you to discover what works best: whirling like a mad Sufi, sitting silently in Zazen like a Buddhist monk, dancing, chanting, humming....

People like Osho, who know the geography of the inner world, can offer guide maps and methods, but you are the one who has to test them for personal suitability. No single method or map will do, because each person's journey is going to be different. There is no super-highway to truth, because every human being is unique.

However, in my experience, individuals can come together and create meditative energy fields, a certain spiritual atmosphere, like a pool of silence, where it is easier to have inner experiences.

Osho has created one such energy field at his meditation resort in Pune.

India, generally, possesses this meditative atmosphere. If you can get away from the chaos, noise, traffic and people, and find a quiet place to sit down and close your eyes, you will soon feel this country still radiates that vibe created by millions of meditators down through the centuries.

In the West, it's a little more difficult to move inwards, especially if you are on your own. Then the individual has to stand against the whole collective psychology, the whole

212

social atmosphere that is pulling outwards – into entertainment, distraction, worldly affairs.

But I know it is possible to create this meditative vibe anywhere in the world. That's what I try to do, every time I lead a workshop or training. Each group becomes a little energy field, or Buddha field, where I help people discover their creativity while at the same time going deeper in meditation.

In fact, both things lie in the same direction. The deeper you go in yourself, the more likely you are to tap into your sources of creative expression. The deeper you go in, the more likely you are to meet silence, emptiness, bliss. It's all part of the same package, and a double bonus for seekers who happen to also be artists.

The best part, for me, is that all these discoveries happen through discovering yourself. It's you that you find, when you go inwards. It's your individuality that you reclaim. It's you that possesses all these beautiful qualities – just you were so busy watching movies, reading magazines and surfing the web that you never went in and noticed them.

As Osho says:

"Inside yourself you will find a tranquility, a serenity, a silence, a treasure unfathomable. And in finding it you will know everybody has got it; whether he knows it or not, that's a different matter. Knowing and not knowing – that is the only difference. But as far as existence is concerned, everybody has all the beauty of the world, of the universe; all the ecstasy and dance of the universe. Yes, in different ways it will express itself.

"There is no need to think that somebody who is expressing it through dance is better than the one who is expressing it through a song or one who is expressing it through his silence. What is being expressed is exactly the same ecstasy."

I think this is where Kandinsky got a little confused, not having the benefit of the Eastern mystical perspective. He seemed to think that a synthesis of art happens through

213

connecting different forms of expression in a specific way, in a matching order or sequence.

For me, synthesis happens when we, as artists, taste the inner world of meditation. That is where we experience oneness, a sense of unity in all things. Then our different forms of expression can come together spontaneously and harmoniously, with unlimited possibilities.

In other words, when art becomes a by-product of self-inquiry, synthesis happens by itself.

Before becoming a sannyasin, I felt very strongly that art was the most important thing in my life – a great cause for which I needed to sacrifice everything. So when I began to learn about meditation I looked on it as an aid, a support, something that could maybe help to deepen my painting.

But pretty soon I got the point: it's really the other way round. Compared to the inner journey, compared the adventure of spiritual self-discovery, art is just a play, an enjoyable spin-off that happens while searching for truth.

The real point of synthesis lies beyond art. There is no need to try and impose a synthesis on art itself. The real harmony is spiritual in origin and is not a serious phenomenon. It is more like playfulness, more like fun.

Strangely enough – and this is probably going to sound very odd – one of the earliest expressions of this playfulness was communicated to me through Osho's signature.

He has a very unusual signature, written, of course, in Hindi. Even Indians say it's strange. It's a kind of flowing movement, not really planned, slightly different every time he does it, using the language and letters of his native tongue but not restricted by them. He just moves his hand across the paper and then, at a certain moment, it's finished. To someone like me, who has trained in calligraphy as well as painting, it looks so balanced and beautiful, so playful and perfect.

Over the years, Osho collected thousands of books – maybe he created the world's largest private library of books on philosophy, psychology and religion – and he signed them all, inside the front cover.

214

But he didn't just sign them. In many books, using color felt pens, or marker pens, he made designs and paintings. For some reason, the pens he used created the same effect as watercolor painting, allowing colors to overlap, blend and merge together, making the overall effect very mysterious.

He never studied color balance, or any art techniques, but to me, looking at these paintings, I see many of the qualities I try to convey to my group participants: balance, playfulness, spontaneity, surprise, creativity.

How did he manage it? The way I figure it, he came to art from the reverse direction: first, he reached the ultimate point in human consciousness, then he came back to art. This means that, for an enlightened being, everything is a play and the qualities that I usually have to teach people come naturally.

For example, you know that, in my groups and trainings, many people are afraid to go into darkness, to use really dark colors. They think, 'If I make my painting so dark, it may destroy the beauty, so it's better to avoid it.'

An enlightened being has no fear, so he experiments with darkness, and then on top of the dark color he puts a lighter one… and suddenly such a mysterious layer enters the painting, because usually one doesn't do that.

Normally, conventionally, you put a dark color on top of a light color, not the other way around, especially when the colors are transparent and merge with each other. In an oil painting, or with acrylics, of course, you can do what you like, but not with watercolor.

So that was an interesting insight into Osho's perspective, seeing how he understands things from a certain height of consciousness.

Until I met Osho, I had the idea that, having become a painter, I would spend my life searching for meaning and fulfillment within a particular form of expression.

The paintings in his books helped me flip the coin to the other side. To see that, "Oh yes, painting is a beautiful form of expression, but it's not that big a deal. It doesn't have to

215

give me all the answers. In fact, it cannot. The answers that I am looking for lie beyond it."

In November 1979, Osho asked me to form an art group in his rapidly growing community of sannyasins in Pune. By this time, he was becoming big news around the world, especially in Europe, and hundreds of people from Germany, Holland and Italy were pouring into the ashram – many of them wanting to stay indefinitely.

One evening, I was sitting in front of Osho, in darshan, and he said, "Now your paintings are beautiful, so you start the art group."

This was a total surprise, for two reasons:

First, I had never shown him any of my paintings. How did he know they had changed, becoming more beautiful?

Second, I'd never dreamed that he would want an art group in his ashram, or that he would want me to lead it – it came out of the blue, like a Zen thunderclap.

I was so stunned that I forgot to ask any questions – how to run the group, what is its aim, what kind of guidelines he would like me to follow, and so on. And then the very next day it was announced that Osho would not be talking with people personally in darshan any more, so the opportunity was gone. Clearly, I had to find my way without detailed guidance from my master.

Fortunately, help arrived in the form of an American painter called Geetesh, a wild-eyed, scraggly-haired, bohemian-looking fellow, with whom I felt an immediate rapport. He had enthusiasm, drive and a vision of how an art group might work, plus some teaching experience, and pretty soon he'd found a place for us in a big old colonial-style house, about five minutes away from the main ashram.

It was already occupied by the ashram's weaving department, including 15 looms and 30 weavers, offering a visual feast to my eyes, with large, colorful skeins of naturally-dyed yarn hanging everywhere from the bamboo roof. The continuous sound of the looms and shuttles was music in itself.

An international group of musicians also took up residence and that's how the house got its name – the Music House. In addition, a silk-screen printing crew began working there, but even with all these creative developments there was enough room to accommodate an art group, so I staked my claim by moving in and sleeping on a plank of plywood, suspended under the roof.

I made an announcement on one of the commune's notice boards that a new art group was happening, inviting people to come to an exploratory meeting at the Music House. About thirty-five people showed up and that, in itself, was surprising. I didn't know there were so many artists in the commune.

At first, I was enthusiastic, but within a short time, after only a few meetings with these people, it became clear that it wouldn't work. I'd forgotten about the artistic ego, the feeling of specialness that we painters have about ourselves. In fact, painters, musicians, dancers – it doesn't matter which area of creativity – have some of the biggest egos on the planet.

In those days, we were in a very raw state, only just beginning to meditate and create a flame of awareness inside ourselves. In no way was I a group leader, in the sense that I could guide people to look at themselves – even if they had been willing for me to do so – and the group soon broke up.

Undaunted, Geetesh and I started again, this time contacting painters individually, talking to them privately, taking time to share our vision of how an art group might work, and in this way we gradually built up a community of about a dozen painters

We decided to be self-sufficient, not asking for money from the commune administration but offering painting groups to new arrivals interested in art and living off the income, and this worked pretty well. We became a self-supporting commune of artists, functioning like a satellite to the main commune, and were supporting about 15 artists, providing food, lodging and painting materials.

Together, Geetesh and I discovered a direction in which to guide the group, and it was expressed in a simple slogan: "Jump into the unknown!" This, we borrowed from Osho, because one of his most basic suggestions for his sannyasins is to keep moving from the known into the unknown, to keep exploring deeper into life.

Life is, essentially, a mystery and it is only our tendency to cling to the known, to the past, to the dead, that makes it become dull and boring.

The Music House became both a laboratory and a classroom, since we were exploring ourselves through painting and at the same time teaching others to do the same. Naturally, it was a rough ride at times, because, as I just mentioned, we were not yet skilled at group leading, nor in seeing our own ego trips, so situations like the ones I described with Ram and Sukhi in the previous chapter were an almost daily occurrence. Usually, at least one of us would be "going through it" in terms of running up against the rock of the ego, hitting a blind spot in our self-awareness, and struggling to find a way through.

We were aided by Osho's daily discourses, in which – in a thousand different ways – he was continually speaking about the growth of human consciousness and what can help or hinder it. We could also seek help from the commune therapists, including some very skilled counselors and group leaders.

Most of the time, though, we could handle it ourselves, and our life together was intense, enjoyable and above all an adventure. Sometimes, too, we combined our art groups with other fields of self-inquiry, such as primal therapy, hypnosis and working with the chakras – the body's seven energy centers. Later, I learned the art of group leading by participating in dozens of groups and trainings.

When Osho left India for America in 1981 it became clear that Pune was finished for us as artists, but we were not ready to see our group split up so we moved to Amsterdam in Holland. There, we rented a concrete barge on one of the city's main canals, which had formerly been a meditation center for Osho's sannyasins.

They moved to a bigger location and we moved onto the barge, ten of us living together trying to find money to pay the rent, feed ourselves and keep warm as the European winter approached. Again, offering groups and trainings provided the main source of income.

It was hard going but personally very rewarding, because I was able to create many beautiful paintings in this new environment, especially working in Amsterdam's botanical gardens. More and more, I was being drawn to nature as my favorite theme and as the place where I could learn most.

Eventually, after nine months, economic reality dawned on us starving artists, and we knew we had to abandon life in the big city. We put a small notice in a sannyasin magazine, asking Osho's global community of disciples if anyone was willing to take us, and to our delight we received four offers, including the one we accepted – a small house in the mountains of Sicily.

There we lived for ten months, twelve of us, painting like monkeys and scratching around for food and fuel – we needed a fire every day because it was so cold in the mountains. We were incredibly poor but mostly happy and cheerful. After all, poverty was a tradition in our field – this was how hundreds of painters had lived before us, sacrificing comfort for the sake of art.

Nature in this part of Sicily is immensely beautiful; we were living inside a wild life sanctuary filled with orchids, morning glories and cherry blossoms, and there I produced one of my best works. There, too, I learned the value of living in an artists' community, for although we painted alone – each seeking a personal form of expression – there was a supportive feeling between us that was strengthening and uplifting.

One night, I remember, we all walked to the top of a cliff, carrying a bottle of whiskey that we had somehow managed to purchase, and watched the full moon rise over the mountains. Sip by sip, we watched the moon rise higher and higher above us, until we were all very drunk, huddled together under blankets and half asleep – a very cozy and heart-warming feeling enveloping us all.

Meanwhile, Osho's international commune in Oregon was growing spectacularly, making waves of controversy in both the USA and Europe. A great deal of the money that financed this huge experiment came from European sannyasins who by that time were highly organized, living in big communes and running successful discotheques – mainly in German cities – to raise money.

Our commune was eventually closed down – "you guys are too poor" was the message we got from one of Osho's secretaries – but Geetesh and I never quit our passionate affair with art. We wandered around Europe for a while, living in other Osho communes, then traveled to California where we established a small art company and started selling paintings in the streets of San Francisco and at fairs in the North Bay area.

By now you have probably realized that Geetesh and I were lovers, my affair with Govind having faded some years earlier. Govind had chosen to spend his time in Japan and the US, rather than in Pune, so naturally we drifted apart.

Geetesh and I became street artists, local artists, painting small scenes of nature that could be sold cheaply, because – as I said before – Americans are not very interested in spending real money on paintings unless they are by a recognized artist.

All this time, my personal style of painting was crystallizing, and looking back on my time in California with Geetesh I can see the value in it, even though we had little money and no public support.

At the time, in order to survive, we began to study what the human psyche is attracted to, in terms of beauty and commercial art. For example, we went into many shops that sold postcards, asking the retailers which postcards sold best and then buying those and making collections of them.

Sure enough, we discovered that people like sunrises, sunsets, ocean views... and nearly always in such scenes there's something in the foreground, some rocks or palm trees, or people kissing, or there's a boat... this kind of thing.

We discovered there's a certain mathematical order, or structure, to the public's attraction to beauty, and this is international, very widespread – Japanese or Chinese, American or European – the sense of beauty is quite universal.

So this we studied, and then Geetesh and I painted together to create our own version of the same thing. I was good at flowers, plants and trees – the foreground of the paintings – and Geetesh was good at backgrounds.

Our rendering of nature was neither pictorial nor abstract, but a synthesis of both. We tried to penetrate immediately to the essence of a particular scene, whether it was a moonlit mountain or a sunlit sea, and let the expression happen effortlessly and spontaneously.

It was more of a happening than a deliberate effort to paint a picture, and in this way my painting took a big jump. I was discovering ways to create something original – giving a new look, a new style, a new definition to ordinary nature – and at the same time to connect quickly and directly with the public, with people's hearts.

Even though we were ruled by the need to make money to feed ourselves, I never felt I was wasting my time, nor did I lose my dignity as an artist.

On the contrary, Geetesh and I felt like two creators, meeting every day and every night, and we were continuously inspiring each other. And although we were the only two remaining from our art group, we still carried the flavor, the spirit, of working, sharing and growing together – as painters and as human beings.

Sometimes we made greetings cards, sometimes paintings with frames, knowing that whatever we produced had to be cheap because otherwise people would not buy them.

We were amused to discover that people liked to buy paintings signed by a couple – of course, because it's an

221

original idea and also rather romantic. We became so practiced at producing this form of commercial art that we could create fifty paintings a day, often selling from street stalls, where I used to cook underneath, making miso soup for Geetesh and myself.

When times were hard, two stories inspired me and kept me going. One, that I heard first from Osho, concerns the famous Bengali poet and Nobel Prize winner, Rabindranath Tagore – the man who wrote Gitanjali, one of the world's most beautiful poems.

Rabindranath's uncle was a master painter and one day, when Rabindranath was enjoying some tea with him, one of his uncle's disciples came to show him a painting, a portrait of Krishna, he had just completed.

In front of Rabindranath, the uncle shouted at the disciple, "What are you painting? This is pure shit that you're doing! It has no meaning. Go and study with the town painters; they are doing much better. Go to the town and paint with them, learn from them."

And he threw the painting out of the window.

The disciple said nothing. He bowed and immediately left.

Rabindranath was horrified and said to his uncle, "This is not right. The painting was beautiful. You're just jealous, because he paints better than you, that's why you threw away the painting."

The uncle went outside, brought the painting back into the room, and he said, "It's true that he is far superior to me."

He took down his own painting from the wall and hung the disciple's painting instead, then added, "But if I said that to him now, in this very same moment he will stop growing and never reach his full potential. I can't do that to him; he is my disciple."

Meanwhile, the disciple went to the town and for years studied and worked with the commercial street artists. He really got the point: all these town painters are so anonymous, yet they are good painters, because they have to amuse ordinary people in order to earn their living – otherwise they will starve.

Most people have no idea about art, but they have heart, they have feeling, so they can recognize simplicity, beauty. This, in turn, teaches the artist to be ordinary and simple in what he is trying to convey, and to let go of his attachment to originality – the desire to be acclaimed for producing something unique.

I remembered this story many times while I was painting in California with Geetesh, because we had to sell paintings to people who were not particularly interested in art. Maybe they just want to give something nice to a friend for a birthday, or for Christmas.

That reminds me: one day, when we had a stall on the street – always checking for the police because we didn't have permission – a little boy about six years old came up to me and said, "I want to buy a painting. I want to give it to my mom as a present."

I was really touched – such a little boy, and yet feeling that one of our paintings was the right thing to make his mother happy.

I said, "Wow, you want buy a painting? How much do you have?"

He said, "Two dollars."

Even as street artists we didn't usually go that low with our prices, but I wasn't going to disappoint him.

"Of course, you're welcome," I said, "take whichever one you like best."

He picked out a sunset over the ocean, with a pine tree silhouetted darkly in the foreground, and I helped him wrap it in the gift paper he'd already bought.

So that's the kind of people we were dealing with. We learned a lot about how to catch the hearts of people without compromising our dignity as artists. We learned to be fast, simple, ordinary painters.

If I look back now, I can see it was the perfect preparation for what came next, but before I tell that part of my story, I need to mention the other historical anecdote that

223

kept me going in California – I told you there were two of them.

In 1868, when he was still very much a struggling artist, Pissarro, with another French artist, Armand Guillaumin, urgently needed money to survive an exceptionally cold Paris winter – Pissarro had a wife and children to support – so they got jobs with a manufacturer of canvas roller-blinds.

Pierre-Auguste Renoir, who later became famous for his paintings of voluptuous nudes, had worked in a similar way in a porcelain factory. He advised Pissarro and Guillaumin not to accept a daily wage, but to insist on a piece rate, and to decorate as many blinds as they could. The owner had given them freedom to paint whatever designs they wished, but clearly the canvases needed to have public appeal or they would not sell.

Pissarro and Guillaumin worked at a good speed, using plenty of blue skies and clouds – having learned that these cover the canvas quickly and are pleasing to the eye – and as an amusement they signed many of their works, some of which are still preserved today.

In this small anecdote I see the same lesson: the opportunity to drop the artist's ballooning ego of self-importance and to discipline oneself to produce quick, simple, satisfying paintings.

As it turned out, this could not have been a more fitting preparation for what was to come. As I told you, it was during my California phase that Taeko, my sister, decided to rescue me from poverty by organizing an exhibition near Tokyo. After that, I visited Pune, where Osho had again taken up residence, having been expelled from the US and refused residence in a total of 21 countries worldwide.

For him, now, India was the only option and his Pune commune the only available location, so it was there that his sannyasins began gathering again in 1987. I felt happy to be there, but didn't stay long and was back in California when my sister became really sick. I abruptly dropped everything to return to Japan and be with her.

Somehow her death made me look deeply at my own sense of priorities, at what was most important and significant in my life, and as a result I left California and came back to Pune to stay. This was the beginning of the end of my being with Geetesh, for although we never stopped loving each other, he did not feel the same pull as I did to stay for a long time in Osho's community.

Not long after I'd arrived, Anando, a cheerful, no-nonsense Australian woman who was now one of Osho's secretaries, asked me to bring all my paintings to Lao Tzu House, a very private part of the campus where Osho was living. Since Anando also lived and worked in the house, I assumed the request came from her own personal curiosity.

"Oh, you want to see my paintings?" I said, a little surprised, because until then she had not expressed any interest in my work.

She shook her head and smiled. "No, it's not for me. Osho wants to see your paintings."

This was a real surprise – one of the biggest of my life.

Recovering quickly from the shock, I asked, "Can I show them to him myself?"

"No. He wants me to do that."

This made sense, because it was rarely that Osho ever invited anyone to his private rooms. But it also posed a practical problem.

"My paintings are very difficult," I explained, "Because sometimes you don't know what is up and what is down. And the main paintings are three or four panels together – they need to be arranged in the right sequence."

Anando thought for a moment and said, "Okay, you can arrange an exhibition for Osho in his library."

Then she said, "But you have only one hour to prepare."

Now, who can prepare a whole exhibition in an hour! But on my travels I always carried a portfolio of my best works, and by chance I'd been sorting through them, preparing for a public exhibition in Mumbai. We quickly arranged three plywood panels in the library, on which I hung my larger paintings, with smaller paintings lying on a table, and more taped to the walls of the corridor outside.

That was an exciting moment for me, working at high speed to create an exhibition for Osho. I was so high. I couldn't believe what was happening.

One of the librarians told me afterwards that Osho spent forty-five minutes looking at the paintings and chose several of them to illustrate the back covers of new books containing his discourses.

Maybe I should explain here: he was giving a discourse every day, and each series of discourses lasted anything from ten to thirty days. Each series had a specific theme, such as answering questions from disciples, commenting on the sayings of Zen masters, interpreting Nietzche's masterpiece 'Thus Spake Zarathustra,' or Khalil Gibran's 'The Prophet'...

Each day, as soon as Osho had finished speaking, the audio recording of that particular discourse would be transcribed by an editorial team, and when a series was complete it would be published as a book, so there was a continuous stream of Osho books being published. Now I was being appointed the 'court painter,' decorating his books, inside and out – jackets, end papers, chapter title pages.

This was the beginning of a very beautiful time for me, because after Taeko's death I'd somehow lost the motivation to paint. For months and months, I'd been painting just for her, to give her happiness, and now she was gone there didn't seem much point in picking up my brushes. Painting for Osho brought back my energy and creative enthusiasm with a rush.

His guidance was simple: 'meditate in discourse while I am speaking, then paint.' By this time, he was talking mostly on Zen, and this made things easy for me because almost always he included in his discourses Zen haikus and poems– by Basho and other masters – and these were filled with references to nature.

Now I could see the value of my time as a commercial artist in California. Producing beautiful paintings at high speed had become second nature to me.

Every night in discourse, I sat in stillness while Osho was speaking on some Zen master – Ma Tzu, Rinzai, Dogen, Hyakujo, Kyozan, Sekeito, Nansen – and I soon found that, while I was meditating, I got flooded with artistic visions.

This was a new and amazing process. I think I must have been the most ecstatic person in Buddha Hall, because I was flying so high as a creative artist. Colors and pictures were flooding into my mind, whole designs for book covers – not for a moment need I worry about being able to come up with a design.

On the contrary, so many colors and visions were coming into my mind that I began to feel guilty. I started to worry that I was not meditating properly. After all, hadn't Osho said a thousand times that meditation was all about emptiness and nothingness?

Just at that very moment, when I was thinking "Now, I really must write to him and ask him what to do about this," Osho recited a Zen haiku in discourse and said to everyone in the hall, "Visualize this! It's not poetry. It's a painting."

So this was my answer – instant feedback to an unasked question.

Several times he gave guidelines how to paint for the jacket covers, which colors to use, and this was an interesting experience because at times it felt like I became just a hand – that I didn't exist as a person. Nor did it feel like the hand belonged to Osho. It was pure creativity, coming from beyond any personal sense of 'I' or 'him.'

I was flying high, but my feet were firmly on the ground. I felt a lot of hara energy, centered in myself, solid and capable, while immensely enjoying the painting – I didn't care about anything else.

One time he said, "Now paint snow." So I painted snow for a week.

Another time I was trying to paint a night scene, with huge mountains looming darkly in the background and a moonlit 'night rainbow' arching across the sky.

Osho commented, "Why are you so miserly, with just one rainbow? The whole existence is filled with rainbows!" So then for a week I painted multiple orgasmic rainbows at night, and that's when a whole new theme of night paintings was created in my mind.

Another time he said, "Why just one sun? Don't be stingy! Go with abundance." So for a while I started painting millions of suns.

As an artist, I was intrigued by Osho's freedom of vision. He wasn't concerned with the usual preoccupations of the painter, like composition – what is going to be in the foreground, middle ground, background. He was much more open and flexible.

This is essentially connected with what I'm teaching these days to my course participants: I teach unlimited abundance in painting, not coming from mental ideas but from a freedom that is connected with your being, your innermost core.

I used to send my paintings to him every two weeks – most of his Zen series lasted between 10-14 days – and I'd submit about thirty paintings every time, nicely mounted for the master to see. Altogether, he chose 500 paintings for 42 books, and I must have produced over 1,500 paintings during that time.

Of course, I needed assistants, because otherwise the mounting business would have taken all my time. So I found myself becoming part of the publishing team.

I worked regular, ordinary hours, starting at nine in the morning and ending at four in the afternoon, with a break for lunch. To some people, this may seem strange, after all, we artists are supposed to stay up late in the night, wrestling with a vision, torturing ourselves to grasp the mystery.... and so on.

But even back in Spain, I'd caught the habit of following workman's hours, never painting in the night, and this habit had continued in Pune. Besides, the flood of creative inspiration that was coming during Osho's discourses meant I was never short of ideas – I never had to stay up late, struggling to grasp a vision. On the contrary, they were falling from the sky like rain. I just moved my hand and immediately painting was happening.

This brings me back to Kandinsky's central theme of the artist's 'inner need,' the impulse for spiritual expression. Living and working in a meditative community, under Osho's personal guidance, I felt so in harmony with my own 'inner need' that the expression of it simply poured out of me like a flood.

Of course, it's not always that easy, but I know the same experience can be felt by anyone who is sensitive enough to search within. It is not confined to art and it is not necessarily recognized as something spiritual, although I think Kandinsky would say – and I agree with him – that any impulse to create is essentially a spiritual experience, even if it is not understood as such.

Understanding is secondary. What counts most is to feel the impulse arising in you, to let it overwhelm you and to give it expression.

As an example, I'd like to talk about Premraj, a 45 year-old artist and traveler who has been a sannyasin for many years. Born in Holland and now living mainly in Australia, he is a lapidary gem cutter and a sculptor. A couple of years ago, while traveling through Asia, he decided to try and find someone who could teach him how to go deeper into the art of sculpting.

He continues:

I was living in Indonesia, wanting to sculpt and find a teacher to go deeper into it. I met a man who said he would show me sculpting only after I had painted with him.

Really, I had no interest in painting before then, at all. A few of my friends were painters, but I never looked at their works. If they asked me to, I said, "Don't bother."

Imagine my surprise: after these two three days of painting it became an obsession to paint, only wanting that, and this obsession has not left me, nor let go of me, since.

I was travelling at the time and at first it seemed difficult, but in the end I got so frustrated that on the spur of the moment I just bought oil paints and started painting.

It gave me great joy.

I discovered, "I need to do this!"

I knew about Meera and her trainings and I waited almost two years to meet her. Up to then, I knew only artists who were stuck, mostly into drugs and alcohol, and using painting as personal vomit – not to create real art.

The training with Meera is a beautiful exploration, taking me into a new world and a new universe of colors. At the same time, it is like walking through my own psyche, facing my conditioning and limitations as well as my qualities.

To see so much paint and paper available to satisfy my inner thirst is an amazing experience. Somehow, I am coming into a playground where I can be myself and explore, without worrying about anything. I feel very much Osho's message to be creative, to enjoy and celebrate life!

The main difficulties I meet are my desires, my judgements, my ideas about how things should be, and especially my wanting to create something. Every time I want to create 'something' I get stuck and start feeling bound, imprisoned.

I lose the free flow in trying to protect an idea, limiting myself.

And the biggest surprise is that, when 'I' do not 'do,' it simply happens.

And then experiencing the joy that comes, seeing something spontaneously arising out of the paper. And the sweet sadness that comes after the bliss, feeling as if something got ripped out of my heart.

Realizing the oneness of everything is another surprise, and realizing that everything is within me. I never look at a tree, while painting trees, because I know the tree. I am the tree. I have to laugh, when I discover that I do not need to look outside myself.

Whatever is 'in,' so it is 'out.' It is a complete mirror, this painting process.

You cannot get attached. Attachment, perfection and goals will kill the painting and everything. They kill all celebration. Strange, that we cannot just enjoy, but always must arrive at some future goal.

Meera is a master. She creates incredible situations for us to discover on our own, without the traditional way of teacher and student. This gives space for great inspiration, joy and fun.

Without her, I would have never met these qualities, and all this, within myself. She makes me jump into the unknown. For one moment, the painting becomes the painter and I am taken over by something else – there is no more 'me.' That is incredible, amazing, it brings tears to my eyes.

Painting is my meditation. I forget all. It is like being with my Beloved. Many times it becomes very late in the night and I want to go home, but I simply cannot. Before I know it, I am back on the painting.

I discover the need to be creative and share myself this way – share Osho, that love, through painting. I am not a man of words, nor of talking, so this makes it difficult to describe the process I am going through.

And I know I am just starting. It is an inner need. Without following it, I turn sour. I have lived my life intensely, I cannot repeat myself, and painting is the only thing left. The joy is, I am possessed by something greater than my personality, which seems so pathetic compared to this other experience.

It is as if God is making love with me... I disappear and the mystery takes over!

No drug, nor any woman, has been able to give me this.

I am no more and life is full and shivering through my body.

It is delicious!

Well, as you can see, I have not spent much time in this chapter talking about the training. But I wanted to give more of the background that has formed my approach to painting, to helping people awaken the impulse for creative expression.

Another reason is that – as I said before – I don't want to focus only on the individual. I have a more ambitious scheme in my head and in my heart: to reawaken the whole spirit of art and rescue it from the desert into which it has somehow lost itself.

This may seem like a monumental task, but I don't see it like that at all. To me, it's an easy next step that should become perfectly clear to everyone who is interested in art, once they have understood the point that I'm trying to make.

After all, when you get lost, have no place left to go, and someone shows you the right direction, it's just natural to start heading that way.

Chapter 10

Fame, Freedom and Fulfilment

About three quarters of the way through the training, I send the whole group into the Lao Tzu walk-way for three days to paint watercolor in that rare and precious atmosphere. Lao Tzu House, you may remember, is the house where Osho lived from 1974 until 1990, not counting the six years he was in the United States and traveling around the world.

In the last few years, when he was frail and often sick, Osho's personal staff wanted to find ways to keep him healthy, particularly to encourage him to exercise, as he was a notoriously lazy man and would sit for hours in his room, eyes closed, doing nothing. He moved so little that even a very expensive, self-winding watch that he kept on his wrist would stop because he didn't move enough to stimulate its delicate mechanism.

His doctors wanted him to walk every day, so a group of sannyasins constructed a long, narrow, marble-floored walkway, that weaved its way through the dense jungle of Lao Tzu garden. Osho loved the feeling of being surrounded by trees, plants and creepers, all growing wildly and freely, so his garden really was, and still is, a real jungle.

The walkway was accessed through a door in Osho's dining room and was about fifty meters long, enclosed with glass on both sides and on the roof, with air conditioning units strategically placed at intervals along the way. It was a perfect, sealed environment with a gorgeous view of the garden, ideal for a morning or evening walk.

Osho, I think, walked it about twice – maybe only once – and then resumed his habit of sitting in his chair, doing nothing. He then invited the sannyasin community to use the walkway as a place for silent meditation courses like Vipassana and Zazen, and this practice has continued ever since.

For me, the place is pure magic: very silent and cool, filled with the vibe of meditation, with a fabulous all-round outlook onto the green jungle of Osho's garden: a painter's paradise. So, every year, I send the training participants into the walkway to experience a synthesis of art and meditation, painting and silence.

My helpers set up places for everyone, covering the floor with plastic and placing cushions so that people can sit looking out into the garden. We bring in the watercolor paint sets, buckets, brushes and so on – it's quite an operation to move all this stuff.

Next morning, the participants arrive with a fresh sheet of paper gummed to their boards and file into the walkway. This is also quite a delicate operation because the walkway is not very wide, less than two meters, and over thirty people have to arrange themselves inside. But when everyone is settled, it looks lovely: all these silent, maroon-clad figures, kneeling or sitting on their cushions in a corridor of steel and glass, surrounded by the multi-colored greens of the garden that crowd in from both sides and above.

I realize that I haven't explained the maroon robes. The idea is that if everyone in the resort wears the same color it helps to harmonize our energy and create a meditative atmosphere. It was Osho's idea, naturally. He also suggested that all buildings should be painted black. The overall effect – maroon people and black buildings surrounded by lots of green foliage – is pleasing to the eye and does indeed create a very soothing, meditative vibe.

The basic instructions for our painting exercise in the walkway are simple: sit for at least ten minutes, meditating with eyes closed, then open your eyes, look at the foliage and begin to paint. Or, if you like, continue meditating for as long as you like, until you feel the impulse to paint.

Bhaven, my Japanese assistant, guides this part of the training, and suggests that people begin by focusing their awareness on the hara, the balance point of the body and the source of our life energy, located in the center of the lower belly.

"Breathe slowly and deeply into your hara, open your eyes and look at the nature," he says, speaking softly into a microphone. "Don't be in a hurry to begin painting. Take time to connect first with your own energy source.

"As you breathe into your hara, feel the energy spreading up through your chest... into your arms... down your arms and into your hands... reaching into your fingers. This is the energy with which you are going to paint.

"When you feel ready to paint, move slowly, silently and gently. Each movement can be done with full awareness. Pick up your brushes and begin..."

What happens to people who meditate and paint in this way? There is no single answer, no particular outcome. It all depends on the person and what is happening to him or her at this point in the group process.

Just to give a few examples, I'd like to invite three of the participants to share their stories, starting with Nisarg, a 34 year-old, handsome Japanese sannyasin who is a theater actor in Tokyo. He did a couple of short groups with me five years ago in Pune and has returned this year to do the training:

When I was a child I had the feeling I was quite a good painter, but since then... you know how it happens... as you grow up, other things become more important and painting gets forgotten.

Still, somewhere in my mind, the idea continued that "Maybe I can still paint, maybe this is something at which I am naturally good." So when the opportunity came to join Meera's training I decided to find out.

But I was very disappointed – disappointed with myself. I thought I already knew how to make forms, how to create depth, how to play with light and dark, but I didn't. And I didn't want to learn from others and copy them. So I became very frustrated. Also, I felt jealous, because I compared my paintings with those around me and mine didn't look as good – not so beautiful.

I wanted to do it my way. I tried so many times by myself, but it was not good to my eyes, so finally I said, "Okay, maybe it's time to learn from other people." I allowed myself to learn from my friend Vijay, another Japanese sannyasin in the group, how to make forms, how to make contrast with shadow and light, but still something was missing. It wasn't coming from inside me.

So, today, as we go into Lao Tzu walkway, I'm hoping this will change something. Certainly, I like the atmosphere. It's cool and peaceful, and we are all much more introspective and quiet than we are on the roof, where often it's like a party scene – a lot of dancing and very social.

I find that Bhaven's suggestion to begin by focusing on the hara helps me very much. It makes me slow down, giving me time to focus inside first, connecting with the breathing, before even touching the brushes and colors.

After this simple meditation, I begin to paint, slowly and in a relaxed way. The painting that unfolds before my eyes is really naïve – no depth, no subtle effects – a kindergarten painting, to my eyes, but strangely enough I am very happy with it.

I ask myself why – how can I be happy with something so simple? And the answer is clear: because for the first time I am being sensitive to what I am doing. The pressure is off, the impatience has vanished, the frustration has disappeared, and this is what has been blocking my creativity.

Slowing down, beginning each session by focusing inside myself, turns out to be a golden key in my hands. All through the next three days I am much more sensitive and careful in the way I paint, always beginning with an inner connection. I realize that, out of this organic feeling, painting is an extension of my own energy, not something separate, not something borrowed from outside.

By the time our stay in the walkway ends, something has changed deeply in the way I relate to the rest of the group. Now I can allow myself to learn from others – from Meera, Bhaven, Vijay, from any of the participants – because now I know that I'm not copying someone else's style. Now I know that I have my own source of creativity.

Nisarg's comment about sensitivity reminds me of an interview I read a few years ago with Henri Cartier-Bresson, a French artist who could rightly claim to be the world's greatest photographer. I think almost everybody has seen his 'decisive moment' pictures, like the one of a man jumping across a pool of water, or a cyclist snapped at the bottom of a spiral staircase... these incredibly powerful black and white images are world famous.

Cartier-Bresson died in August, 2004 but the interview took place in 1994, when he was eighty-five.

One of the first things he said was that he disliked giving interviews, mainly because he was fed up with answering questions about the techniques of photography.

"Everything I have to say about my work is in 'A Propos de Paris,'" he told a reporter for the New York Times, referring to a book containing his best photographs of Paris. "It's like a rear-view mirror of my life. What counts for me is the visual attitude and motion. And the visual attitude is structure, geometry. And you have to have sensitivity. You can learn everything nowadays – there are even books teaching people how to make love – but there is no school of sensitivity."

When I read these words, I would have liked to jump on a plane, fly to Paris and give Cartier-Bresson a big hug. This is my attitude exactly – why I don't spend much time teaching techniques in my trainings.

Any art school can do that, and if you can't make it to college, then there are a hundred 'how to' books on the subject that teach everything you need to know about painting technique.

My emphasis is on teaching those things that others do not, such as sensitivity, spontaneity, self-trust, following the creative impulse, being guided by your own flow of energy, learning how to look at things as they really are rather than from memory.

By the way, Cartier-Bresson was an interesting man. His first love was painting and he studied for two years in a Paris studio, which helped to develop his subtle and sensitive eye for composition – one of his greatest assets as a photographer. That must have been around 1930, when he was about 20 years old. Then he bought a Leica camera and his passion for photography caught fire.

He said, many times, that he was strongly influenced by the Surrealist movement of art, with its emphasis on the density and magic of every day life, and also by Cezanne – of course, because of his emphasis on structure and composition.

Cartier-Bresson visited India, taking some of the most classic pictures ever to be published about life in this ancient culture, and during his stay was influenced by Hindu philosophy. After his retirement from photo-journalism, he practiced meditation and followed the Buddhist teachings of a Tibetan rimpoche.

One of the most interesting things about him, however, is that in the last years of his life he dropped photography and took up sketching and drawing. Even though his sketches could not be compared in quality to his photographs, he declared quite emphatically that he found drawing a more rewarding and fulfilling experience.

"Photography is immediate action. Drawing is a meditation," he replied, when asked why he switched mediums.

It's an important point and one that can answer those commentators and critics who, during the past few decades, have pronounced that painting and drawing – having once dominated the art world – are now dead.

It's probably true that painting will never again rule the world of art as it once did, because so many new media have been developed in the last century: photography, film, video, kinetic art, computer graphics, multi-media installations and so on.

But drawing and painting have a simplicity and immediate creativity that almost nothing else can match. Your instrument, like a pencil or a brush, is a direct extension of your hand. There is no division, no separation between the creator and his work. It's right here, with you, simultaneously inside you and in front of you.

With a medium like photography or film, there are many steps: preparing your equipment, setting up your location, shooting, developing and printing… So I don't find it surprising that an artist like Cartier-Bresson would be pulled back to drawing and sketching.

After all, Pablo Picasso, throughout his life – during which his paintings became steadily more bizarre and outrageous – would periodically return to sketching, which he did in simple and classical way. Clearly, it provided something for his artistic soul that nothing else could supply.

Now I'd like to introduce Urmila, whom you may remember from the self-portrait chapter, and let her talk about her time in the walkway. As you will see, each participant has a different story, yet there is a common thread running through their experiences: -

We go into the walkway, sit down and do a type of Zazen meditation, looking out through tall glass windows at nature. In accordance with Bhaven's suggestion, I'm not fixing my gaze on a single point in the garden, not looking at specifics, like the form of a leaf, or the way sunlight hits a branch. I'm just watching in a soft, unfocused way, in a mood of receptivity.

After a while, as I'm sitting here, something unexpected starts happening to me. Normally, my way of looking is rather hard and direct. It's the same, I think, for everyone,

239

using the eyes mechanically to identify objects: people, food, a magazine, a toothbrush... anything we come across that needs attention.

But as I sit here, gazing into the garden in this unfocused way, I find myself becoming aware of the spaces between the objects. Instead of putting my attention on specifics – the trees, the branches, the effects of shadow and light – I'm seeing the space between them all. The space in which all things grow and intermingle, the space that creates the background, the context, for everything else to exist.

Suddenly, I find myself connecting with the same space inside. Instead of my usual experience of myself – feelings, emotions, thinking this and that – I'm aware of an inner space and a silence that I've not really known before.

Awareness of outer space is provoking an experience of inner space. I don't know how this happens. It's a mystery, but I know the two things are joined, are the same. When I look between the branches and the leaves, I feel connected with the space inside me.

I pick up my brushes, dip them in the paint and start to move my hand slowly across the paper, and I'm delighted to find I can keep my inner connection while I'm painting.

In a way, I'm not painting differently than before, because the objects appearing on the paper are the same: leaves, branches, trees, plants... But my attention is not fixed on particulars. I'm not so focused. I'm not saying to myself, 'okay, now I'm going to paint a leaf.' It's not a 'doing' on my part. It's more like a happening, coming from the empty space inside.

It reminds me of what I've read about modern physics: the deeper you go into matter, the more space you find. Something that seems so solid and hard, like a table or chair, is made up of atoms, which themselves are made up of even smaller particles – electrons, protons, neutrons – that exist within huge amounts of space.

I feel it's the same inside myself. If I go deep inside my body, inside my mind, I find lots and lots of space and silence. This changes the way I look at myself, because

240

before I was putting all my attention on my daily preoccupations and problems.

Now I'm feeling something else as well. It's like saying, 'Okay, those things are there, I am still caught up in them, but I have a lot of space inside, too, which I can connect with at any time, and this is also me – who I am, at a deeper level.'

Before introducing my third and last participant to talk about the walkway, I'd like to say something about Andy Warhol. Because it seems to me that whatever we can find inside ourselves through meditation – the inner need, the creative spark, the empty space that is full of creative potential – is exactly what Warhol did not succeed in finding at any point in his life and career.

This is interesting to me. I feel it's important not only to study people like Kandinsky and Cartier-Bresson, artists who acknowledged a spiritual dimension in their work, but also to look at those who fail to find it – those who maybe are not looking for it, or even aware of its existence.

I realize that I'm going to make some controversial statements now, and probably offend many people who admire Warhol's approach to art, but it can't be helped.

Andy Warhol is so closely associated with the term 'Pop Art' that many people think he began that particular trend – in much the same way that Salvador Dali is linked with Surrealism. But in fact it began at least two years earlier than his first public exhibition, which was held in 1963.

Roy Lichtenstein was already exhibiting comic strip paintings in New York art galleries in 1961 and the roots of Pop Art are said to stretch much further back – some say to Britain in the 1940s and '50s.

Warhol's famous exhibition of all 32 flavors of Campbells' soup was launched in Los Angeles in 1963 and it was in this year that the collective phenomenon known as Pop Art acquired its public identity. It became a movement, an artistic trend – "the next big thing," as they say in Hollywood.

241

At about this time, Warhol also saw the potential of silk-screening photographic images onto canvas – although here, again, I don't think he was the first artist to do it – and he used it create ironic portraits of famous people like Marilyn Monroe, Elvis Presley and Jackie Kennedy. His combination of satire, glamour and mass-produced imagery hit exactly the right spot, mirroring American values back to the public, who soon welcomed Warhol as the guru of the new cultural trend.

Anything can be 'Art' – this, in essence, was Warhol's message.

One reason why it could be received and accepted was that it relieved the public of the need to look any deeper than the surface of its own culture for significance, for meaning, for answers to life's mysteries.

Just think about it for a moment. Art, for the general public, has always been an enigma. It beckons people to that which is beyond the norm, outside the conventional way of seeing life. It stirs up feelings of wonder and longing. Because of this, art has always made people uneasy, giving them the feeling that there is more to life than their daily experience has to offer.

That's why the Parisians crowds who came to the Salon des Refusés of the Impressionist painters in 1863 had to laugh and jeer at what they saw, because if these artists were right, then their whole way of looking at life was wrong. And this uneasiness with art, especially modern art, has continued, right up to the present day.

Warhol changed all that, at least for a moment in time. Suddenly, here was a champion of the common man who was saying, 'Don't worry about all that nonsense. Art is just like you. Art is cheap, ordinary, mundane. There is nothing hidden in it, nothing above you, nothing mysterious.'

Of course, he was being ironic, sarcastic, and this is why I say that Warhol never managed to find his own inner need, his own creative source. He was a satirist, an ironic observer, and both satire and irony are perverted forms of anger. The real emotion behind them is rage.

That's what I see when I look at photos of Warhol and read his statements about art and society: a man filled with suppressed anger, hidden rage, at not being able to tap into his own creativity. Rather than having the courage and determination to go within himself and find fulfilment, he decided it was easier to make art as superficial as his own experience of it. And he succeeded. He was really very successful. Hence, Pop Art.

I don't say that Warhol is not an artist. Art can be satire, social commentary. It can be popular. It can be – as he himself said – almost anything.

For example, in 1975, Warhol stated, "Being good at business is the most fascinating kind of art. Making money is art and working is art and good business is the best art."

If he had simply said that being good at business is an art, I would have agreed with him, because making money is a useful and important form of creativity. I don't have a problem with it at all. It's only when he says it is 'the best art' that he reveals his shallowness.

For me, Warhol is an example of an artist who missed the point, who failed to find what he was really looking for. And, contrary to his own philosophy, I think he knew it – that the mundane can never be fulfilling unless it is set on fire by the flame of inner need.

You can look at a sunflower by Van Gogh, or a pine tree by Hasegawa Tohaku. In a way, they are also mundane, common objects. But the way they have been painted, the passion and depth and mystery that they exude, transforms the mundane into the sacred. Nothing like that happens with Warhol's work. That was his secret anguish, his private hell – because I'm sure he was aware of his own inner poverty as an artist.

Now, back to the walkway.

This next report, told by Rajanila, illustrates an important point. It shows what happens when you have an idea that you are supposed to be painting in a certain, particular way, but your energy, or mood, leads you to do it differently – and the unexpected benefits that may arise out of it.

243

Rajanila is Japanese and 38 years old. She is a bodyworker by profession and an artist by temperament – she has that kind of passionate intensity. At the time of the walkway sessions, she was not feeling satisfied with the way her painting was going, and this, naturally, was affecting her mood. She continues:

We are sitting Zazen style, being guided by Bhaven to look out at the garden, but I am feeling so sad and depressed that my body is sitting in a collapsed position, my head drooping down, my shoulders hunched forward.

I know that if I look up I will see the trees, the leaves, the sunlight, but somehow I just can't bring myself to do it. Instead I am looking downwards, my eyes gazing at the ground just outside the window. I see only small stones, pebbles and gravel, with dead leaves resting on them, rotted by the rain and mixed in between them.

Bhaven indicates that we should start painting, but still I don't feel like looking up, because somehow that would mean running over myself, pretending this sadness inside does not exist. So I think to myself, "Okay, I'm supposed to paint now, so I'll just paint these stones and leaves."

As I do it, something happens. In a way, it's nothing extraordinary that I am seeing – just stones and leaves – but as I paint, colors and shapes are coming onto the paper by themselves. I know I am directing my painting a little bit, with my mind, but the main feeling is that I am painting from inside.

It has a magic. Energy is circulating between my inner feeling and the stones outside, and finding expression in the painting. What I see appearing on the paper, with the watercolors, is so beautiful that I feel overwhelmed, a bit like crying. The misery doesn't matter any more. It's replaced by a space of deep happiness.

When the session is over and the painting is complete, I take my painting home with me. I don't want to leave it behind. I stick it on the wall above my bed and decide that as soon as the training is over I am going to frame it.

It's fascinating to see how people access the creative impulse in unexpected ways, sometimes – no, better make that often – against their own ideas and expectations. If Rajanila had tried to suppress her feelings, sit up straight, look out at the greenery and paint the way she was 'supposed to do it,' she would have missed the entire experience. But because she accepted the mood she was in, accepted the fact that she was sad, she was able to relax into her own energy and this opened a door inwards.

All three participants had a similar experience: the sensation of feeling connected inside at a deeper level than we normally allow, and this in turn created a parallel sensation of feeling more connected with the outside, with nature. A cycle of energy started to happen that gave a whole new insight into creativity and painting.

It sounds easy, but one thing you need to remember is that all of them have been meditating regularly since the beginning of the training. They have immersed themselves in an atmosphere of meditation and I'm sure this was partly responsible for their experiences – plus, of course, the silent and peaceful vibe of the walkway itself.

Oddly enough, it's easier for beginners to have these kinds of experiences than people who've already developed their gifts as artists. Having led many trainings over the past ten years, I can say without hesitation that it's the professionals and talented amateurs – people who already know they can paint – who have most trouble opening to the new and the unexpected.

In this context, I want to talk about Salima, whom I mentioned in chapter two. She is a successful painter, selling well in Australia during the past few years, creating abstract oil paintings that appeal to the public's taste.

One morning, I am walking around Buddha Hall, where the course participants are sitting on the marble pathway, painting nature with watercolor. I stop to look at Salima's painting and am surprised to see it's like that of a five-year old child.

It's a patchwork of unrelated objects: a tree standing here, a cluster of bamboo there, small plants, grass... like a pencil drawing filled in with colors. A bit like Warhol's 'Do It Yourself Sailboats', half-painted and the rest left blank, with numbers to indicate where the rest of the colors should go.

Not surprisingly, it looks flat, and then, of course, it has no power, joy, or mystery.

"How're you doing?" I ask Salima.

"Fine, but I don't know what is the next step, how to go on," she replies, hesitantly.

"Do you remember the demonstration I gave yesterday about overlapping the colors – creating different layers to give dimension, to give the jungle feeling?" I ask.

She nods. "Yes, but I have difficulty putting it into practice."

I sit down beside her.

"Okay, let's try something new. Maybe we mess up the painting, but maybe we can get more understanding that way."

Immediately, she gets tense.

"But I'm afraid to lose what's already there," she objects.

"Yes, I know, that's what keeps you stuck. What I see is that all this..." I wave a hand over her painting to include everything, "...is basically background. You need to put a big tree or bamboo in front to create dimension, depth."

Still she is hesitating. I can see that explanations are not going to help – you can discuss for hours, but if you don't take a jump then nothing happens. In painting, you grow through action, not talking.

I take a deep breath, because in this moment I realize I am going to break all my own rules. Everything I've said about not interfering, about giving people freedom to explore in their own way, at their own pace, is about to be thrown out of the window.

Yet in my heart I feel this is the right thing, both for Salima and myself. It's a gamble, of course. It could turn out to be a negative experience, but still I have to trust my

246

impulse, my intuition. I see her potential as an artist, and I love her, so I don't mind going through this turmoil with her.

I take a big sponge, soak it in water and make a big washing movement, diagonally, right across Salima's paper.

She gasps, "Ah! You're destroying my painting!"

Of course, I'm not destroying anything. But I can't help noticing the difference between Salima's horrified reaction and how Sukhi was so willing to let her painting go to Deepak. This, typically, is how it goes: the more of a painter you think you are, the less willing you are to experiment, take risks – you think you've got too much to lose.

"We're just learning how to create dimension, that's all," I assure her. "You've been putting plants here and there, like a classroom exercise, but this is only a preparation for the real painting. Look at the nature surrounding us here: everybody's dancing together; space and light and trees and grass. There's no idea of 'you are here... I am there.' They're all celebrating in one dance, in harmony with your own inner dance.

"You look in one direction... this isness is happening. You turn your head and look in another direction... that isness is happening. Always and everywhere... isness is happening, and you have the freedom to put it together."

Salima says nothing, just looks confused.

"Well, okay, let me do it."

I continue washing with the sponge. Things start appearing, disappearing, and pretty soon a mysterious feeling enters her painting. Forms on the surface fade away and traces of other plants begin to show underneath.

Then I give the sponge to Salima.

"Look at this big wash here. It's an indication of a tree. Why don't you put a stroke of darkness along the side of it, so the tree gains more definition."

Timidly, Salima does as I suggest, and the tree starts gaining solidity, but her movements are half-hearted and soon she loses her nerve, stops in the middle, and starts crying.

247

"It was such a fantastic painting," she sobs. "And I lost it. I lost it!"

Here, in this delicate moment with Salima, I see how deeply we cling to the known and refuse to welcome the new and unfamiliar. In essence, it is the fear to lose one's own identity.

I put my hand gently on her shoulder and say, "Okay, it's lost. But we're not going to regret what's gone, hmm? We're not here for that. You are much more than your painting and there's no need to stay attached to it. We need to go forward, because this is our only way of learning."

Still she is crying and then I realize that Salima is one of the biggest challenges for me in this training. How to communicate with this person? How to support her essential beauty to come out?

I take her hand and say, "If you don't feel like painting, why not come with me? We'll look at what other people are doing, because you are here to learn something more than what you already know."

She nods. We stand up and take a walk together, hand in hand, along the marble pathway that encircles the meditation hall.

Each person is working with two nature paintings, both of which are done on vertical sheets of paper. One is in color, the other in black and white.

When you work with two paintings like this together, on one sheet of plastic, you can move from one to the other, as the feeling takes you. It's a great way to learn how to translate colors into black and white, and black and white into colors.

If you really want to be an artist, this translation has to be accurate, because only when you understand the importance of contrast, in black and white, will your color painting gain dimensional quality.

For me, it's also interesting to observe people working in this way, because it's easy to see where they are stuck, or where they have gained new understanding.

I pause with Salima to look at Halima's paintings. This morning, she is working on her black and white.

"You remember how Halima was struggling with the colors?" I ask Salima, referring to a sharing we'd had a couple of days earlier. "She was saying that she likes to put nice colors next to each other, but she doesn't like to overlap with dark colors. That's her weak point.

"Look there, you can see it in her watercolor painting. She puts a little bit of yellow, then on top of she puts transparent red to define a tree. So, again, it's nice colors. You can see her fear of facing radical change from light to dark.

"But look what she's doing now, with her black and white! Suddenly, she understands how important it is to say 'yes' to form, to strength, to contrast. She has captured the feeling of painting nature – what it is – through black and white.

"Now her trees are standing excellently, just because of contrast. Now she can paint big trees quickly, with many branches, other trees overlapping... you can see her Japanese quality, the calligraphic hand movement, which helps her to create all these branches."

Halima is happy with herself. She smiles and says, "I still don't understand one thing, Meera. Can you teach me how to paint those leaves... the ones farthest away, against the sky? They're very delicate, almost transparent. I don't know how to do it."

I am pleased at her question. This kind of longing to express the beauty shows that her real journey as an artist has started.

"It's a good question, Halima. Tomorrow, I can try."

We walk on, Salima is still crying, and we pause next to Naveena.

"Look how she puts three tree trunks on top of each other, almost filling the whole painting with these big, solid shapes," I say to Salima. "It has an organic feeling, almost Tantric, three separate trees yet all becoming one, with a great sense of dimension and depth.

249

"You see, Salima, when your inside says 'yes,' it's not a technique that happens. You just allow the energy to express itself, in this moment. When the 'yes' happens, such a big thing…" I point to Naveena's inter-twined tree trunks, "…can happen without any hesitation.

"So it's not a question of how to do it. It's not a question of technique. It's the totality of your inner that is manifesting on the painting."

I've never done this before, taking one participant around with me, pointing out the issues that people are facing in their painting. I'm not sure that Salima has the space to receive it, but she is crying and this indicates to me that some kind of release is happening. Her façade is breaking down, so I trust that something creative will come out of it.

Later, in the instructors' sharing session, she tells the group how difficult it was for her to walk around the path with me.

"Everyone could see that I was crying," she whispers. "And Meera was showing me how beautiful this person's painting is, how beautiful that person's is. I know she was offering me opportunities to learn, but I could only compare and think how bad my own painting is.

She sobs, "I don't know what to do… I feel terrible… I don't want to paint for the rest of my life!"

Coming from a successful artist, this is quite a statement! But I can understand, because it reveals something of a dilemma that many artists find themselves in – especially with modern and abstract painting. I'll come back to this point a little later.

The sharing is over and the participants are getting ready for another session around Buddha Hall, but Salima is still deeply affected. I can see she needs more personal attention than I am able to give right now, so I ask Devena, my co-leader, to stay with her.

Devena, a warm-hearted English woman in her mid-fifties, has been a sannyasin for a long time. She has certain qualities that are rare. For example, she never tries to conceal what's happening inside her. Even when she is instructing she doesn't come across as a teacher, she only shares herself.

For me, this is important, because as soon as an instructor starts to play a role – 'I am the teacher, you are the students' – nothing of value can reach the participants. Only sincerity makes a bridge.

I feel, too, that Devena has an immense longing to disappear into the nature – into the beauty of the early morning light, into the songs of the birds, into the magic of moonlight. She is still exploring with her painting, because what she feels in her heart doesn't yet find expression in her art – it doesn't reflect the depth of longing that she experiences inside herself.

"This is the best teaching," I told her, when she raised this point in a group sharing. "If you can teach only this much, then you can lead people to far away stars, or to the very roots of their being."

So I am happy when Devena offers to stay with Salima in the group room, while the rest of us depart for the pathway around the meditation hall. Perhaps better than anyone, she understands Salima's predicament, sharing her own doubts and fears, and when a course leader can do that, creating such empathy, the participant can't help but relax.

Next day, Salima doesn't come to the resort. She is hiding in her room – I heard from one of her friends. But the following morning I see her at breakfast. It is a day off from the training and I am wearing a maroon robe like everyone else, so this is a good opportunity to meet in an informal way.

I walk over to her table, ask her if I can sit down, and she nods.

"Today, I want to meet you as a friend, I'm not wearing a black robe," I tell her. "If I hurt your feelings the other day, I'm sorry. I was trying to communicate something – that if you're open, there's no problem in exploring and experimenting with your painting.

251

"But maybe I pushed you too hard. Maybe I got carried away with trying to teach something that you weren't ready to receive."

Salima gives a sad little smile.

"Meera, I think you've been seeing my stuckness since the beginning of the training. You just didn't say anything until now"

I shake my head. "Hey, come on, you're doing fine. It's a fragile business, getting in touch with your creativity. I never said anything before because it was all flowing along nicely for you – especially when we were painting abstract. Then, of course, when the need for form enters, when the challenge of painting nature enters, you start to compare with nature's perfection and feel crushed."

But I can see she is not convinced. She thinks I'm trying to cheer her up.

"I think there are two things going on in the human heart at the same time," I tell her, shifting away from the personal. "One is our willingness to grow, our willingness to learn – that's why we are sannyasins. The second thing is just the opposite: we don't want to grow. Somewhere, deep down, we're saying 'no' to coming out of our familiar cocoon, our cozy shelter.

"It comes from childhood," I continue. "There's something very comfortable about being taken care of by others, by adults, and this can become a habit and an obstacle. When I really look at people's paintings, mostly I see that their mental age stops around five years old…"

To my surprise, Salima agrees.

"That's right," she says, emphatically. "That's exactly what I was thinking yesterday, when I was staying in my room. I realize I have no memory connected with painting from the time I was five years old until I was fourteen. It's just blank. Maybe, some time around five, my creativity got blocked. But I can't remember how it happened."

I shrug. "It could have been a choice you made yourself: to remain the protected child, rather than taking the risk of breaking away and growing on your own. But this is a

252

general condition – everybody has it, more or less. There's something else I'd like to share with you..."

I tell Salima the story of an Italian painter, already quite famous in his own country, with exhibitions of abstract art in well-known galleries, who came to one of my courses. I'd arranged a life drawing session, with a naked model. We were sitting in a circle around her, and he was drawing from a position where her feet were closest to him and her head was farthest away.

Usually, when drawing from such a position, the feet become the biggest part of the body and the head becomes small, because that's the way perspective goes – that's how you give three-dimensional effect to a two-dimensional drawing.

I couldn't believe what the man did. He drew a big head and small legs! I really got a shock, because naturally, if someone comes to me and tells me he is a successful painter then I assume he knows the basics – the ABCs of drawing and painting. And then I realized, 'This guy can't draw at all! He can't see how to translate what is in front of him.'

"With modern art you don't need to learn all these things," I tell Salima. "You can know very little about art and yet sell paintings to the public. You may have a certain sensibility for color combinations and abstract patterns that appeals to the public's taste – and that's enough. You can become a successful artist.

"Before, to be an artist meant that you had to study your craft. You had to go to a master craftsman and be accepted by him as a student. You had study with different painters for ten, fifteen years, just to learn the basics.

"All that has changed. In the modern world, everything needs to be cheap and quick. But it's also okay. I can't turn the clock back to the Renaissance and Michelangelo, and I don't think I would if I could.

"If you want to go on the way you are, I'm not putting you down for it. I'm just trying to show you the predicament that modern abstract painting creates. If you really want to be a professional painter, using the language of painting in

253

all its dimensions, then you need to master things like drawing and depth, painting form and painting nature."

Salima is not offended by my words. In fact, she wants to share something with me that she has been reluctant to tell anyone.

"It's true what you say," she confides. "Even when I became successful, I couldn't really relax with it. I couldn't trust myself. Everybody was admiring my paintings and deep down inside I was always sweating, thinking 'When are they going to find out that I can't paint?' I was shaky all the time."

Having let out her secret, Salima starts to feel better. Next day, she is back in the training with a new willingness to explore, to take risks. This is what I want for all my participants. The real learning starts when they get in touch with the fire to express; then it follows naturally as a by-product. If Salima can allow herself to connect at a deeper level with her own creativity, that is enough.

This is the bottom line for people who want to be creative: fame is one thing, fulfilment something else. Both can be satisfying, especially when they come together. But, if you get attached to your public image, you are going to find yourself in trouble as an artist, because then you lose your freedom – freedom to explore, to try something new, to go into the unknown. And in my experience the creative impulse is always pointing towards the unknown. That's just the way it is.

Sakaama is another successful artist, selling seascapes in the Greek islands during the tourist season, but he is a totally different kind of person than Salima. Relaxed, centered, with a neatly trimmed white beard, he looks a bit like a jovial Greek god – one of the good guys in the heavenly pantheon.

One day, I am walking around Buddha Hall and stop to look at his painting.

"My god, it's so pretty!" I exclaim, and we both laugh, because he knows this is his weakness. He just can't make a mess. He can't let the colors mix, merge, overlap and reveal mysteries amid the chaos.

He's using watercolors, but in gouache style, with thick paint, almost like a knife painter, in a very exact and professional way. His plants look perfect and his colors are almost psychedelic, like the jungles of naïve artist Henri Rousseau, but without Rousseau's tigers and other animals. Now, as I watch, he's adding his own fantasies to the nature he sees before him: little pink flowers here and there, to make it even more pretty.

"Can you make any suggestions about my painting?" he asks.

"What am I going to do with you?" I ask, jokingly. "If you were depressed, unhappy, then I'd have an excuse to interfere, but I can see you are enjoying what you're doing."

I have my own weak point, as you must have realized by now: I always want to provoke people, to challenge them, stirring things up, causing chaos. But I also have a good excuse – it's my job.

"Look at these leaves, you are only trying to copy nature," I say to him, pointing to a bright green plant that dominates the foreground of his painting. "All these bends that you put in, you know, unnecessary wrinkles – as if, when you get angry, you can see all the wrinkles on your face or something!"

Again, we both laugh. Somehow it's impossible to be serious with this fellow.

"I am not teaching that," I continue. "I'm teaching the effect of water. It's a surprise, yes? The way that water plays among the colors, mixing them, and when it dries the patterns happen on their own – complementary colors, darkness on top of light, light on top of darkness, all on one leaf.

"In nature, every leaf has unique patterns and texture, which you can never imitate. It's like marble: when you look at the way marble tiles are cut, all the surfaces are different although the colors and patterns are very similar.

"You can't copy it directly, but you can get this quality when you let the colors and the water play together on their own. Then you're surprised. When it dries you just say 'wow!' because the patterns appear on the leaves by themselves. And you can see there's a similar quality of play happening inside and out – in you and in the painting."

Sakaama listens attentively to my discourse, then lays a warm hand on my shoulder and says sincerely, "Meera you're right. I respect your way. I hear you. I say 'yes.' I try to do it the way you suggest, but what can I do... after ten minutes I find myself painting the way I like to paint!"

Here, I have to leave teaching behind and the rest is not in my hands. I do my part and then step out. He is free to take it or leave it, and I respect his freedom. I know that Sakaama is enjoying the training and, in spite of what he says, is showing increasing flexibility and openness.

For example, early in the course, when I asked people to work on each other's acrylic paintings, I deliberately sent Nirvikalpa to partner Sakaama. I told her to make a real mess on his picture, which was supposed to be abstract but – not surprisingly, considering his background – looked very much like a Mediterranean seascape. I wanted to see his reaction when she totally changed his painting.

She did a good job, using dark colors, destroying the formal prettiness, infusing the picture with chaos, but when Sakaama returned and looked at it he was not offended. He was surprised, maybe a little shocked, but accepted it and continued to paint. And this has been my feeling about him all the way through the course: a man of habit, but not inflexible, not stuck in some ego trip; a little bit stubborn, but basically a good artist and a happy man.

Well, I can see that I am already approaching the end of this chapter and there is only one more ahead of me, so I will conclude by telling you the rest of my personal story, after I'd become the 'court painter' for Osho at the commune in Pune.

In fact, there is not much more to tell. As I said before, by 1989 Osho was speaking only on Zen anecdotes. For him, Zen was the purest form of spiritual teaching, because it avoided all scriptures, doctrine and belief systems, and it was my job to illustrate the book covers.

A few months into the year, Osho stopped speaking entirely, and this proved to be a portent, an indication of his failing health. He died in January 1990.

To my surprise, his death didn't affect me very much. Of course, I missed his beautiful eyes and his smile, his jokes, his physical presence, his personal influence on my work as an artist, but the atmosphere in his 'buddhafield' – the meditative energy of his commune – remained delightful and filled with potential. Energy-wise, it didn't seem like Osho's enlightened consciousness had gone anywhere, so in terms of getting on with my spiritual growth it was very much 'business as usual.'

By that time, I'd already begun to lead painting groups and trainings in Pune, and this gradually expanded to include Europe, Japan and Mexico. Now I was leading them by myself. Now there was no commune of artists, no soul mate like Geetesh to partner and support me.

This, I learned, was not a bad thing. It has given me strength and integrity, pushed me to stand alone, on my own feet. It has challenged me to offer whatever I've absorbed about art and meditation, and to see whether people appreciate it.

I'm happy to say that, so far at least, many people have found it a valuable and rewarding experience. This is especially true of the training in Pune, the last days of which I will describe in the final chapter.

Chapter 11

ReAwakening of Art

There is an ancient story about a Chinese emperor who arranged a painting competition to see who was the greatest artist in his kingdom.

Many people entered the contest, but one of them, who was known as something of a mystic and a rather strange fellow, told the emperor that he must insist on one condition.

"My painting will not be ready for one year. If you can wait that long before judging the contest, I will enter. If not, I will return to my home," he said.

The emperor hesitated, but was intrigued by the man and eventually agreed.

The painter requested that he be given a large room in the emperor's palace, and that an order should be given throughout the court that no one must enter the room for a year. His request was granted.

After a while, all the other artists completed their entries. Only the artist inside the room was still working.

After one year, the artist came out of the room, bowed before the emperor and invited him to come and see his work.

As the emperor entered the room, he gasped. One entire wall had been painted, filled with natural scenery, beginning in the foreground with a thick forest and then rising through cascading hills towards snow-capped mountains in the far distance.

"It is magnificent! So alive! So lifelike! I can almost smell the pine leaves. You have surely won the first prize," said the emperor.

Then he saw a small path, just at the edge of the forest, winding its way into the woods and disappearing around a hillside.

"Tell me, where does that path go? he asked the artist.

The painter shrugged. "I don't know," he said. "Why don't we find out?"

And he took the emperor by the hand and led him onto the path. The two men walked into the painting, following the path through the forest, and were never seen again.

Osho has told this story several times in his discourses. It comes to my mind now because it contains a truth that I would like to share with you: life is a mystery and a true artist is one who can convey some flavor of this mystery to the public.

I would love the last chapter of my book to be a little bit mysterious, but words have their limitations, especially for me. I am not really a person of words. I am a painter and sometimes a dancer. I can show you one of my paintings and help you see the mystery in it, but to write about such things is a different kind of challenge.

So I will just tell you what has been happening to me and hope that some flavor of mystery weaves its way into these pages.

A whole year has passed while this book was being written, so the training I am going to talk about is the one that is ending just now. I can't look back at last year's course, because so much has changed, is still changing, and I am changing with it.

The Meera that was telling you everything in the last ten chapters is not the one that sits before an empty sheet of paper now, ready to splash a few fresh colors onto the receptive purity of its whiteness.

During this past year I have traveled the world, leading

groups in Europe, Japan, Mexico and also visiting Australia, and I return to Pune for the winter season to find that the Osho Meditation Resort is also changing.

The roof covering Gautam the Buddha Auditorium, our old meditation hall, has been taken down and the whole space is open to the sky. So this year, in addition to our usual space on Krishna House roof, we are offered one end of the hall's oval-shaped floor as a working space for our group.

"Just cover the marble floor with plastic and this can be your second group room for the next six weeks," I am told by one of the resort administrators.

This is a really touching moment for me, and one of the best things I've done in my life, because this is the space where Osho used to have his discourses and I feel his energy very much when I am working here.

Still, in the beginning, I hesitate.

"How can this be used as a group room when it has no roof? How will we protect ourselves from the sun? How can we keep a sense of unity among us, in such a large space?" I muse.

But the hall is ringed with trees that lean and reach towards the center, doing their best to make a covering of leaves and branches. When we work, we are always under the shade. For the first time, too, we can all paint on a single plastic sheet, working together and yet visible for everyone to see.

The resort's daily meditation program has shifted to a new, fully enclosed, pyramid-shaped auditorium, and so all kinds of other activities are taking place here, in the open space that was once Buddha Hall. Whirling, dancing, singing… people just hanging out, chatting, reading, sitting quietly… there is a continuous stream of people and activities, swirling around the borders of our painting area.

But still, among all the colorful chaos, the feeling of a protected group space remains and our training flourishes in this new environment.

I want this year's training to be a different from other trainings. I want people to get more deeply into the basic system of creativity, which includes flexibility, spontaneity and easiness to move without getting attached. The participants need to become a pool of energy so that they can go in any direction.

The first section of the training, ten days of primal painting, has a new flavor. Instead of beginning with formless, abstract painting and then moving into form, I invite everyone to stay with the formless.

For years, I have been carrying a *koan* within me – a question about form and no-form – that I hope to solve during this first section.

Jackson Pollock, in his action painting, didn't want to paint from a preconceived idea. He wanted to get deep into the painting before he could even begin to figure out what it was going to be. Rather than impose form on the canvas, he wanted it to emerge from the action of painting itself.

For me, it's the same. I want to create a painting that comes not out of the head, or intellect, but through action, playfulness and the energy of the present moment.

The idea of action painting is not new. The ancient Zen masters of China and Japan did it through calligraphy, emphasizing *this*, the present moment, the spontaneous flow of energy as it finds expression through the movement of the hand and the arc of the brush as it moves across the paper.

Either you are here and now, present and alert in this moment, or not – that's all that counts. If you are here and now, you are not thinking about form. You don't carry an idea of what you are going to do.

That's the essence of the Zen approach to calligraphy. Jackson Pollock accidentally discovered the same principle and it became a 'big deal' in the evolution of Western Modern Art, something new, a breakthrough. But essentially it is the same thing.

One thing my participants soon discover is that, when there is no intention to create form, it's easier to stay out of the grip of the mind. It's just like that, because form is more connected with mind than no-form. It is mind that conceives form, thinks about it – what am I going to paint today, a tree, a face, a landscape? – squeezing shapes out of past experiences, memories, borrowed ideas, learned techniques.

My challenge is to introduce form to painting without using the mind and this is what I invite people to explore during the 'primal painting' section, using acrylics, inks, and our special handmade paper.

Sometimes it's not easy – also not for me – because any movement of the brush, any juxtaposition of color, starts to create form. And, as I've mentioned before, when you work on the floor, the paint tends to move around the paper by itself – naturally seeking the lowest point – and this creates accidental shapes.

So form is continually arising out of the action of painting. This is a natural aspect of our work and perfectly okay. What I am guiding people to avoid is recognizable, common forms that start to illustrate or describe the world of objects that surrounds us.

When you allow such forms to enter, immediately it starts to look more like a painting and this is what the mind wants – a result, a goal, a product, a recognizable process with some kind of concrete conclusion.

To not go into that, to stay all the time in a state of not knowing, needs lots of courage and, of course, it's easier when you are part of a group, with everyone moving, sharing and exploring together.

So our common discipline is that we never allow any shape or form to become recognizable. We are always ready to let go of anything that is emerging.

What we discover during these ten days is that the longer we linger in no-form, the more the act of painting comes from the body, not from the mind.

The longer we stay free of form, without collapsing in frustration, without falling into a routine, without quitting – 'this is useless, this just goes on forever, whatever I do seems pointless' – the more the act of painting comes as a memory from within the body system.

Perhaps 'memory' is not exactly the right word; because it implies that something has been learned and absorbed, whereas really it is a reflection of our natural inner sense of harmony that finds its way onto the paper.

This is what I mean by 'mystery.' It's already there, hidden inside us. It comes with the package of being human. We just have to find ways to bring it out.

Modern dance – one of my secret passions – is also like that. As a student, I want to memorize the steps my teacher shows me, because in this way I feel safe. I am learning 'how to dance.' But, gaining confidence in myself, I find that when I stop thinking about the correct steps and dance from my guts, the body remembers and the dance unfolds on its own.

Like this, I invite the training participants to get in touch with painting: brushing aside the mind and allowing the body system to remember.

Originality, as I've said before, comes from deep within yourself and if you want to go inside and discover it, then the body offers a better doorway to pass through than the mind.

Once your body system takes over, painting becomes an ongoing process. You find that you've got everything. You can go in any direction without any attachment. Even if you create a beautiful form you know that you can keep moving.

I do many exercises with partner painting and with groups of people painting together on a single, large piece of paper, because this is the easiest and fastest way to learn. When you paint with so many people you automatically absorb many different styles and techniques through your in-built body memory. Everyone is doing something different. Everyone is constantly trespassing on each other's territory, overlapping, integrating, and so there is tremendous aliveness and vitality in group work.

When you can work with so many people without conflict, then it's easy to do it alone. You can pull out all kinds of techniques at any moment.

Now, naturally, when you work like this for ten days, the question arises: if you are not attached to any form, how and when does the painting become complete? If you are drowned in an ongoing process, watching forms come and go, how can you stop?

If you ask me, I will say that it is a matter of spontaneity, not completion.

For example, Fulwari, my longtime Japanese helper, is in the training again this year and she has a tendency to take a long time with each painting and not agree that it is finished until everything looks exactly right.

But this time a real easiness happens to her. When there is a feeling of life in the painting she recognizes it and, in the very same moment – in the lively look of the painting – she decides, 'okay this is completed.'

One morning, I am really surprised, because she had started a new painting just the day before and this morning, when I come and look at it, I say spontaneously, "Just leave the painting like this. It's complete." And she agreed!

So in this year's training one of the new elements is that I am more aware about the vitality of the painting and, using this as my basic criterion, to spontaneously decide at which moment the painting is finished.

Of course, this is subjective, because personal taste changes and personal understanding shifts all the time, so I can't say any decision is forever. But once you start to recognize the element of life in the painting you can see it has truth in it.

You can call it life, or beauty, or truth, or mystery, but there is something that, when you look at it, brings you into the different space. Something hits you. When you look at the painting it transports you into another dimension and when that happens, in that moment, for me it is finished.

To help the participants learn this way of looking at a painting, I encourage them to make little window frames,

265

made out of white paper, and to go around the whole painting, looking through the frame at all the corners, asking themselves "Is this part conscious? Is this part conscious?"

If you can say that all the areas are done consciously, and in balance with each other, then it's finished. This is important because ordinarily, when you look at a painting, you receive only an impression of the strongest part – the part that has the most visual impact. That's what grabs your attention.

Then your eyes don't go into the corners or the areas that are more subdued. But if you make a little window frame, then you can check each area... this corner, that corner. Later, you don't need any frame because you get the knack of seeing how conscious each part is.

What do I mean when I say 'conscious?'

Conscious, in terms of painting, is connected with a feeling of beauty, aliveness, silence, with seeing that there is no mechanical movement. In every corner, the painting has some spirit – I don't know what else to call it.

In the first part of the training, Fulwari is painting next to Premraj. These two cannot be more different in their styles. Fulwari is a perfectionist, moving her brush slowly, carefully and gracefully. Premraj is the opposite. He is like an animal when he paints, totally afire, splashing colors here and there, working fast, not at all careful, not hesitating in any way.

When I met Premraj for the first time, he told me that he stayed more than half a year in India waiting for our training to happen. During that time, he was just moving around the Himalayas, killing time.

When he said that, I thought, "My god, I am fortunate to have a participant like this."

From the beginning, he is like a sponge, absorbing everything, every word – how I am guiding people each day. The first stage of primal suits his style, but when we move to the second stage, it isn't easy for him. Here, we begin to allow form to emerge, to let shapes arise spontaneously from the painting, from nowhere, not imposing anything,

266

just helping them to come out with the use of contrasting colors.

Premraj wants to give expression to creative shapes that are buzzing around in his head and put them on the paper.

"No, it's not like that," I say to him. "Form is already there, in your painting. Just bring it out through contrast, through using darkness and light."

And then he gets it. The good thing is that he is ready to learn, in spite of all his ideas, and is able to slowly let go of them. He stays with the process. He really gets involved physically and psychologically.

For three days, he partners Nartan, from Taiwan, who has a similar dynamic approach and together they create such a mess, paint flying everywhere.

The scene reminds me of a Japanese rice field, where you have to plant the rice in mud that is covered with water. Of course, the mud is stirred up when you work and pretty soon you are covered with it. That's how they look – two rice planters in the middle of a muddy field.

What I notice about Premraj is that he is so speedy. He is ready to create any aspect with the colors, use any movement, with no attachment, but it all happens too fast and so one of my aims is to encourage him to slow down and bring more awareness into his actions.

"If you can combine your flexibility and dynamism with awareness, this is one of the most excellent things one can imagine," I tell him. "Then you won't do any stupid move, like letting go of everything, scratching it all out and starting again from zero."

One day, in the nature painting section of the training, I am looking at Premraj's work and see that something is missing in the front of his painting – in about a quarter of the foreground area. It has an empty feeling.

I mention this to him and ask, "So, what are you going to do?"

He looks thoughtfully at the painting and says, "Let's look around."

I take his hand and we walk around Buddha Grove – as Buddha Hall is now called – looking at all the plants. What he needs is not an ordinary, decorative plant, not something pretty to fill the space, but something wild, some plant with an extraordinary shape, almost like something out of the primal section of our training.

I have a particular plant in mind, with big leaves full of holes, but when we arrive at the spot... surprise! It's not there. Some gardener has removed the offending leaves and what is left is really much too ordinary.

Together, we find another plant that looks exactly right, but it grows in the middle of the busiest street in the resort and you can't sit and paint there.

So I leave Premraj and for the rest of the day I don't see him on the plastic in the Buddha Grove. I assume he has met some friends and is drinking coffee somewhere, and next day I jokingly ask if he enjoyed spending the afternoon in the local coffee shop.

He says, "No, no. I was talking a walk among the plants and trees."

This surprises me, because up to now he has never waited a moment to paint. If I say, "Something is missing," I expect him to find something and fill the gap within minutes.

When I share this with him, he smiles and shakes his head. "No, it's not like that anymore. I have learned how to wait."

I am happy that Premraj understands my feeling – that just because you think something is missing in your painting you don't fill it up with any old thing that comes to mind. Some people tend to do that, out of desperation, just to finish a painting. But to me it's an invitation to silently wait for what really fits, from inside and outside. It's a meeting of both.

"So the front part of your painting is still empty?"

He nods. "Maybe that's the way it needs to be."

As we talk, we come to a new conclusion: maybe this idea that something missing in his painting is also just an idea.

"When I really put my consciousness in the painting, accepting the gaps as well, then I see it is finished. I don't need to do anything," he explains.

Talking with Premraj, I realize how much I orient myself to what is missing and what is not missing in a painting. This makes me examine my way of teaching, my general approach.

In Premraj, I have a really good student. Sometimes, a teacher needs a good student from whom to learn. It's a mutual kind of learning, from each other, because what the student offers is his ignorance, a kind of child-like innocence. He is more free than the person who knows and so he brings freshness to the subject.

I am happy to have this new understanding. Even in a split second, your awareness can expand and change the whole gestalt. You don't do anything to the painting, rather, you do something to yourself, and in that moment you see it's finished.

Maybe other people will say, "Hey, something is missing in your painting."

If you are wavering, uncertain, and people say something like this, then you can be crushed. But when you are centered in yourself, in your awareness, you know you have the only argument that matters. You understand that this is your creation, not anybody else's, so all that counts is how you decide – from your mind or from your consciousness, your awareness.

As the training continues, I feel the urge to test Premraj's non-attachment to his work. You may recall, from earlier chapters, that this is something I love to do – it's such an important quality if you are going to move beyond your limitations.

Premraj makes an incredible black and white nature painting that reminds me of the native forests in Australia: huge trees standing side by side, jungle in front and more jungle behind.

Casually, I ask him, "Can you leave this painting with me, after the course is finished, as a sample for the next training?"

He hesitates. "Yes, but first I have to take it to Goa and show it to my mother, because she paid for me to do this training."

"That's fair enough," I agree.

On another occasion, I see that one of his acrylic paintings is finished, but I want to test him again, so I say, "Hey, Premraj, let's wash this painting under the tap."

He doesn't hesitate for a moment.

"Okay."

So together we carry this big painting to the sink and I turn on the running water and look at him. I can't believe it! He is really ready to wash the whole painting.

So then I smile and say, "Premraj, we don't have to do anything to this painting. It is finished."

And we both laugh.

Now it is finished he has nothing to do, so I go to a corner and pull out an old, dirty-looking painting from last year's training and give it to him. I keep a stock of them for occasions like this.

"Now I'd like you to convert this painting into beauty," I tell him. "I want to see how much you have understood."

He agrees and when I come back in two hours I am surprised – another painting is finished.

So I gave him another painting from the pile and in this way we continue. This is a rare moment, because I can see that there is no separation between him and the action of painting. He is totally in it, so everything he does contains the quality of oneness.

This quality reminds me of Henna, a silent and graceful 42 year-old woman from Japan. Like Fulwari, she has been with me for many years and is one of my best students.

Henna comes from Yamagata province, the cherry blossom country. Her home is on a mountain, by a river – maybe that's why she is so pure in her approach to painting, because she comes from a region of such virgin natural beauty.

Some people are really meant to be creators, that is their destiny, and I feel it with Henna. She has a very feminine approach and an immensely elegant dance in the movement of her hand. She doesn't go along the path of Premraj, but her paintings also have this quality of oneness, of no separation between art and artist, of disappearing into mystery. Primal painting, nature painting, portrait painting... it is all coming from her source.

But even Henna, whom I think I know so well, can surprise me.

For example, on many occasions she is working next to Margaux, a middle-aged woman from Australia who is a prominent artist.

Margaux wants to throw away all her knowledge as an artist and start again from zero, so she creates a real mess, making everything dirty, changing everything around, painting this way and that – even lying down and rolling right across her painting with her robe.

Henna paints quietly by her side, a complete contrast in style. You could not find two painters who are more opposite.

One day, in the water color section, I look at Henna's painting, which is following her usual style, and I think, "Hmm, this is almost finished. Just one or two more delicate touches and that's it."

Five minutes later, I come back and get a real shock: Henna is covering one third of her painting with thick black paint.

"What happened?" I ask.

She smiles and shakes her head.

"I myself don't understand. But I feel the energy coming from Margaux and I find myself moving with it. It's really new for me. For the first time, I am not insisting to finish my painting in a certain way. It feels good. When I sit next to Margaux I become like her and this gives me so much freedom."

This really touches me, and I realize I have grown accustomed to 'Henna and Henna's style.' It is something fixed in my mind. Now, suddenly, it has disappeared and later on, when Henna returns to her own style, I can see that she has gained more strength, new dimensions, because of this experience.

A few days later, I go to her and look at a painting that she began only three hours earlier. I see the painting is already complete and this is a good opportunity to test her new openness, because in earlier times Henna could never even conceive that something could be finished in such a short time.

"I think this painting is finished," I tell her.

"Yes, I think so," she replies and in this moment I feel more close to her than in all the seven years we have been painting together. We are synchronized. She understands the same visual language and we are very much in tune.

From these examples, you can to see how important it is to have creators as friends to inspire each other. You discover something, I discover something, and pretty soon it's clear that each of us has something to offer.

Artists need other artists to grow, like the Impressionists who gathered in Pere Tanguy's shop, like the avant-garde painters who joined the Blue Rider School in Munich. Something similar is happening to us here in Pune.

Sometimes, I see very clearly that if I didn't do this training, if I didn't share my vision with these participants, my own painting wouldn't happen with such vitality and vigor. So I'm really receiving back what I share, I'm drinking it, taking it in.

And maybe this is a good time to say what is happening to my own style, as a result of what I have been teaching and learning.

For one thing, I am filled with a tremendous amount of energy. I just want to paint and paint. The energy for painting is here in abundance and nothing else matters – my hectic schedule, my personal difficulties in love relationships – none of these things can stop me.

My hands want to move, my hands want to create. This is the basic feeling. And it doesn't matter what – I can paint almost anything. For example, whenever I have a spare moment in the training I pull out one of the old paintings that some student threw away – maybe black and white, maybe color – and I start to work. Whatever I touch, whatever I see, is becoming a painting easily in my hands.

Then I fall in love with a particular tree in the resort, which turns out to be a very interesting experience.

You see, once upon a time, maybe two or three hundred years ago, this area of Pune called Koregaon Park was a huge jungle, with tigers roaming freely.

I have always loved the jungle, the wilderness. That's why I liked visiting Byron Bay, on the East Coast of Australia, because it has a dense, jungle-like rain forest that inspires me.

When I meet nature like that, I remember what it is that I really want to express with my painting. My inner vision hits the outer nature, and vice versa, and from this collision the creative urge wells up inside me, spilling over onto the paper.

This tree reminds me of those bygone days in India. It looks old, ageless. It looks wild. This tree has everything that I was dreaming about: you don't know where the roots are coming from, or to where the branches are disappearing. You don't know what is the tree and what is a creeper that twists and snakes around it, disappearing into the earth and coming back again.

Maybe that's why I like this tree so much, because somehow it is a reflection of my love for chaos, of the wildness and mystery of existence – all these creepers weaving in and out of nothingness.

Then, on the way into this chaos, you meet beauty. You meet form and non-form, disappearing into each other and re-appearing again.

Basically, when I look at this tree, I can't figure out what's happening. And that's what I'm looking for, because when I can't figure out nature then I want to bow down to it in awe and appreciation.

Really, the mind is so limited. Again and again, I see that human beings are limited and this is really a wonderful quality. Without this quality, human beings would become so arrogant: you conquer nature, you borrow from nature, you paint nature on a piece of paper, sign it, show it to your friends and you think you are a great artist.

For me, this is a wrong approach. I am always seeking something new to learn, as if I am just a student. I'm always a learner from nature. And I can bow down to nature because whatever I do is just a little stuttering, a pale shadow of the beauty of nature itself.

Each moment, the light is changing during the day. Each moment, the wind is stirring the leaves, swaying the branches. When I paint, all I can do is capture and express this moment, because the very next moment the sun's position changes, the breeze changes, everything changes... and you can't wait for permanency in nature, because it never happens.

This is good for me, because I have to keep on moving. This teaches me what life is, and that's why painting continues to be interesting for me, because I have to be always ready to move. If I stick with the past, I kill the life of the painting and myself.

I used to figure out about proportions, dimensions... why, how, what. But now, in these paintings, something different is happening. Now it's more like calligraphy movements. I see the tree, I fall in tune with the tree, I feel my hand dancing with the brush on the paper and there the essence of the tree appears.

I also paint in my studio, but the memory patterns in my mind are limited. Nature gives so much more freedom. I'm constantly intrigued how nature can so generously create each moment new, so fresh, with such incredible dynamism and variety.

Sometimes, when I look at my paintings and feel their hidden harmony, their secret dance, their musical quality, I find myself wishing that I could show them to Paul Klee.

His quest as an artist was similar to mine, seeking to embrace child-like elements such as freedom, spontaneity and playfulness, yet at the same time his work was very refined and sensitive.

Like Kandinsky, Klee wanted his paintings to have melody and rhythm, which has also been my quest – even though, as you may recall, I was criticized for it by my Tolmo colleagues while working in Toledo.

Klee was a contemporary of Kandinsky. He was born and raised in Switzerland and, like Kandinsky, was passionately fond of music but chose to make painting his first love.

In 1898, at the age of 19, he went Munich and studied at the same art schools as Kandinsky – although they didn't meet at this time – then he traveled around Europe to view the works of the great masters.

Klee knew he had talent, but was aware that he was just beginning to develop it and didn't want to fall into the trap of being pretentious or over-ambitious:

"I have to disappoint at first," he stated. "I am expected to do things a clever fellow could easily make. But my consolation must be that I am much more handicapped by my sincerity than by any lack of talent or ability.

"I have a feeling that sooner or later I'll arrive at something valid, only I must begin not with hypotheses but with specific instances, not matter how minute. I want to be as though newborn, knowing absolutely nothing about Europe; ignoring facts and fashion, to be almost primitive."

In these words by Klee, I could hardly hope for a better definition of the child-like approach.

Nevertheless, he hungrily absorbed all the influences of his time, including the Impressionists and Cézanne, and here I'd like to make another important point: having the attitude of knowing nothing, being primitive, new born, doesn't mean that you don't learn from others.

It simply means that you don't borrow from here and there, in an intellectual way, then patch together a superficial style that has no roots in your own being. You wait for the real thing to arise spontaneously from within.

Klee did a lot of sketching and drawing before he graduated to painting, which to me is further evidence of his determination to develop a solid base for artistic expression.

He had a quirky sense of humor. One of his early and best-known etchings is titled 'Virgin in a Tree,' consisting of a small tree in whose branches sits a bony, naked and rather ugly woman. Another is called 'Two Men Meet, Each Believing the Other to Be of Higher Rank,' showing two men obsequiously bending over while greeting each other, keeping eye contact yet somehow trying to outdo each other in humbleness, until their heads are almost touching the ground.

In 1911, Klee joined the Blue Rider group in Munich, making his first acquaintance with Kandinsky. In 1914, a trip to the deserts of North Africa became an almost spiritual experience for Klee as an artist, and confirmed his passion for light and color:

"Color has taken hold of me," he declared. "No longer do I have to chase after it. I know that it has hold of me forever. That is the significance of this blessed moment. Color and I are one. I am a painter."

His paintings reflect his passion. To me, they vibrate with a sense of harmony, the colors merging easily, the forms neither wholly abstract nor realistic, and almost always presented with child-like simplicity and freshness of vision.

After the First World War, Klee joined the Bauhaus in Weimar, Germany, which was to become the Mecca for European design. During the next few years, while setting down guidelines for the students he was teaching, Klee compiled three volumes of principles that form the whole basis of modern art.

"Art does not render the visible; rather it makes visible," he asserted, and used the symbol of a tree to describe the creative process as it occurs in the individual artist. Klee's description of this symbol is worth quoting here at length:

"The artist has busied himself with this multiform world and has in some measure got his bearings in it, quietly, all by himself. He is so well oriented that he can put order into the flux of phenomena and experiences. This sense of direction in nature and life, this branching and spreading array, I shall compare with the root of the tree.

"From the root the sap rises up into the artist, flows through him, flows through his eye. He is the trunk of the tree. Overwhelmed and activated by the force of the current, he conveys his vision into his work. In full view of the world, the crown of the tree unfolds and spreads in time and space, and so with his work.

"Nobody will expect a tree to form its crown exactly the same way as its root. Between above and below there cannot be exact mirror images of the each other. It is obvious that different functions operating in different elements must produce vital divergences.

"But it is just the artist who at times is denied those departures from nature which his art demands. He has even been accused of incompetence and distortion.

"And yet, standing at his appointed place, as the trunk of the tree, he does nothing other than gather and pass on what rises from the depths. He neither serves nor commands – he transmits. His position is humble. And the beauty at the crown is not his own; it has merely passed through him."

All this is very well said and I find myself in harmony with Klee on most of his points, especially with his understanding that creativity cannot be forced. Like sap moving upward, it needs to be a natural overflow of energy arising from the source.

And what is that source?

Klee doesn't really answer the question with his tree symbol, because the 'phenomena' that make up his roots are not the source of creativity, but merely raw material for its expression. And the artist, as the trunk, is not really

277

overwhelmed by the current rising from the roots, but by the vision he brings to it.

So, where does the creative impulse come from? Western culture has no answer for this question, except to attribute it to the unconscious part of the mind, or to take refuge in conventional religious terminology, like 'soul' or 'spirit.'

This is why I feel an urgent need to introduce eastern mysticism to western art. Without meditation, we are never going to get beyond this point, and if we don't get beyond it then art has no future, no significant direction in which to move. It will just circle around upon itself, going nowhere, as it has been doing for the past half century.

Meditation is the method to move towards the source, penetrating through the layers of the mind to the consciousness that resides behind them. Creativity springs from consciousness as naturally as water from a freshly dug well. This is the essential understanding that I want to convey.

Klee is right when, describing a painter's artistic expression, he says, "the beauty at the crown is not his own; it has merely passed through him."

This is because the source of creativity lies beyond the 'I' and the 'me.' It is rooted in consciousness. And if you have trouble understanding why consciousness is creative, then perhaps we need to borrow Osho's vision that every human consciousness is part of cosmic consciousness, part of the universal life force.

This force is continuously involved in creativity. How else does this beautiful planet exist? It is a continuously changing dance of creative energy, an ongoing 'leela,' or play, in which invisible consciousness seeks visible forms of expression.

By the way, when I say 'meditation is the method' to access your own consciousness, I don't mean there is only one technique available. As I've said before, there are hundreds of techniques that can be used.

I'm not trying to sell a particular brand product – that's a misunderstanding created by the way religion has tried to monopolize these techniques and turn them into private property.

That's why, perhaps, all intelligent people have an aversion to orthodox religions, because they have been claiming exclusive rights to something that should be common to all.

Well, I don't want get up on my soapbox, because really this is Osho's work, not mine. He spent most of his life attacking religion for exploiting humanity and, as a result, he became a very controversial figure worldwide, making enemies as fast as I can make sushi rolls – which, if you have ever been to one of my Japanese dinner parties, you will know is really, really fast.

My job, as I see it, is to demonstrate, if I can, the way meditation, creativity and art can be brought together in a beautiful synthesis. And this is one of the reasons why I end my training with an exhibition of all the paintings that we have created over the previous six weeks.

Before talking about the exhibition, however, there are a few more things I need to explain about my meditative approach to art, which might otherwise be misunderstood.

For example, a painting that contains the flavor of meditation doesn't need to be pretty or beautiful. I'm not like Renoir, who broke away from his fellow Impressionists in order to indulge his personal passion for painting pretty children, sensual naked women, beautiful flowers and elegant scenes.

There are no conditions on a meditative painter. There are no limitations. It is not a question of choice of subject or attitude. It is, essentially, a question of depth. It is a question of connecting with your own unique individuality and giving it creative expression.

This, however, brings up another relevant issue:

How to know? How to tell the difference? How can you distinguish a meditative painting from a non-meditative one?

This is like the dilemma that for several decades has faced modern art and especially abstract painting. Standing in a gallery or a museum, looking at a swirling mixture of blobs of color on a canvas in front of you, how can you know if this is the work of a genius, an idiot, or a charlatan?

Kandinsky, the father of abstraction, was determined to ensure that every color he used, every line he drew, every stroke of his brush, was filled with deep symbolic significance. It was almost as if he could see, looming ahead of him, the danger that abstract art could deteriorate into something arbitrary and meaningless.

"Beauty of form and color is no sufficient aim by itself," he warned. "If we begin at once to break the bonds which bind us to nature, and devote ourselves purely to combination of color and abstract form, we shall produce works which are mere decoration, which are suited to neckties or rugs."

Here, I must relate a strange coincidence. On the same day that I was reading this statement by Kandinsky, I'd asked a friend to come over and help me with web research – I'm hopeless with computers.

He was using an internet search engine and happened to enter the words 'Guggenheim,' 'modern' and 'art.' Imagine our astonishment when the search engine came up with an advertisement for rugs with Kandinsky's paintings on them!

It appears that a leading rug manufacturer in America had obtained the blessings of the Guggenheim Museum of Modern Art in New York to use its paintings, including several by Kandinsky, for a series of rug designs. His words were indeed prophetic.

Part of the reason why Kandinsky put so much effort into developing a whole theory of art was – I suspect – to prevent abstract painting from being reduced to 'mere decoration.' But his effort was in vain. It happened anyway. And this relieves me of the burden of trying to prevent the same thing happening to meditative art.

From my perspective, the worst has already happened. Art has become meaningless. There is no need to try and prevent it. All that is necessary for me to do is point the way out of the desert and walk that way myself. If others decide to join me, so much the better – I will enjoy the company.

Looking ahead, I can guess that, if a sufficient number of artists move in this direction, then slowly, slowly, a deeper understanding will arise in the art world in general, and gradually this understanding will spread outward to include the general public.

Everything depends on the quality of the art that is produced – this is the bottom line, and it has always been so. If I am right, if connecting with your own depth through meditation is the best way to find your unique form of creative expression, then the art that arises from this connection will speak for itself.

Which brings me back to the exhibition that we stage at the end of the course. This, in our small world in Pune, is our collective statement of what a six-week creativity training can do for people. It's our way of saying, "Look! This is what we did. Come and see for yourself."

Preparations for an exhibition are always very hectic. In fact, this year I decide not to have an exhibition, just to take the pressure off the participants who, naturally enough, are desperate to get everything finished in time.

But the exhibition happens anyway. A few days before the end of the training, Mukesh, one of the resort administrators, comes to me and says, "Meera, why don't you have your exhibition this year in Buddha Grove?"

He knows that, normally, we exhibit on the roof of Krishna House.

I shake my head.

"There is no light in the evening," I reply.

"Don't worry, I can arrange that," he says, and the next day three Indian workmen arrive carrying huge bundles of fairy lights. Pretty soon, all the trees surrounding the hall are draped with fairy lights, creating a sparkling, magical garden. And in the middle, a tall post holds four floodlights that shine out toward the periphery.

So now we are in a mad rush, hanging paintings from ropes tied between the trees, surrounding the entire hall with paintings.

Everyone gets to exhibit. Here, there is never going to be a Salon des Refusés. We group the paintings by type: black and white nature paintings at one end, vertical watercolors next to them, abstract acrylics along the side, energy ecstasy paintings at the other end, and so on.

Self-portraits don't form part of the main exhibit. They are hung opposite the bookstore, facing the main pathway that leads through the resort. This is my way of catching the public's eye and perhaps startling them as well. Because it really is an impressive sight: more than thirty naked faces – beautiful, but with none of Renoir's prettiness – looking out at you from the depths of their being.

The big group paintings also face the bookstore. These colorful abstract acrylics are used as billboards, eye-catchers, with attached notices announcing the dates of the exhibition and its location.

This year, we have too many, so I wrap one large painting around a stand of bamboo trees, hoping that the resort's gardeners will appreciate this spontaneous blend of nature and abstraction. Alas, they don't; the painting is detached, rolled and politely returned within hours. Pity, I think the bamboos rather enjoyed it.

One more touch and our preparations are complete. You may remember our multi-media night sessions in the pyramid, when we invited guests and painted little cards with our partners, passing them back and forth.

Now we create similar-sized cards and turn them into personal invitations, handing them out to friends, strangers, administrators, fellow artists.

In short, we do everything we can to make a splash and turn heads. "When Meera has an exhibition, the whole resort knows it," jokes one friend, and I accept it as a compliment. After all, art museums all over the world have in recent years learned how to stage glitzy 'cultural events' to capture the public's interest, so why should I be an exception?

When all is ready, we stage a grand opening, offering our guests Japanese tea, rum punch and soft music from a live band. Four Japanese women from the training, including myself, are dressed in traditional kimonos and conduct an elegant tea ceremony in the middle of the hall.

Buddha Grove is ablaze with color, open to the moon and stars above, glittering with fairy lights on all sides. It's an overwhelming visual sensation to walk in here and see these paintings surrounding the whole space. There is so much color, so much abundance of expression, so much energy, vitality, life.

Reactions, of course, vary wildly. Some guests, who have friends among the participants, simply cannot believe that these paintings are by people they know. They never thought of them as artists or painters. It's a secret side that hasn't been revealed until now.

Other guests are familiar with this riotous scene of form and color. They know me well and come regularly to enjoy the annual exhibition.

Some, of course, have reservations. They don't often express them to me directly, but here are two typical objections:

"All the paintings look the same."

"Why does Meera teach them to paint only trees?"

There is some truth in these remarks.

Painters in all the great movements that have given birth to different epochs in art share a certain similarity with their contemporaries. For example, whenever I go to the museum in Munich where works by the painters of the Blue Rider School are exhibited, I can feel this similarity, this common energy – the color scales they use, the treatment of certain motifs, and so on.

I can feel their common passion to create according to certain essential values they hold dear to their hearts.

What, then, are the essential values of our new movement?

Art which makes us sane.

Art which makes us remember that we have everything we need inside us – our creative impulse, our original expression.

Art which connects with life.

Art which makes us more aware and more conscious.

Meditative art has existed before, giving birth to the Taj Mahal in India and a whole series of Zen artists and mystics in Japan, including Basho, Sengai, Hakuin, Ikkyu.

Here, we are doing something more. We are creating a new synthesis, bringing the passion and zest for life that exists in the West to meet and merge with the consciousness and meditation that exists in the East.

This opens the door to re-awakening art, giving it a rebirth.

As for the emphasis on trees in my training, they fulfill a multi-dimensional purpose. They represent the whole spectrum of life, from the earth to the sky, from the deepest roots to the highest leaves and flowers.

Being with them, absorbing their qualities, you learn patience, movement, harmony, blossoming, surprise...

Painting them, you learn the basic ABC of art: form, dimension, contrast, proportion, distance, space. And you learn about the human body, too, because really the forms are very similar, with the tree's central trunk imitating our body, and its branches our arms and legs.

I teach painting, but my work is not limited to this art.

Basically, I awaken the power of creativity in the individual and share my understanding of how this creativity can be sustained and continued.

This is my main job, which I do through the medium of painting. Through this approach, people learn to express their inner vision – something that, knowingly or unknowingly, everyone possesses.

It is just a question of discovering it and bringing it out.

Once this has been accomplished, the joy and of being creative can be applied to any area of life, whether it is painting, cleaning the floor, cooking a meal, making money or raising a child. It's the same creativity, the same flood of energy, the same experience of saying 'yes' to life.

Those participants who fall in love with painting will continue to develop their art, and many have done so. And, of course, they are not limited to the themes I have chosen for the training. They can branch out in any direction. Several of them, over the years, have become successful artists, while many more continue to paint just for personal satisfaction.

Now I see that I am really running out of time and space, so I will end by relating one more personal anecdote that somehow, for me, captures the essence of what I am trying to convey. Well, maybe not the real essence – that's just not possible in words – but an important aspect of it.

About fourteen years ago, when Osho was still alive, I got a message through one of his secretaries: "Come to my dining room, I want to show you something."

I was very curious. I thought for a moment I was going to have lunch with him, but it was not like that. In fact, when I arrived, he was not there and there was no message, no indication of what he wanted to show me.

Still, I received his message, because as I stood there I saw what he had invited me to see.

His dining room was actually a balcony, with big glass windows, and outside was the jungle of his garden – he wanted it like that, he didn't like his gardeners to cut anything, just to let everything grow naturally.

The grass and plants were dark green in color, so it was rather like looking into an aquarium, as if these plants were living at the bottom of the ocean.

The light was subdued, because the trees and bushes were so dense they blocked out most of the sunlight. But individual rays of sunlight were shining diagonally into the garden, as if penetrating softly through still, clear water.

Behind the garden, some construction work was happening and a big plastic sheet, sky blue in color, had been hung in front to screen it off. This sheet was moving and swaying in the wind, making ripples like waves.

As I stood there watching, I also noticed that a black and white photo of Osho, hung on a wall of the balcony, was being reflected in the glass window.

The overall effect was absolutely beautiful: layers of translucent light and movement, overlapping each other, shifting and changing. Each moment that I looked I was getting more and more drunk, because a deep understanding flooded into me that this life contains beauty upon beauty, layer upon layer of mystery.

I realized in that moment there is no end to the expression of this ongoing, ever-changing mystery. All the artist needs to do is empty the mind, be open, and say 'yes' to the abundance existence is offering.

I remembered the earlier message I received from Osho, about overlapping the whole existence with multiple rainbows. Why just one rainbow? Why just one moon, or one sun? There are millions of suns, so don't be stingy.

Today, I feel that everything I received from Osho is coming closer and closer to my expression in the paintings I create.

It is painting without effort. It is so easy and so accurate, because when you paint with awareness you don't make a mistake. This awareness also contains a sense of freshness and aliveness, a child-like innocence, so each painting is always fresh.

It's not dead. It's alive, throbbing with energy and life. I'm so excited that sometimes I can't sleep because I want to get up early in the morning and paint.

Each day is filled with a sense of newness. Each day, I'm intrigued by the discoveries I make as I throw myself into the unknown. I feel like scientist, constantly developing new methods, and new techniques. It's on ongoing process and there seems to be no end to it.

Paintings coming out of this approach are a surprise to my own eyes, and I want to bow down to every new painting that is born in front of me. In such moments, I feel the significance of being alive, and if I can share this thrill with others, so they can make their own unique footprint on this earth, giving birth to their own creativity, then I am most happy.

If you happen to see me working on Krishna House roof, under the trees and the sky, splashing colors on the paper, totally absorbed in my creativity, the chances are you will see only a painter.

But meditation is happening at the same time, inside me. It's not visible to the eye, but it's there all the time – a silent, secret undercurrent, present in every stroke of my brush.

These are my two great love affairs: art and meditation. To be able to combine them in my own life, and then to mix them in a delightful fizzy cocktail and offer this drink to others, is the greatest joy imaginable.

About the Author

Meera (Kasue Hashimoto) was born in Ishikawa, Japan, in 1947.

Beginning in 1966 she studied for three years at the Musashino Art University, Tokyo, and in 1970 visited Europe, touring the major art museums and eventually settling in Toledo, Spain.

From 1970-72 she studied drawing at the Circulo De Bellas Artes, Madrid, and Escuela De Arte, Toledo, where she became a co-founder of the Grupo Tolmo and Galeria Tolmo.

In 1974 she travelled to Pune, India, and became a disciple of the mystic Osho.

In 1979, at Osho's suggestion, she established the Osho Art School, together with Geetesh Gibson, an American artist, and began leading art groups and trainings all over the world.

She developed new methods for helping people discover their creative expression and founded art communities in Amsterdam, Sicily and California.

More than 40 books by Osho are illustrated with Meera's paintings.

Currently, she leads painting trainings at the Osho Meditation Resort in Pune, and also in Ibiza, Bremen and Tuscany. She offers workshops in Creativity and Art Therapy in many places in Japan and Europe.

Her unique way of working is documented in three videos:

1) The New Man, The New Art.

2) Birth of Creativity (Osho Master Painter Training in Pune).

3) Osho Painting Training, Ibiza.

Also, in 'Blossoming,' an art book with 160 full-color paintings combined with poetry by Meera's friend and colleague, Satyam Anand, a Japanese farmer-poet.

Videos and copies of 'Blossoming' can be ordered from Doris Schneider, Meera's secretary in Munich, Germany, email: SchneiderDoris@t-online.de

For information about Meera's schedule of trainings and workshops, please consult her website:
www.meera.de

Questions about Meera's groups – timings, prices, etc. -- need to be directed to the organizations and agents shown on the schedule.

For more information about Osho, his meditations, and the Osho Meditation Resort in Pune, India:
www.osho.com

Exhibitions

Japan
Tokyo: Japan Art Academy, Tokyo City Museum, Nikaki, Sanko Gallery, Jujiya Gallery, Kinokuniya
Osaka: Toho Gallery
Kyoto: Seiho Gallery
Toyama: Daiwa Gallery
Ishikawa: Kanasawa City Culture Center, Renaissance Gallery
Kiryu: Shima Gallery
Nara: Nara Culture Center
Fukuoka: El Galle

Spain
Madrid: Palacio del Crystal, Galeria Tebas, Galeria Ifa
Toledo: Galeria Tolmo, Caja de Aorros, Sala Cindical, Galleria Armas 51
Barcelona: Fundacion Joan Miro
Zaragoza: Galeria Leonardo
Lerida: Colegio de Arquitectos

Portugal
Lisbon: Fundacion Caconste Gulbenkian

Germany
Munich: Gallerie Meera
Cologne: Gallerie Klaus, Osho Uta Institute

Switzerland
Basel: Gallerie Munsterberg
Lugano: Villa Margherita

England
London: Osho International

Holland
Amsterdam: Gallerie Scheenjes

USA
Santa Rosa: Lawrence Gallery

India
Mumbai: Taj Art Gallery, Jehangir Art Gallery
New Delhi: Gallery Art Today
Pune: Osho Meditation Resort

www.ingramcontent.com/pod-product-compliance
Lightning Source LLC
Chambersburg PA
CBHW020604270326
41927CB00005B/175